HOMOSEXUAL
SAINTS

THE COMMUNITY OF CHRIST EXPERIENCE

© 2008 by the John Whitmer Historical Association. Published by John Whitmer Books. Printed in the United States. John Whitmer Books is a trademark of the John Whitmer Historical Association.

ISBN 978-1-934901-05-2

View our complete catalog online at www.JohnWhitmerBooks.com.

Learn more about the John Whitmer Historical Association (JWHA) at www.JWHA.info. Learn more about Gay and Lesbian Acceptance (GALA) at www.GALAweb.org.

Cover design and typesetting by John Hamer.

john whitmer books

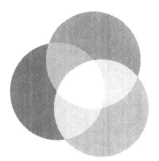

HOMOSEXUAL
SAINTS

THE COMMUNITY OF CHRIST EXPERIENCE

edited by william d. russell
with a preface by d. michael quinn

Dedicated to Bob Swoffer

CONTENTS

PREFACE

D. Michael Quinn

A MIDWESTERN COLLEAGUE and friend of mine for many years, Bill Russell has compiled a very important collection of essays about alternative sexualities in the Community of Christ, formerly the Reorganized Church of Jesus Christ of Latter Day Saints, headquartered in Independence, Missouri. It is a series of stories about repression (first institutional, then cultural, then familial, and finally self) and about liberation (first self, then familial, then cultural, and hopefully institutional).

At the institutional level, the editor's introductory essay describes his denomination's silence about homosexuality, followed by its efforts to punish, its reassessments, its internal conflicts, and its struggles in ministering to those who regard themselves as homosexual or who love someone who is "queer" (GLBTI—gay, lesbian, bisexual, transgender, or intersexual). Members and activists within the Restoration Movement have expressed disappointment that the church's leaders have not acted sooner, or more liberally, or more compassionately in public on the issues. However, there is value in the cliché about a half-full glass.

Beyond what the introductory essay presents, I find an interesting correlation between the larger national context and certain developments within the Reorganization/Community of Christ. The First Presidency of this conservative denomination appointed a "Human Sexuality Committee" in 1978 and established a "Task Force on Human Sexuality" in 1980. The church's leadership showed remarkable sensitivity and vision in these initiatives.

Compare those institutional developments with a conservative church in one of the centers of activism. Not until this same time-period did the Roman Catholic Archdiocese of San Francisco establish its "Task Force on Gay/Lesbian Issues," which issued its first report on *Homosexuality and Social Justice* in 1982.

Likewise, the acronym GALA first emerged on the national scene in 1982 when Yale University established its Gay And Lesbian Alumni association. Shortly afterward, members of the Reorganization adopted this acronym in forming Gay And Lesbian Acceptance, a one-word change that was even more supportive.

RLDS/Community of Christ leaders can be faulted for not investigating the subject sooner, for not publicly endorsing a compassionate ministry to GLBTI members sooner, for not reaching out to suicide-prone youths sooner, for not adopting social-justice resolutions sooner, for failing to do many things sooner and with more gusto. But it takes time to right any wrongs, and the process must begin somewhere, sometime. In comparative context, the institutional concern at Independence has been noteworthy.

At a personal level, I approach these essays from a somewhat different worldview than Bill Russell, even though we are both American middle-class, white, male academics. As a lifelong member of the RLDS Church/Community of Christ, he is a heterosexual male who has become an activist for GLBTI people as a compassionate extension of the civil-rights activism that consumed his thoughts and energies on behalf of peoples of color in the 1960s and 1970s. This book's essays resonate with me as a seventh-generation "Mormon" and a self-defined homosexual (since the age of twelve) who chose to live a heterosexual life in order to serve my homophobic LDS Church, headquartered in Salt Lake City, Utah. There are personal overlaps, academic commonalities, continuities of empathy and compassion, but there are also the differences that separate groups and distinguish individuals.

That applies to the other contributors, as well. For example, some recognized themselves as sexually different in early childhood, or in young adulthood, or in middle-age, whereas I did at puberty. In itself, a significant difference in the age of self-awareness creates different experiences of life, differing worldviews.

No matter when self-awareness emerged as G, L, B, T, or I—*we* recognize ourselves as having the common ground of a minority, a sexual minority. Our sexuality is difficult for the vast majority to imagine or understand as "normal," just as left-handedness and ambidexterity are difficult to imagine or understand for the 90 percent of humans who are "normally" right-handed (myself included).

Others, through no fault of their own, have always fit the "normal" heterosexual stereotypes of the 90 percent majority in sexual orientation. However, such contributors to this collection are "normal" people who love those who are in that 10 percent minority for whom "normal" is "different." This vast majority deserves tolerance, acceptance, consideration, and patience from those of us in a sexual minority, just as we deserve their tolerance, acceptance, consideration, and patience. That is the meaning of family, of religious fellowship, of social pluralism, of human diversity, of being children of God. It is the purpose of this book.

D. Michael Quinn
Rancho Cucamonga, California

FOREWORD

In 1999, my wife, Lois, and I attended our first retreat of the organization called GALA (Gay and Lesbian Acceptance), we heard the heart-wrenching personal stories of gays and lesbians in the Community of Christ. About one-third of those in attendance were their friends and family members. Such sharing of personal stories has been a staple in GALA retreats since the organization first began in the early 1980s.

Soon GALA members like Forrest and Donna Swall, Sharon Troyer, and others were encouraging me to collect and publish a book of stories such as these. My work began in earnest in the fall of 2001 when Graceland University granted me a one-semester leave to work on some writing projects that were already well underway. The result is this collection of personal stories, along with a historical introduction in which I trace the evolution of how the church and church-sponsored Graceland University have dealt with the issue of homosexuality.

My deepest appreciation goes to Lavina Fielding Anderson, president of Editing, Inc., of Salt Lake City, who donated her editing to this book as well as to the authors who shared their stories herein. It is my conviction—and that of the GALA organization—that the ignorance and prejudice regarding homosexuality that is so common in many societies is best addressed, not by debate, but by sharing the life stories of those who have been either directly or indirectly affected by the issue of sexual orientation.

William D. Russell
Graceland University
Lamoni, Iowa

INTRODUCTION

A T THE BIENNIAL General Conference of the Reorganized Church of Jesus Christ of Latter Day Saints[1] in April 1954, C. George Mesley re-signed as an apostle to avoid dealing with allegations from his native Australia that he was homosexual. It was the first instance I'm aware of in which homosexuality became an issue that the general officers of the church had to deal with.

Cyril George Mesley (1900-94) was born in Bairnsdale, Victoria, Australia. He met and married Blanche Edwards at Graceland College in the United States. Blanche's brother, F. Henry Edwards, served as an apostle (1922-46) and as a member of the RLDS First Presidency (1946-66).

George Mesley became an apostle in 1938 and resigned from the Twelve under pressure in 1954, when critics were threatening to "out" him. The First Presidency at that time consisted of President Israel A. Smith and his two counselors, F. Henry Edwards and W. Wallace Smith, the half-brother of the President. I have no informa-tion about what happened behind the scenes. Perhaps Edwards en-couraged his brother-in-law to resign to avoid an embarrassing pub-lic disclosure. Some measure of the official discomfort being felt is that Mesley's resignation is nowhere mentioned in the minutes of the 1954 General Conference and that the process of replacing him included a sharp departure from tradition. President Israel A. Smith presented to General Conference a revelatory document approved by the delegates and added to the Doctrine and Covenants as Section 143 calling Donald V. Lents to fill "a vacancy" in the Council of the

---

[1] Prior to April 6, 2001, the Community of Christ was known as the Reorganized Church of Jesus Christ of Latter Day Saints. Independence, Missouri, has been the headquarters of the church since 1920.

1

Twelve. Normally, such revelations are filled with praise for the out-going apostle's service, but this revelation did not mention Mesley's name.

At the time of Mesley's resignation from the Twelve, his priest-hood status reverted to high priest. Two months later, however, he was "silenced"[2] because of the charges about his sexual orientation.

He and Blanche moved to Sacramento, California, where they lived until they moved to Resthaven, the church-sponsored nursing home in Independence, in 1986, where George died in 1994. During those forty years, Mesley remained active in the Community of Christ and was very highly respected as a person and as an able church lead-er. Mesley had made a significant contribution to the Community of Christ in the Stockton-Modesto District in California. For example, he took the lead in creating the outdoor redwood chapel at the Happy Valley campgrounds. In 1974, he was reinstated in the priesthood as a high priest, and he was elected pastor of the Stockton Branch in 1976, serving in that capacity for several years. Don Compier, Dean of the Community of Christ Seminary in Independence, Missouri, re-calls that George and Blanche Mesley were "very important mentors for me" during those years.[3]

Where has the Community of Christ come on the issue of ho-mosexuality since 1954? This introduction provides an overview of significant events as a context for the personal accounts that follow. Although both the historical and the personal accounts overlap the change on April 6, 2001, in the church's name from Reorganized Church of Jesus Christ of Latter Day Saints to Community of Christ,

---

[2] In the Community of Christ, to be "silenced" is to have one's authority to act as a priesthood member in the Church removed. She or he is still a member of the church. Grounds for silencing and procedures for appeal are outlined in World Conference Resolution 1192, adopted in 1986. "Excommunication" means that the person is still a member of the church but is not in good standing, and therefore cannot partake of the sacrament, hold an office in the church, and cannot function in the priesthood, vote in business meetings, or be a delegate to church conferences. To be "expelled" is to be completely removed from the church and "should only be inflicted in cases of most flagrant violations of church law and standards." World Conference Resolution 922 (1932).

[3] Don Compier, email to Bill Russell, April 13, 2004.

I have standardized the name to "Community of Christ" for the reader's ease in reference and also to avoid the fussiness of switching back and forth between terms.

The 1961-62 Standing High Council's Consideration

Early in 1961, the First Presidency, then consisting of W. Wallace Smith and his two counselors, F. Henry Edwards and Maurice L. Draper, considered the need to revise church policy on divorce. The most recent policy was General Conference Resolution 412, adopted at the 1896 General Conference, which recognized adultery as the only grounds for divorce, based on Matthew 5:32. The First Presidency, finding the policy "more and more difficult to administer,"[4] proposed a new policy at the 1962 World Conference which, after considerable discussion, passed with minor amendments as World Conference Resolution 1034 (1962). The new policy recognized as acceptable grounds for divorce "adultery, repeated sexual perversion, desertion, [and] such aggravated conditions within the home as render married life unbearable for the party petitioning or for the children of the marriage."[5]

While the issue of divorce had been troubling Church leaders for some time, by early 1961, the related matter of homosexuality also needed attention. The First Presidency asked the Standing High Council to study the problem of homosexuality in the church, specifically considering whether male homosexuality would call into question a man's priesthood and/or membership, and also whether homosexuality would be grounds for divorce. George Mesley had continued to attend and be active in church following his 1954 silencing, no additional accusations of homosexuality had surfaced, and his marriage had survived. Thus, the First Presidency, particularly his brother-in-law, may have wondered about whether he should be reinstated in the priesthood at some level.

---

[4] *World Conference Bulletin, 1962* (Independence: Reorganized Church of Jesus Christ of Latter Day Saints, 1962), 17.

[5] Ibid., 104. World Conference Resolution 1034 is also published in various editions of the church's *Rules and Resolutions* (Independence: Herald House, various dates).

The Standing High Council is composed of twelve high priests chosen by the First Presidency and approved by the World Conference. It is chaired by a member of the First Presidency and advises the First Presidency on moral and ethical issues when the Presidency asks for its advice. It does not have the power to initiate policies on its own, and the First Presidency is free to accept or reject the advice of the council. None of its policies becomes official unless the First Presidency approves, and none of the policies, whether approved or not, may be published unless authorized by the First Presidency. A member of the First Presidency always chairs Standing High Council meetings, and usually all three members of the First Presidency attend council meetings. The council has sometimes addressed such controversial social/moral issues as adultery, abortion, and capital punishment.

Following the First Presidency's request, the Standing High Council formed a subcommittee of its own members consisting of Charles Grabske Sr., a physician; Arthur B. Taylor, an attorney; and Clifford P. Buck, director of the Church's Department of Religious Education and a former high school chemistry teacher. When I interviewed Buck in September 2000, he recalled that the late Dr. Grabske took a traditional medical view, contending that people can change their sexual orientation. "I read everything I could put my hands on," Buck recalled, "and I took the point of view that it's in the genes." Buck also confirmed that the George Mesley case was in the back of people's minds during the discussion and added that, unsurprisingly, "among the First Presidency, F. Henry Edwards was the most interested in the subject."[6]

Five months after the 1962 World Conference revised the Church's policy on divorce, the Standing High Council approved a policy on homosexuality and forwarded it to the First Presidency. The conservative views of Grabske and Taylor prevailed over Buck's more liberal stance. In essence, the policy allowed that people might experiment with homosexuality in their youth without serious consequences, but if it became a "persistent practice," then it should be regarded as a sin and an illness for which treatment should be sought.

---

[6] Clifford P. Buck, telephone interview, September 19, 2000.

4

If the homosexual did not repent, he or she should be excommunicated. The policy also recommended that, if an excommunicated homosexual is readmitted to good standing in the Church and is again found guilty of homosexuality, he or she should be expelled from the church. Certainly a homosexual could not be in the priesthood, the council held, concluding: "Members of the priesthood found to be practicing homosexuality and persisting therein, should be placed under silence until the responsible administrative officers have all reasonable assurance that the practice has been abandoned."[7]

After the Standing High Council completed its work, the First Presidency sent a letter to all pastors, instructing them that homosexuals should not be ordained. A former assistant in the History Department at Community of Christ headquarters, Daniel T. Muir, recalls the reaction of Joe Campbell, who was pastor of a small rural congregation near Lamoni, Iowa. Unimpressed with the administrative ultimatum from Independence, Campbell queried, "And what if God calls a homosexual?"[8]

Naturally, as individual cases came up, word spread about the instructions to pastors. But the policy was not published in full for nearly four decades. Only gradually did portions of it become public. Nearly nine years after the policy was formulated, the *Saints' Herald* of September 1971 carried a "Question Time" answer from Fred L. Young, the World Church Secretary, responding to the question: "Is homosexual behavior fornication or adultery or what?" Young replied that it was neither fornication nor adultery, and after citing Romans 1:24-28 and 1 Corinthians 6:9, 10, 13, he wrote, "The Standing High Council has given this matter careful consideration and urges leaders to advise 'on the dangers of continued homosexual practices and the possibility that one may become so habituated to the homosexual pattern that in later adult years he may not be able to enjoy normal family relations . . . . The essential requirement in effecting a cure is that

---

[7] Major portions of the 1962 Standing High Council policy were published in Fred L. Young, World Church Secretary, "Question Time," *Saints' Herald,* September 1971, 53. (See Appendix A.)

[8] Daniel T. Muir, email to Bill Russell, May 18, 1999.

the individual himself have a strong desire to be cured.'"[9] Questions for this column nearly always come from the magazine's readership, but the questioners are not named. The managing editor, or sometimes the First Presidency, selects the letters that will be answered; the respondent is nearly always someone whose expertise qualifies him or her to give an insightful, if not authoritative, answer. Young wrote that practicing homosexuals should first receive "ministry," but if they refuse to repent they should be brought to church court.[10] Child molesters should be reported to the civil authorities. Although Young described the Standing High Council's "consideration," he did not tell readers that the council had, in fact, drafted and approved a policy statement.

Three months later, the *Herald* published a rejoinder by Joe A. Serig, a World Conference appointee minister serving as the Church's director of Christian Education. Serig felt that the council's position was much too simplistic and legalistic. "The classification of homosexuals as 'sinners' to be expelled provides a convenient but unchristian method for dealing with the problem," Serig noted. He pointed out that the Community of Christ retains members who are alcoholics, adulterers, child abusers, etc. "Surely our understanding of this problem has been enlightened since the 1962 statement by the Standing High Council," he urged.[11] This protest was a significant one. Serig was a prominent leader who, eleven years later, would be ordained an apostle after having been recommended by President Wallace B. Smith and approved by the vote of the delegates at the 1982 World Conference (D&C 155:5). Immediately following Serig's letter in the same issue was another letter to the editor, this one signed "name withheld for fear of excommunication." The author wrote:

"As a homosexual and a member of the Church, I was stunned at the directives . . . . I find it most distressing to think that I can be dismissed from the fellowship of the Saints because—through no fault of mine—I find a strong and romantic attraction to another man. All this time I have thought that the Church existed for sinners (al-

---

[9] Fred L. Young, "Question Time," *Saints' Herald,* September 1971, 53.
[10] Ibid.
[11] Joe E. Serig, "Lingering Legalism," *Saints' Herald,* December 1971, 8.

though I feel no guilt because of my God-given feelings)." He closed with a plea for understanding: "I would not want to be denied the sacraments of Christ."[12]

Three months later in the March 1972 issue of the *Herald,* Charles Grabske and Arthur Taylor, two of the three members of the 1962 Standing High Council's subcommittee, replied to Serig.[13] They asserted, "We know of no new medical science or social technique since 1962 that has thrown any new light on homosexuals." Comparing homosexuality with adultery, they added that the 1962 policy was "in accordance with the Three Standard Books of the Church," and cited a number of scriptures including Leviticus 18:22 ("You shall not lie with a male as with a woman; it is an abomination") and Romans 1:27 ("men, giving up natural intercourse with women, were consumed with passion for one another"). They concluded, "We still believe those guidelines to be true."[14]

This was where matters stood in 1974 when Mesley's priesthood was reinstated. The guidelines made no provision for gay men who do not engage in homosexual acts to hold priesthood offices in the church, but presumably, any accusations against Mesley were in the far distant past by that point, allowing church administrators in California as well as the First Presidency in Independence to feel comfortable about reinstating him in the priesthood.

The topic did not surface again in the *Herald* or any other official publication for the rest of the 1970s.

---

[12] Name withheld for fear of excommunication, "New Legislation Needed," *Saints' Herald,* December 1971, 8-9.

[13] The *Herald* does not solicit people to write letters to the editor although the editor, of course, chooses which letters actually are printed. By this point, Buck, the more liberal member of the subcommittee, had withdrawn from Church activity and had moved from Missouri to Ohio.

[14] Charles F. Grabske Sr., M.D., and Arthur B. Taylor, "Individual Permissiveness," letter to the editor, *Saints' Herald,* March 1972, 8-9.

World Church Committees, 1978-82

Meanwhile, society at large paid increasing attention during the 1970s to the issues raised by discrimination against homosexuality. For the gay rights movement, the Stonewall Rebellion that began on June 27, 1969, was a trigger to activism similar to Rosa Parks's refusal to yield her seat to a white man on a Montgomery bus in December 1955. The New York City police were on a routine visit to a gay bar, the Stonewall Inn, in Greenwich Village. When they began arresting patrons, a crowd formed and began resisting the arrests. Three nights of rioting ensued. According to historian Byrne Fone, "For those present, it was intoxicating and overpowering. For the first time in American memory, gay people had refused to accept the law, which indicted them as second-class citizens, as sick, perverted criminals, as undeserving of its protection as they were of the compassion of the righteous."[15] The Gay Pride movement, with its personal encouragement to gays to accept their orientation, its educational outreach to defuse homophobia, and its political activism to claim the rights of other citizens, was launched.

During the 1970s, the Community of Christ was also moving closer to mainstream Protestantism in its theology and away from its sectarian "one true church" self-understanding. A greater tolerance of human behavior usually accompanies such a sociological shift. Some church members, including Joe Serig, realized that the medical and psychological disciplines had concluded that the old orthodoxies about homosexuality failed to account satisfactorily for the evidence.[16]

Possibly the ordination of Dr. Wallace B. Smith as president of the church in April 1978 was the most significant factor in causing the First Presidency to begin a reconsideration of the issue that year. A physician who had practiced ophthalmology for fourteen years, Smith had also served as president-designate (1976-78) and had shown himself open to theological change in keeping with the

---

[15] Byrne Fone, *Homophobia: A History* (New York: Metropolitan Books, Henry Holt and Company, 2000), 407.

[16] Joe E. Serig, telephone interview, September 21, 2000.

developing shift of the church from sect to denomination. His thinking at the beginning of his presidency was reflected in his presentation in January 1979 of what came to be known as "The Presidential Papers." Approximately two hundred fulltime appointee ministers and their wives were invited to Independence where Smith and his two counselors read papers reflecting their theological positions. The papers were shockingly liberal for many of the more conservative appointees.

On June 7, 1978—two months after Smith became president—the First Presidency appointed a ten-member Human Sexuality Committee (seven men, three women) who were psychologists, counselors, medical doctors, educators, etc. It was chaired by another physician, Wallace's brother-in-law, Otto Elser.[17] "The committee was charged with the task of exploring the area of human sexuality and recommending to the First Presidency ways in which the Church can be ministerially responsible and responsive in this area of life."[18] The First Presidency at first indicated to the committee that its assignment did not include alternative lifestyles, singleness, or homosexuality. But committee members, including people from the fields of psychology, counseling, education, the medical sciences, medical practitioners, and college and university professors, were saying, "This is unrealistic. We deal with this everyday; and if we're going to help the church, we've got to help people come to terms with some of these issues." So they insisted that they needed to be free to look at all areas of human sexuality, especially since the First Presidency could endorse or withhold its recommendations as it saw fit. The presidency relented and the committee was given the freedom to go forward as it saw fit.[19]

The committee gathered information on how other denominations dealt with the issue. Serig, one of the members, took a theo-

---

[17] Other committee members were Bernard Butterworth, Barbara Higdon, Richard Hughes, Linda Koehler, Margaret McKevit, Kenneth Robinson, Roy Schaeffer, Joe Serig, and Parris Watts.

[18] Joe E. Serig, interviewed by Paul Davis, Independence, May 7, 1998; typescript, Library-Archives, Community of Christ, Independence.

[19] Serig, email to Russell, September 21, 2000.

logical perspective. He recalls that Catholic conceptions of grace were particularly helpful. He felt that a church that believes in an open canon of scripture cannot hold rigidly to what was said thousands of years ago and that the scriptures must be looked at contextually because it is difficult to know what the Apostle Paul had in mind in his brief statements that are often quoted on this issue.[20] Serig thought that a more productive theological approach was the sacredness of human sexuality as a gift of God. He recalls that the committee read materials from other Christian denominations and that the Catholics "with their doctrine of grace, have a very high theological reflection of the sacredness of human sexuality."[21]

There were no openly gay or lesbian people on the committee, and none were officially consulted for input. Serig told me that individual committee members got feedback from gay and lesbian friends and acquaintances or had significant contact with homosexuals in the course of their professional careers. Serig recalled that gays were generally happy the issue was being studied but were "pretty sure it would be a fairly limited perspective that came out."[22] Kenneth Robinson recalls that President Smith's two counselors—Howard S. Sheehy Jr. and Duane E. Couey—were generally conservative on this issue, Sheehy more than Couey.[23] On the other hand, President Smith seemed willing to allow the exploration of such sensitive issues as ordination for gays and communicating respect for them, or even kind of recognition of committed relationships.[24]

---

[20] New Testament scholar Victor Paul Furnish has noted that Romans 1:26-27 is "the only place in the New Testament where there is as much as one complete sentence about same-sex intercourse—and the only place in the entire Bible where female relationships, as well as male, come into view." Quoted in Jeffrey S. Siker, *Homosexuality in the Church,* 1994, as quoted in RLDS Temple School, *Homosexuality and the Church* (Independence: Reorganized Church of Jesus Christ of Latter Day Saints, 2000), 43.

[21] Serig, interviewed by Davis, 8.

[22] Ibid., 9.

[23] Kenneth N. Robinson, interviewed by Paul Davis, Independence, May 25, 1998, 2, typescript, Library-Archives, Community of Christ, Independence.

[24] Robinson, interviewed by Davis, 6.

The committee's report has not been made public. Joe informed me that it was submitted in June 1980 and was more than a hundred pages long. The nine-page section on homosexuality was written by Kenneth Robinson, who, before going under appointment as a full-time salaried Community of Christ minister, had been a clinical psychologist with a significant number of homosexuals among his clients. Robinson had also done quite a bit of professional study in the area.[25] Robinson later served as an apostle (1980-96) and then as a member of the First Presidency (1996-present).

Among the Human Sexuality Committee's recommendations were that the First Presidency continue study of this issue by appointing a Task Force on Human Sexuality. That same year, in November 1980, the First Presidency appointed the recommended task force, chaired by Joe Serig, who was then serving as the Church's Program Planning director. The thirteen-person task force carried over eight members from the previous committee and added five new members: Wayne Ham, Karen Ritchie, Duane Graham, Charlene Sears, and Cassie Cline.

This task force, in turn, created a subcommittee on homosexuality chaired by Otto Elser, which submitted an interim subcommittee draft report on April 21, 1981. Serig recalls Elser as open-minded on the issue of homosexuality.[26] This document was very progressive, as Emeritus President Wallace B. Smith recalled in 1998, "advocating acceptance of homosexuality and responsible homosexual expression." It also left open "the possibility of ordination of gays under those circumstances" and "called for civil rights advocacy for gays by the church."[27]

But a later, undated report from the same task force, while retaining the first and third recommendations, revised the second, saying that only celibate gays could be ordained.[28]

---

[25] Kenneth N. Robinson, interviewed by Paul Davis, Independence, May 25, 1998, Community of Christ Library-Archives, Independence.
[26] Serig, email to Russell, September 21, 2000.
[27] Robinson, interviewed by Davis, 2.
[28] Ibid.

On May 26-30, 1981, the Church sponsored a High Priests/Seventies Conference at Graceland College to foster better understanding on how to minister to the modern family. A total of 445 priesthood members attended, including representatives from Europe, South America, Asia, and Australia. The program included nineteen different classes and several plenary sessions. Roger Bauer, president of Blue Valley Stake (Independence and area west of the city), taught a class on "Homosexuality and the Family," and Joe Serig, in a plenary session, presented a report from the Task Force on Human Sexuality.[29] The First Presidency had approved the presentation of information in a revision of the interim report.[30] The task force had asked Elser to respond if the issue of homosexuality came up during discussion in the plenary session. It did, and Serig recalls "quite a hostile reaction" to the fact that the task force "had even dealt with the issue of homosexuality." Further hostility focused on the fact that the task force had made a distinction between homosexual orientation and homosexual acts.[31]

It seems probable to me that the First Presidency would have rejected the committee's liberal recommendations, even if they had not received a negative reaction from this high priests/seventies conference. Wallace B. Smith recalled in 1998 that the First Presidency simply wasn't willing to move "too far, too fast" on this issue.[32] Instead, ten months later, with input from the First Presidency, the Standing High Council adopted a compromise policy on March 18, 1982, that represented only a modest step forward from the 1962 policy.

Again, the full policy was not published at the time it was adopted. Three years later in March 1985, W. B. "Pat" Spillman, the Director of Adult Education for the Temple School, responded to the question, "What is the Church's current stand on homosexuality?" in the "Question Time" column of the *Herald.* The first two thirds of

---

[29] "High Priests/Seventies Convene at Graceland,"*Saints' Herald,* June 1981, 297, 307.

[30] Robinson, interviewed by Paul Davis, 5.

[31] Serig, interviewed by Davis, 3.

[32] Wallace B. Smith, interviewed by Paul Davis, May 27, 1998, 2, typescript, Library-Archives, Community of Christ, Independence.

the council's document contained history and other background information with the policy in the last third. This was the section that Spillman quoted in his response.

The policy differentiated between homosexual orientation and homosexual actions: The former "is accepted as a condition over which a person may have little or no control; the latter is considered immoral and cannot be condoned by the church." Homosexual acts were equated with heterosexual promiscuity. "In the critical matter of ordination," the policy read, "the church should not admit a practicing homosexual to the priesthood. It cannot sanction homosexual acts as morally acceptable behavior any more than it can endorse heterosexual promiscuity." Celibate homosexuals could be ordained under the new policy, but practicing homosexuals should be silenced "according to church law."[33]

The 1987 edition of the *Church Administrator's Handbook,* included those portions of the 1982 Standing High Council statement that Spillman had quoted in his *Saints' Herald* column, again without the preliminary history and background.[34]

During the 1990-92 inter-conference period,[35] the First Presidency appointed an eight-member Human Diversity Committee, chaired by Gwendolyn Blue Hawks, an African American elder from Kansas City and including an openly gay member, Curtis Filer of San Francisco. I also served on this committee.[36] We drafted a resolution that was adopted by the 1992 World Conference as Resolution 1226. It

---

[33] W. B. Spillman, "Question Time," *Saints' Herald,* March 1985, 30.

[34] *Church Administrator's Handbook* (Independence: Herald Publishing House, 1987), 68; also printed in *World Conference Bulletin, 2004* (Independence: Church of Jesus Christ of Latter Day Saints, 2004), 143-45. The entire 1982 Standing High Council statement has also been published in the Temple School's course on homosexuality (discussed below). See Appendix B.

[35] More technically, from the adjournment of the World Conference held March 31 through April 8, 1990, to the convening of the World Conference held April 4-12, 1992.

[36] Hawks is now a high priest and member of the Standing High Council. The other five members of the committee were Nellie Chun-Ming, Charlotte Willis Graham, Barbara Moore, Thomas Peterson, and Hazel Scott. "Report of the Human Diversity Committee," *World Conference Bulletin, 1992,* 256-62.

acknowledged that "human beings often fear, hate, and abuse each other because of factors such as socioeconomic status, culture, race, gender, age, sexual orientation, and mental or physical disability." Affirming the love of God for all persons, the resolution declared that "all are called according to the gifts of God to them" and urged congregations to create a spirit of openness and peace "where all persons may find acceptance and the opportunity to share their giftedness." (See Appendix C.)

We consciously decided not to recommend priesthood ordination for homosexuals in the resolution itself; but we left the door open for the possibility by including "sexual orientation" and by our strong assertion that "all are called according to the gifts of God to them," and our urging congregations to allow all persons "to share their giftedness." In the 1992 World Conference legislative hearing on the resolution, several speakers complained that this resolution was calling for accepting gays in the priesthood. However, when the resolution came to the floor for discussion and vote, no one raised this objection, and the resolution passed easily with some very minor amendments on April 10, 1992.[37]

World Conference Resolution 1226 is the most relevant official policy statement by the Community of Christ on discrimination. Not only does it supersede the 1982 Standing High Council policy on homosexuality, but it comes from a higher authority—World Conference legislation.

Seven months after the World Conference adopted Resolution 1226, the *Herald* published an article by Leona Barwise, a retired nurse, entitled "Bruised and Brokenhearted." The title is a quotation from Doctrine and Covenants Section 153 (1978), brought to the conference by Wallace B. Smith : "Let the word be preached to the bruised and brokenhearted ... " Barwise recalled the negative comments about homosexuals she had heard from childhood on and her "battle of Jericho" struggle, when her son came out to her, to accept

---

[37] World Conference Resolution 1226 appears in the *World Conference Bulletin, 1992,* 239-40 (amendments, on p. 386) and in Community of Christ, *World Conference Resolutions, 2002* (Independence: Herald Publishing House, 2003), 85-86. It is reprinted in this volume as Appendix C.

the fact that he is gay. She recalled the "spirit of love" among the delegates that she felt during the conference's deliberation of Resolution 1226, contrasting it with the shame and shunning associated with mental illness in earlier years.[38] Controversy erupted over her article. Nine critical letters to the editor were published in 1993 issues of the *Herald.* Kathryn Sacry cancelled her subscription. Duane Porter accused Barwise of asking us to excise Romans 1 from the Bible. E. T. Rockwell advised the editors to not discuss the subject further. Irean Cox asserted that homosexuality is a choice and a sin, while Lorna Smith praised Exodus International, which claims to convert homosexuals to heterosexuality through prayer, Bible reading, and counseling.[39]

The *Herald* also published seven supportive letters. Gary McLean said the Barwise article was long overdue. Enid S. DeBarthe said that "the Levitical and Deuteronomic laws related primarily to sexual exploitation and not to committed, loving relationships." Ray Biller of Los Angeles, a leader in GALA (Gay and Lesbian Acceptance, a support group for Community of Christ members and their families), explained this support and fellowship organization, the first time it had been mentioned in the *Herald.* (See his story, chapter 8, in this volume.) Melba Jean Dixon said Barwise "summons us to free ourselves from antiquated religious laws and concepts," adding, "Christ's example calls us to view others through the eyes of love." (See her son, Mark's, story, chapter 21.) Hal and Rozie McKain thanked the *Herald* for publishing Barwise's article and mentioned their own gay son (See chapter 2). David Baux identified himself as a gay man who had not chosen his orientation and regretted the negative letters about Barwise's article. Damien Scott Markland pointed out prob-

---

[38] Leona Barwise, "Bruised and Brokenhearted," *Saints' Herald,* November 1992, 461.

[39] The critical letters published in the *Saints' Herald* in 1993 in response to Barwise were: Duane Porter, "Paul Bashing," January 1993, 19; Glenn A. Carlson, "Lack of Editorial Balance," January, 19; Kathryn Sacry, "Stand like a Rock," February, 63; Mary C. Bacon, "Condemn Sin, Not the Person," February, 65; E. T. Rockwell, "Leave Subject Alone," March, 106; Irean Cox, "Bruised and Brokenhearted," April, 151; Lorna Smith, "About Exodus," April, 150; Robert L. Wilkinson, "March Letters," May, 195; and Miriam L. Gilstrap, "Preach the Scriptures," July, 287.

lems in Exodus International's claims. Some of those who entered the program "wanted it to be true" because "they had so much self-hatred" but found that "it wasn't" and abandoned it, having only worsened their situation. He also asserted that Paul was wrong on some things.[40]

In the fall of 1993, the First International Women's Forum was held at the recently dedicated Community of Christ Temple in Independence. I have heard women who attended this conference recall it as akin to the Pentecostal experience recorded in the book of Acts. Gail Biller, Ray's mother, presented a well-attended class on "Loving Someone Gay" in which she talked openly about her gay son. Letters to the editor of the *Herald* followed, which furthered the dialogue on homosexuality in the Church press.

In late 1995, the First Presidency appointed a new committee: the Human Sexuality Task Force, chaired by a highly respected retired apostle, J. C. Stuart. Stuart chaired the committee until 1998, when Kenneth N. Robinson of the First Presidency became the chairman. For the first time a gay man (Ray Biller) and a lesbian (Cyndi Sears) were asked to participate in this discussion at the World Church level.[41] At the April 1996 World Conference, the delegates directed this task force to report to the 1998 World Conference. At that 1998 conference, J. C. Stuart, its chair, led a discussion on homosexuality in a delegate session on the last full day of the conference. The comments from the delegates were mostly positive. Don Wiley from the San Diego District, for example, told a moving story about how, when his gay son came out to his parents, he already had his suitcase packed and his jacket on, sure he was going to be expelled from the family. (See Wiley's story, chapter 4.) At one point, Stuart asked all

---

[40] The seven supportive letters in the 1993 *Saints' Herald* are: Gary McLean, "Taking a Risk," January, 19; Enid S. DeBarthe, "Two Touching Articles," February, 64; Ray Biller, "Regaining Wholeness," February, 64-65; Melba Jean Dixon, "In Praise of November *Herald,* February, 65; Hal and Rozie McKain, "Thank-You for Article," March, 106; David Baux, "Firsthand Condemnation," April, 150; and Damien Scott Markland, "Open Debate," July, 186-87.

[41] Stuart's task force included Carolyn Brock, Dennis Clinefelter, Phil Craven, Clive Davis, Jeanne Earnest, Ray Hogue, Sue McLaughlin, Mathew Naylor, David Schall, Jim Slaughter, Blake Smith, and Forrest Swall.

those who had homosexual relatives or friends to stand. I was sitting in the first row of the balcony where I could see most of the delegates; although no count was taken, I'd guess that approximately half stood or raised their hands. Forrest Swall, a member of the task force (see chapter 3), has described this moment in various conversation as the "outing" of the Church. He felt that the discussion and standing acknowledgement "left me with the impression that there is a large body of support from the influential Saints who serve as conference delegates."

Six days earlier on the opening day of that conference, President W. Grant McMurray lifted the spirits of many when in his "World Conference Sermon" he briefly addressed the issue, saying:

> We struggle today with the proper way of expressing the sense of calling and giftedness of persons with varying lifestyles and orientations, including those who identify themselves as gay and lesbian. We often do not speak openly of this issue. Tonight I will. Let me make a heartfelt plea with all of you, whatever your views on this difficult issue may be. In a world that cannot come to common ground on any of the medical, psychological, cultural, and social issues that swirl around this topic, the church cannot be expected to have those ready answers.
>
> But here is what we can expect—that every person who walks through our doors will be received with open arms. We will listen to the life stories of each person who graces our fellowship and embrace them in love. On this there can be no compromise.[42]

Just before the April 2000 World Conference convened, the Task Force on Human Sexuality completed the writing and testing of the lessons that became the Church's Temple School course, *Homosexuality and the Church*.[43] This 102-page collection of materials became

---

[42] W. Grant McMurray, "The Vision Transforms Us," 1998 World Conference Sermon, *Saints' Herald,* June 1998, 232.

[43] Human Sexuality Task Force, *Homosexuality and the Church* (AL365), (Independence: Temple School, Reorganized Church of Jesus Christ of Latter Day Saints, 2001). Temple School courses are designed for leadership education in the Church. Since new priesthood guidelines were adopted in 1985, persons being ordained, whether for the first time or not, are expected to take three Temple School courses considered to be foundational, including a course on their specific priesthood office. After ordination priesthood members are expected to take additional courses from

widely available shortly after World Conference concluded. It contained eight personal stories from gays and lesbians and a section on scripture with analyses from non-Community of Christ New Testament scholars Richard B. Hays from Duke University and Victor Paul Furnish from Southern Methodist University.[44] A section of documents included the 1982 Standing High Council policy (Appendix B), World Conference Resolution 1226 (1992) (Appendix C), and the reports of the Human Sexuality Task Force to the 1998 and 2000 World Conference.

The course also included three videos. One was a conversation with Brian McNaught, *Growing Up Gay and Lesbian,* distributed by Motivational Media, Los Angeles, and the second was *Straight from the Heart,* distributed by Cinema Guild, Inc.[45] A key interviewee in this second video was Wayne Schow, a Latter-day Saint who became an outspoken proponent of gay acceptance after his son became the first man to die of AIDS in Idaho.[46]

The third video, *A Passage Out of Homosexuality,* was a twenty-six-minute production by Exodus International, espousing change therapy. One third of the personal stories and one-third of the videos were from the Exodus perspective. Even though both sides should naturally be presented in an educational course on such a controversial topic, and even though it would be possible to argue that, at

time to time but may select them from a wide variety of offerings. The typical course involves ten hours of in-class instruction with the use of a course book supplied by the Temple School at headquarters in Independence. The Temple School, directed by Paul M. Edwards from 1982 to 1997, tried to maintain quality control by certifying teachers for the various courses. They tried to see to it that teachers of the *Homosexuality and the Church* course were knowledgeable in the area of human sexuality. Temple School courses are offered at locations throughout the church. Local Temple School coordinators are appointed who work with the staff at church headquarters to arrange for courses to be taught.

[44] Four of the stories were from Community of Christ members, and four were from other denominations. Five of the stories could be characterized as affirmative, including all from Community of Christ participants. The three negative stories were from the Exodus ministry.

[45] McNaught is the author of a college textbook, *On Being Gay: Thoughts on Family, Faith, and Love* (New York: St. Martin's Press, 1988).

[46] See Wayne Schow, *Remembering Brad* (Salt Lake City: Signature Books, 1995).

least numerically, gay acceptance had the edge, the inclusion of the Exodus material was offensive to nearly all of the gay members of the Community of Christ with whom I have discussed this course. GALA sponsored this course at a retreat at the Church's Samish Island camp-ground near Bow, Washington, in September 2001; and the response of gay members there was also negative about the Exodus materials. Participants pointed out that even without going beyond other mate-rials in the course, the Exodus claims can be easily refuted. A stron-ger reaction came from some participants who asked if the church would include Ku Klux Klan materials in a Temple School course on racism to "give the other side of the issue." Still others pointed out that the pressure to "become straight"—from family, friends, the Church, and the gay person him/herself—has caused untold anguish, often leading to rejection, self-loathing, and even suicide attempts.

While it is easy to understand why the Exodus materials are up-setting to some Community of Christ members, especially if a teacher chooses to emphasize the Exodus materials as support for the notion that the Community of Christ affirms reparative therapy to make gay people straight, it seems to me that the course, on balance, favors the pro-gay side. I believe that it has probably resulted in fostering an en-vironment of greater acceptance of gays in the Church. I have taken the course twice, once with liberal teachers and once with conserva-tive teachers. Both times, I think that course participants left with the same general orientation they came with, although many seemed to appreciate getting better educated on the subject.

Some gays have told me that they are upset that Community of Christ leaders will issue direct instructions to the Saints on issues they consider important—such as baptizing polygamist men in non-western cultures, ordaining women, or changing the Church's name[47] —but on this issue of basic human rights, the leaders seem willing to appear neutral or only slightly supportive. As a civil rights activist during the late 1960s, I see a parallel in the church's official timidity in both settings. One high church official recently expressed to me his

---

[47] These measures were approved by the World Conferences of 1972, 1984, and 2000 respectively.

own opinion: This issue is sufficiently important that the leadership elite should expend their political capital.

One member of the Human Sexuality Task Force, High Priest Jeanne Earnest of Independence, was concerned about the slowness of church officials to respond to the work of their task force. The 2000 World Conference was billed as "The Jubilee World Conference," in honor of the ancient Jewish "Year of Jubilee" in which every fifty years debts were forgiven, land returned to its original owners, and captives freed.

Earnest recalls waking up in the middle of the night early in the conference week. She began writing a resolution on homosexuality that she would present to the High Priests Quorum meeting at the conference that day, the last day resolutions could be proposed to the various quorums. "The resolves I wrote were fairly mean-spirited," recalled Earnest four years later. That morning she shared her draft with three other High Priests who were also on the Human Sexuality Committee—Matthew Naylor, Sue McLaughlin, and Paul Davis. (See his story, chapter 26.) The consensus of their discussion was that the best immediate resolution of the matter would be for the church leaders to announce a moratorium on enforcing the 1982 Standing High Council policy while the needed dialogue took place. They felt that it would be impossible for real dialogue to occur if some people faced the danger of being penalized (silenced) for speaking the truth from their heart.[48] Many gays and lesbians in the church also believed that a moratorium was the indispensable first step.

When the resolution came up for discussion in quorum meeting, Earnest, as mover of the motion, spoke first. "Then a lot of people flocked to the microphone to speak. I was afraid they were going to be very negative. But almost all of them were standing up to speak in support." Earnest recalls only two or three speakers who took an opposing view, but their criticism was mild. The motion passed "with at least 75 percent approval," she told me.

Gay rights supporters of the moratorium were heartened by the news of the High Priests' resolution and the strong support it had received. They have since been disappointed by the fact that the First

[48] Jeanne Earnest, interviewed by Bill Russell, Lamoni, Iowa, August 5, 2004.

Presidency has never acknowledged receipt of the resolution, much less acted upon it. "It is rather ironic that during the conference of 2000 the word was coming down from the higher authorities that they didn't want this issue brought up because they didn't want to spoil the Jubilee conference," Earnest regretfully told me.

As the April 2002 World Conference approached, two local jurisdictions approved resolutions on homosexuality and forwarded them to the World Conference for action. One was from the Greater Los Angeles Stake and the other from the British Columbia District. The Los Angeles resolution cited various previous declarations of President McMurray and of past conferences, called for a review of the Standing High Council policy of March 18, 1982, and asked the First Presidency "to work with appropriate councils or quorums of the Community of Christ to implement a policy on homosexuality that is consistent with the principles of inclusion, wholeness, acceptance, and the worth of persons."[49] The resolution from the British Columbia District went further and called for the church to "set aside the [Standing High Council] document on homosexuality dated March 1982 and adopt a policy, either written or unwritten, that will permit the full participation of homosexual persons in the life of the church, including, without limitation, the option to join same-sex couples in marriage, where local laws permit, and to ordain homosexual persons who give evidence of living a moral lifestyle under the same criteria applied to . . . monogamous, long-term relationships."[50]

Those supportive of gay rights in the Community of Christ saw few encouraging signs of headquarters leadership as conference approached. The First Presidency had not acted on the resolution submitted by the High Priests Quorum at the 2000 World Conference. The Human Sexuality Task Force appeared to have been shut down by the First Presidency before it could make a recommendation for a change in policy to the World Conference.

But the pro-gay faction was heartened when President McMurray, in his sermon on the first day of conference, addressed the issue at length. He commented:

[49] *World Conference Bulletin, 2002*, 73.
[50] Ibid., 74.

Gay and lesbian brothers and sisters are walking with us on the path of the disciple. They have chosen to be there because they feel God's call to them. Some have struggled throughout their lives with questions and uncertainties about their identity, their acceptability, their status as children of God. Some have dared to tell their story, resulting at times in warm acceptance and other times in cold rejection. Some have come to understand that God loves them unconditionally and embraces them as valued members of the human family; others are not so sure.

Our church, like all churches, has struggled with how to be inclusive, agreeing that God's love comes to all persons, but differing on what behaviors and lifestyles are deemed acceptable. Because there is no social consensus, no moral agreement, no definitive psychological explanation, we have all cast about in search of answers. For some, that answer is provided in one of the seven biblical passages that seem to condemn homosexuality as a sin. For others, the answer is in compassion upon seeing the face of a man or woman who simply says "this is my story." For our brothers and sisters in some cultures of the world, it is not something to be discussed nor is it thought by them to exist in that culture to any appreciable degree. For families and friends the answer comes only in the call to love a loved one, which has precedence over virtually every other call.

Because of these many differences, our church stands in the midst of much ambiguity and inconsistency. We have a twenty-year-old statement from the Standing High Council that serves as official guidance, but that has not been universally adhered to throughout the church. I will be totally honest and acknowledge that I have myself participated in situations where its provisions were not honored. I have been present in conferences where persons I knew to be in long-term, committed homosexual relationships were approved for priesthood in jurisdictions where their lifestyle was known and their ministry was accepted. The conflict within me was between lawgiver and pastor. To enforce the policy would have required me to intervene and prevent the ordination of someone whose call to ministry I could not deny. This I could not do. This I will not do.

In fairness, you should know the hearts of those of us you uphold in leadership. I read scripture contextually. I believe that scripture carries a powerful witness of the love of God but that it has to be read in its totality and not in phrases and fragments here and there. When it comes to people and our many differences, I will always choose to love rather than to judge. My instincts are toward inclusion and not exclusion.[51]

Homosexuality often generates heated debates between church people, with both sides claiming truth on their side, very much like the earlier struggles over race and gender. Therefore McMurray expressed a pastoral concern, reminding the Saints: "This is not a dialogue between faithful and unfaithful people. It is not a dialogue between saints and sinners. It is a dialogue between believers, between disciples, over differences that are real and honorable. I ask us, as members of the Community of Christ, to be willing to share with each other in that exploration."[52]

Some people are not comfortable with a situation in which church policy is not consistently enforced—meaning that some leaders in some jurisdictions support known homosexuals in committed relationships in their priesthood callings, while leaders in other locations are so hostile that homosexuals would not dare come out of the closet if they wanted to be in the priesthood. McMurray asked for patience:

> I ask the Community of Christ to be willing to live with us on the boundary for a while. To do this means that we may not have a policy that guides every decision, but we will have to trust the Holy Spirit to accompany us in our choices. It means that some parts of the church may function differently from other parts of the church and there will be distinctions that are occasionally unsettling but representative of the diversity of our body, both in terms of viewpoints and cultures. We recognize that certain national governments have requirements that our local church leaders in those nations will need to respect and interpret in accordance with their own cultural understandings.

McMurray asked the delegates not to act on either of the proposed resolution [from Los Angeles and Vancouver]. "I will ask the Standing High Council to participate with others in looking anew at

---

[51] W. Grant McMurray, "Called to Discipleship: Coming Home in Search of the Path," 2002 World Conference Address, *World Conference Bulletin, 2002;* reprinted in the *Herald,* June 2002, 8-21. The *Saints' Herald* became the *Herald* with its April 2001 issue, the month the church's name was changed to "Community of Christ."
[52] Ibid., 183.

this matter, seeking issues on which we can surely agree (God's love for all people, fidelity, the value of family, the sacredness of sexuality as part of creation), and shaping dialogue in areas where we do not agree (the blessing of same-sex relationships, standards for ordination, the interpretation and authority of scripture)."[53] In effect he was asking the conference to do what the more moderate Los Angeles Stake resolution was asking for but thereby avoided a debate on the conference floor that could have become rancorous.

Probably McMurray's biggest mistake in his conference sermon was his statement that he had allowed practicing gays to be ordained, contrary to the official policy. McMurray traveled extensively around the Church that summer, including areas of the greatest discontent, thus setting an example of open, though heated, discussion. Perhaps it is not surprising that there was a strong reaction to McMurray's statement from some conservatives, especially in the southern United States, where he was personally jeered during one visit, and in Haiti, where the Church is well established and where at least one congregation threatened to leave.

In September, he attended GALA's annual international retreat at a campground near Jackson, Ohio. For McMurray, this visit was part of his call for dialogue. But some GALA members felt betrayed when, in late September, the Church Leadership Council, after discussion with the Standing High Council, issued a statement entitled "Community, Common Consent, and the Issue of Homosexuality," circulated via the internet on September 27, announcing their decision reached at a retreat on September 15-19. They assured conservative Saints that the 1982 Standing High Council policy was still the Church's official position and that it would be followed.[54] This development was clearly a setback for the pro-gay cause in the Community of Christ, for dozens of openly gay members, some with partnership commitments, had been ordained in recent years; and very few practicing gays had been silenced. It seemed obvious that the Church's leaders had decided to backtrack on the issue, much to the disap-

---

[53] Ibid.

[54] World Church Leadership Council, "Community, Common Consent, and the Issue of Homosexuality," *Herald,* November 2002, 28. See Appendix D.

pointment of supporters of the gay cause. However, this decision did not include silencing any already ordained gays nor taking Church court action against practicing gays and lesbians.

The First Presidency and the Committee on Homosexuality in the Church have adopted the strategy of forming "Listening Circles" in local jurisdictions, in which people engage in dialogue on homosexuality in a mutually respectful manner. Apostle David R. Brock, the committee chair, says the committee "has focused on developing a Spirit-led process to reach common consent in a climate of trust and respect." The Listening Circles are designed to "provide a way for all of us to hear each other. Listening Circles can help trust and respect take priority over disagreement.... The circles are designed for understanding, rather than changing another's point of view."[55]

At the biennial World Conference held in Independence March 27-April 4, 2004, resolutions were proposed from three southern United States districts (Alabama, Southern Mississippi, and Pensacola, Florida) calling on the church to make the 1982 Standing High Council policy "the law of the church."[56]

The First Presidency moved a substitute motion, "Dialogue on Homosexuality," which resolved that these proposed resolutions "be referred without prejudice or specific action to the First Presidency so as to not hinder or limit the continuing dialogue on this issue within the church," that the conference "encourage the use of Listening Circles within all jurisdictions of the church where it is culturally appropriate," and that "the First Presidency report to the 2006 World Conference on the progress of the Listening Circles, along with recommendations as to further steps that may be appropriate to the mission and ministries of the church."[57]

The First Presidency's motion passed and became World Conference Resolution 1279. Therefore the current policy of 1982 tacitly re-

---

[55] David R. Brock, "Listening Circles Implemented to Foster Dialogue on Homosexuality,"*Herald,* March 2004, 28-29.

[56] *World Conference Bulletin, 2004,* 127-30.

[57] Ibid., 291. The 2006 World Conference was postponed until 2007 in light of the special 2005 World Conference, which had the very limited agenda of installing Steven Veazey as church president.

mains in place while dialogue continues. Clearly, the First Presidency is patiently working to build consensus by providing time, space, and opportunities for members' hearts, communicating respect to both the liberal and the conservative factions in the church, and keeping options open while that consensus develops.

GALA's Contribution

Despite the First Presidency's conservative positions taken in its Standing High Council policies of 1962 and 1982, the years following 1982 saw considerable change in the hearts and minds of many Americans, including church members. During those two decades, the larger society began to pay more—and more compassionate—attention to the issue of homosexuality. One force that focused some church leaders and members on the question was the creation of an organization called Gay and Lesbian Acceptance (GALA), which for the past two decades has done much to educate church leaders and members as well as provide support for gays and lesbians within the church.[58] Persistently it has reminded the church that gays and lesbians claim a place in the church and merit being treated with dignity and acceptance.

If one person can be identified as the "founder" of GALA in the Kansas City-Independence area, that individual would be the late Bob Swoffer of Independence. In 1982 Swoffer and a neighbor, Arthur Butler, discovered that they were both RLDS. A friendship developed and Swoffer invited Butler to a meeting at his home. Swoffer had met a former Mormon high priest, Tony Feliz, the Assistant Director of Housing at Park College in Parkville, just north of Kansas City. Five years later Feliz wrote a book, *Out of the Bishop's Closet,* the story of his life as a married Mormon and closeted gay who had served on his stake high council and participated in excommunicating members

---

[58] I am indebted to Allan Fiscus of Lansing, Michigan, for loaning me what may be the most complete set of the newsletters produced by GALA. The first newsletter in his collection is the *Affirmation/GALA News,* a two-page newsletter aimed at Gay/Lesbian Mormons and Gay/Lesbian RLDS.

who were gay and unrepentant. Finally Feliz came to terms with his own sexuality, divorced, and was excommunicated.[59]

Swoffer was an RLDS priesthood member was the primary co-ordinator for the Kansas City chapter of the LDS support network called "Affirmation." In a November 27, 1983, letter to a friend (see Swoffer's account, chapter 9), Swoffer noted that the Affirmation group met twice a month with twelve in the group, ages twenty-one to forty. He identified eight as RLDS and four as LDS, adding, "I personally know about a dozen more local gay RLDS members who are not yet interested in our Affirmation chapter." When Swoffer invited Tony Feliz to a meeting at Arthur Butler's home, the only people who showed up were Swoffer, Butler, and Stephen Hackett, who also played a major role in the creation of GALA. Soon several other people expressed interest and a group began meeting in Butler's home for worship and social events.[60]

Meanwhile, David Gilfillan and others had begun meeting in the Bathurst Congregation in downtown Toronto. Gilfillan and several other Canadians who came to the biennial World Conference in 1984 made contact with the Independence area GALA people. This was the first opportunity that gay and lesbian saints had had for gathering from diverse geographical locations. Invitations were spread by word of mouth, inviting people to a celebration at Arthur Butler's home during conference week. Thirty people attended, about one-third from Canada. "We decided to do some organizing," recalls Ginger Farley. "Some of our friends were dying. The AIDS epidemic spurred us forward. This church we love was ignoring that we have homo-sexuals and some have AIDS."[61] In GALA's early years, two or three retreats were held at the Bathurst Church in Toronto.[62]

In the mid-to-late 1980s, a reasonable-sized group had formed in Toronto, with fifteen to twenty people at most social gatherings.

---

[59] The *GALA Newsletter* for February 1989 included a review of Feliz's book.

[60] Arthur Butler, "GALA History," *GALA Newsletter,* October 1995, 9.

[61] Ginger Farley, telephone interview by William D. Russell, January 2, 2005.

[62] James William ("Larry") Windland, telephone interview by William D. Russell, December 22, 2004.

Most, but not all, were gay. There was some talk of organizing a congregation, but nothing came of it.[63]

During the 1984 World Conference in April, these GALA members arranged to meet again in the fall in Independence. About forty people attended, again including a significant contingent from Canada. In addition to Swoffer, Butler, and Hackett, key leaders included Ginger Farley from Independence, Allan Fiscus from Lansing, Michigan, and David Gilfillan from Toronto. "It was at this retreat that the GALA name was chosen," recalls Butler.[64]

More meetings were held in Canada and in the Kansas City area. Larry Windland, the RLDS Region President for Ontario, was very supportive of the GALA group, and used David Gilfillan and others in various leadership roles, in worship, in church camps, and so forth, "trying to raise the profile in the Toronto area and establishing an attitude of normalcy: that homosexuality is part of who we are."[65]

Memories of those pioneering years are poignant. "Larry [Windland] was fantastic," recalls David Gilfillan. "He began awareness sessions in the church in the area."[66] Ginger Farley recalls being overwhelmed by how loving the GALA people were. "We had all been thrown away by family, friends, the church, etc." She was speaking from experience in making this statement: "My biggest disappointment was with the church. We talk about being loving but we won't love our gay and lesbian members. The church had always been my external family; and when I came out, I lost my family. That is a very ugly feeling—to lose your family over something you can't help. That's the way God created me. That's who I am. Once they found out who I am, I lost them. I lost my sense of belonging. I am fifth generation."[67]

As the group developed in the Kansas City area, Bob Swoffer initially envisioned a Kansas City chapter of Affirmation that included

---

[63] Ibid.

[64] Butler, "GALA History," 9.

[65] Windland, interview, December 22, 2004.

[66] David Gilfillan, telephone interview by William D. Russell, December 23, 2004.

[67] Farley, telephone interview.

mostly RLDS members. In January 1986 the Kansas City people began publishing a newsletter entitled *Affirmation/GALA News.* This newsletter announced that two meetings would be held each month, one a social gathering and the other for worship. Meetings were often held at Arthur Butler's home. The association with the Affirmation organization soon faded away, and the group identified itself merely as GALA.

By the end of 1986, it had become apparent that the worship services were well attended but the social events were not, so the group decided to have monthly worship with a light social event afterward. This first newsletter reported that GALA is "a group formed by RLDS members in Kansas City and Toronto, Canada, to deal with issues unique to them. This includes dealing with the World Church at all levels from the First Presidency to the local congregations."[68] The February 1986 newsletter announced that on March 5 "we will gather to worship and share our prayers and testimonies around the theme of God's purposes for our lives. Many of us have struggled for years with inner turmoil over how we as gay persons fit God's plan."[69]

Causing inner turmoil for almost everyone was the agonizing question of whether to come "out" as a gay man or woman, and to whom one might safely reveal one's sexual orientation. In the early years, newsletters would typically use only first names, to maintain a reasonable level of anonymity. Some participants weren't "out" to all of their acquaintances, and some didn't want to jeopardize their relationship with the church. The group maintained a confidentiality policy: no one would reveal who was participating nor what anyone had said at a GALA meeting. News photos of the meetings were used only with the permission of all those who appeared in the picture.

The 1984 World Conference had been a beginning, and every World Conference since then has been a significant opportunity for GALA members and supporters to meet for fellowship, for worship services tailored to their needs, and to develop strategies for relating to the church. It was at the 1984 conference that delegates accepted

[68] "In Other News," *Affirmation/GALA News,* Kansas City, January 1986, 1.
[69] Bob, "Dear Brothers and Sisters," *Affirmation/GALA News,* February 1986, 1.

what became Doctrine and Covenants 156, calling for women to be ordained and for the soon-to-be-built temple in Independence to be "dedicated to the pursuit of peace" and "for reconciliation and for healing of the spirit."[70]

GALA members were accepting, even enthusiastic, about both of these changes, which seemed revolutionary for a conservative church. After the 1986 World Conference, David Gilfillan, a prominent GALA leader, commented:

> The many events and encounters of the past seven months confirm the process of prayer, Holy Spirit direction, and personal and group response. We know that now is the time for our action in ministering to gay and lesbian persons, their families, and their friends. Many gay, lesbian, and non-gay RLDS members have approached our group and individuals with words of support and desires to help.
>
> Our "visible" members have been led to speak to Apostles, District Presidents and Pastors. These individuals have stated a willingness to spread the word that a support network exists. As a result of our meeting and sharing together, bruised persons are being made whole. Emotional, spiritual, and physical healings are taking place in the nurturing, loving, spiritually positive atmosphere of the group. Healed persons are now responsible for reaching out to others.
>
> We must continue to grow in order that one day all bruised persons are healed. Only upon the healing of all will there no longer need to be an ACCEPTANCE group.[71]

Gilfillan added that Canadian supporters had been found in British Columbia, Alberta, Manitoba, and Ontario; while in the United States, supporters had been located in Missouri, Michigan, Minnesota, North Dakota, New York, and Kansas. The three major geographical areas of GALA at this time were Kansas City, Toronto, and southern Michigan; but before long, California would become a major source of GALA members and leaders. GALA was small, and a

---

[70] Community of Christ Doctrine and Covenants 156:9c, 5a.

[71] David-Toronto, "A Challenge," *Affirmation/GALA News,* May, 1986, 1. At that point, early issues usually listed only the author's first name and city. This author is David Gilfillan.

few people were carrying most of the work and financial burden. Some were getting discouraged and feeling burned out.[72]

A major source of frustration and internal tension throughout GALA's history has been selecting strategies of relating to the church and its leaders. Church leaders are far more open and supportive of gay and lesbian members now than they were during GALA's beginnings in the mid-1980s. In the early years, meetings were held in private homes rather than in church buildings, partly because permission to use a church building was difficult to obtain, and partly because GALA members often wanted more privacy. David Gilfillan recalls, however, that all of the church officials who met with them treated them courteously. None showed hostility.[73]

A meeting on the disheartening side, however, occurred when some GALA members met with Howard S. Sheehy Jr., a counselor in the First Presidency, in 1986 or 1987. The GALA people wanted to communicate the sore need for ministry to the gay population in the church. They described how badly some homosexual people had been treated in the church and argued that homosexuality is an issue we need to be able to discuss publicly. GALA members recall Sheehy telling them that the most important thing in the church at that point was to get the temple built in Independence. He told GALA not to use the church name, including the acronym "RLDS."

The newsletter was using the designation "GALA-RLDS," so Sheehy's instructions not to use the church's name since GALA was not officially recognized by the church had immediate practical consequences. In fairness to Sheehy, the church was then engaged in legal disputes with fundamentalist RLDS groups which had split from the church but who contended that they were the true continuation of the RLDS Church that has existed for more than a century and who still wanted to use the name "Reorganized Church of Jesus Christ of Latter Saints" and the acronym "RLDS." In GALA's April 1988 newsletter, Rod Caldwell defended the use of the "GALA-RLDS" des-

---

[72] "Dear Friends," GALA, Kansas City and Toronto, *GALA: Gay and Lesbian Acceptance,* November 1986, 1. The newsletter's title went through several developments before stabilizing.
[73] Gilfillan, telephone interview.

ignation. He contended that the acronym "RLDS" is not a legal name and that "GALA-RLDS" merely makes it clear that it is an organization whose members are mainly RLDS.[74] But by August 1988 the newsletter dropped "RLDS" from its name, likely due to pressure from church officials, becoming just "GALA," a solution that made no differentiation between the organization and its publication.

GALA suspended publication of the newsletter between May 1989 and winter 1991-92, when Ray Biller, as newly elected president, revived this important communication tool. In the fall of 1997 under the editorship of Jim Barry and Reggie Jasper from Tulsa, Oklahoma. As of this writing, GALA has been publishing a newsletter for more than twenty years; and 587 people received the July 2006 issue.[75]

Tragedy struck early and often in the history of GALA. Bob Swoffer died of AIDS on August 20, 1986, at age thirty-seven. (See his story, told by his sister, and his letter, chaps. 8-9.) "He had been the backbone of GALA and the key person pushing us to organize," recalls Ginger Farley.[76] His funeral was held at the Community of Christ's historic Stone Church in Independence.[77]

Swoffer's death was a major blow to GALA. Associated with Affirmation, he had made the initial contacts with Arthur Butler and Tony Feliz that had led to GALA's formation. Swoffer, Butler, and Steve Hackett were the three men most responsible for getting GALA up and running. Swoffer had helped found the Kansas City Interfaith Coalition, an interdenominational organization formed to support gay men and women of various faiths. On November 22, 1987, the Kansas City Interfaith Coalition had a worship service which included tributes to three who had died of AIDS, one of whom was Swoffer.[78]

---

[74] Rod Caldwell, "If Not 'GALA-RLDS,' Then What?" editorial, *GALA-RLDS Newsletter,* April 1988, 4-6.

[75] Carol Cabin, *galaNEWS* editor, telephone interview, July 18, 2006.

[76] Farley, telephone interview.

[77] Arthur Butler, telephone interview by William D. Russell, October 25, 2004.

[78] "Interfaith Coalition Service," *GALA-RLDS Newsletter,* Kansas City, December, 1987, 2.

One of Swoffer's best friends, Eddy Liedtke, gave the tribute to Bob and concluded with these words that Bob had shared shortly before he died: "The God I believe in is a God of love and great compassion. Homosexuality is not a sin; promiscuity and sexual exploitation between human beings is what we should regard as sinful. God is still the Great Physician, the real Healer for what is wrong between us. We should concentrate on that."[79]

Two other important leaders in GALA died of AIDS in June 1993. Steve Hackett, thirty-five, one of the organization's founders, died June 18. His funeral was held in a Kansas City area funeral home. Two days later Reggie Jaspar, thirty-three, who with his longtime companion Jim Barry had been editing the GALA newsletter, passed away. Reggie's funeral service was at the Tulsa Central Congregation of the Community of Christ.

Possibly as a result of Swoffer's death, GALA encouraged its members to work with the Good Samaritan Project in Kansas City. David Elrod, a GALA member, was assistant director of the Good Samaritan Project. An RLDS member and graduate of Graceland College, David's connections with the college led to "AIDS Awareness Days" there April 4-6, 1989. Speakers included Dr. Laverne Wintermeyer, Iowa's state epidemiologist; Dr. Pat Iverson, pharmacologist with the University of Nebraska Medical Center; Denise O'Neil, R.N., a specialty nurse in the AIDS Ward of Sherman Oaks Hospital in California, and Anthony Baptist, a person with AIDS from Kansas City. There was a large student turnout at many of the activities held during those three days.[80] Especially impressive was Anthony Baptist, who spoke at a large assembly and then again in my sociology class on racism. Baptist was a thirty-two-year-old fashion consultant from Kansas City, who later died of AIDS.[81] Two years later, Graceland held an "AIDS Update '91" on April 8-10. Dr. Wintermeyer and

---

[79] Ibid., 2-3.

[80] Jill Harrington, "Campus Active in AIDS Awareness," *Graceland Tower,* April 7, 1989, 1.

[81] Jill Harrington, "Anthony Baptist lives with AIDS," *Graceland Tower,* April 7, 1989, 2.

Denise O'Neil returned. Tim Gladden, a person with AIDS, was also a guest speaker.

Weekend retreats that were open to all GALA members and their supporters became perhaps the association's most important activity for most of its members. The World Conferences were the other major opportunity for significant gatherings of GALA people from a wide geographical area. Occasional retreats were held in Toronto and in the Kansas City area. Beginning in 1987, regular annual retreats began to be held. They were designated "national" retreats to differentiate them from occasional local or regional retreats that have been held irregularly in Toronto, California, Michigan, Washington, Colorado, Kansas, Missouri, and Illinois. By the mid-1990s, the "national" retreats had become "international retreats." Annual retreats have been held in Ontario, Missouri, Florida, California, Washington, and Ohio.

Permission for the use of church facilities for GALA gatherings was often difficult to obtain; but from GALA's beginning, the Bathurst Congregation in downtown Toronto was used local and regional GALA gatherings, thanks to Larry Windland, the church's regional administrator. In those years, GALA people were sometimes able to meet at the Kansas City Stake office.

A bigger breakthrough came when Allan Fiscus of Lansing, Michigan, received permission from the Michigan Regional President Gary Beebe to hold a retreat at Camp Manitou, near Cassopolis in southwest Michigan, September 5-7, 1987.[82] Beebe has been a consistent supporter of gay rights in the church. Interviewed in late 2004, he did not recall having received any criticism for having let GALA use the campground.[83] As regional president he asked June Freeman, a high priest on the executive council of the Michigan Region, to attend the retreat as a laiason for the regional leadership. Freeman and her husband, Ron, attended and had a wonderful time, became strong supporters of GALA, and remained in touch, sometimes traveling long distances to meetings. June Freeman had an excellent reputation in the church in Michigan, so her enthusiastic support may have

---

[82] "Hello, Friends," *GALA Newsletter,* June 1, 1987, 1.

[83] Gary Beebe, telephone interview by William D. Russell, December 22, 2004.

discouraged incipient expressions of opposition against the church letting GALA use the campgrounds.[84]

A feature at most GALA retreats has been the sharing of personal stories, many of which are painful to tell and to hear. Ray Biller recalls the healing that occurred at the Camp Manitou retreat for the twelve attendees: "We were bruised and brokenhearted as we shared our stories of hurt and alienation experienced within the so-called loving embrace of the church. I cried as they described the destructive paths they had taken after they felt abandoned by this church they loved so much. I saw a group of people who were very fragile and who needed to rebuild from this pain. New appreciation for the worth of each person emerged. The group united in God's love, basking in the healing powers of redemption." (See chapter 7.)

Biller recalls that some wanted GALA to be a activist group in the style of the militant, disruptive, and aggressive group, "Act Up." But cooler heads prevailed, and the group agreed upon three goals for GALA: (1) to accept and affirm the worth of all persons without regard to sexual orientation, gender, race, or religious origins, (2) to offer spiritual ministry to other gays and lesbians through retreats and worship, and (3) to work with the church and help educate it to the awareness of the gay and lesbian members.[85]

Allan Fiscus has been a major player in GALA from its early days until the present. (See chapter 21.) The June 1987 newsletter reported that Fiscus had written and mailed a letter introducing GALA to all branch and district presidents and pastoral care leaders in the Michigan Region, as well as to all evangelist-patriarchs in the church. The introduction went out with a cover letter from Regional President Beebe, explaining the reason for the letter.[86]

Fiscus also helped "open up the work" in California. In June 1987, he and David Gilfillan from Toronto flew to California to meet Ray Biller from Long Beach, who became a major leader over the next decade. Biller served as GALA president from 1991 until 1996, and edited the GALA newsletter for several years. He also planned

---

[84] Ibid.
[85] Ibid.
[86] "Hello, Friends," *GALA Newsletter,* June 1, 1987, 1.

and led many retreats and shared the responsibility with John Billings of planning and leading the AIDS Awareness meetings at World Conference from 1990 until 2000. Many other Californians both gay and straight, also got involved in the GALA organization.[87]

Nick VanAtter's first experience at a GALA retreat was typical of many. Traveling from his home in New York to Berkeley, California, for the 1994 Labor Day weekend retreat, he recorded this testimony:

> If I were to sum up what I received from the retreat it would have to be the word HOPE! As a young man who just came out a few months ago, my comfort zones are not fully developed. I had reservations and anxiety about attending the retreat. I only knew two individuals before arriving, but boy, did that ever change. From the moment that I was picked up at the airport to the time I stepped on the plane to return home, I felt loved! True and sincere love. Practically everyone I met had lowered their inner barriers and allowed me to see who they truly were inside. It was like going to church camp when I was a little rugger, except it didn't take half a week to get to know everyone.[88]

The 1987 retreat held over Labor Day weekend at Camp Manitou in Michigan was important, not only because it was GALA's first time to use a church facility, but also because the group decided to formally organize, elect officers, and approve a constitution and by-laws. Allan Fiscus was elected president and Bobby Phelps from Tulsa became the secretary. Regional facilitators were chosen for the four major geographical areas: Don Weiss for the Midwest, David Gilfillan for Toronto, Ray Biller for the Pacific Coast, and Allan Fiscus for the Great Lakes area. They decided that GALA's "primary purpose [is] ... spiritual—to offer ministry, support, [and] group worship—within the context of connection to the R.L.D.S. Church."[89]

When an oppressed people begin meeting together for support in their troubled world, deciding whether to include people from the dominant group in their meetings can be a difficult question. Cer-

---

[87] Ibid.

[88] Nick VanAtter, "My First Time—With GALA, That Is!" *GALA Newsletter* 5, no. 3 (Fall 1994): 6.

[89] "Consistency," *GALA-RLDS, Midwest Region, Newsletter,* November 1987, 1.

tainly, many gays, especially those who still feel it necessary to stay "in the closet" are uncomfortable discussing their personal stories with straight people. In January 1988, the Midwest region of GALA decided to have an additional monthly meeting which would be "gay only" to see if that attracted people who would not attend an open meeting.[90]

GALA adopted a similar two-meeting strategy for the 1988 World Conference. On Tuesday, April 12, Merrill and Karen Nissen hosted an open house and potluck dinner at their home. On Friday April 15, a closed meeting for gay and lesbians only followed.[91] Twenty-one people gathered at the home of Arthur Butler.[92] However, despite GALA's willingness to be sensitive to members' need for confidentiality, most meetings have been open to heterosexual supporters.

Also at the 1988 World Conference, the Central Washington District proposed legislation on AIDS that acknowledged this severe worldwide problem and stressed the urgent need for "the caring ministries of support reflecting the love of Jesus Christ for all." This legislation also noted: "Great damage is being done by cruel and ignorant statements which interpret AIDS/ARC [ARC: AIDS-related complex] as a divine judgment upon disapproved life-styles." The resolution called for the First Presidency to appoint a broadly based committee to educate the church on the subject and report to the 1990 World Conference.[93]

The fourteen-member committee appointed by the First Presidency included Merlene Swoffer Brush, Bob Swoffer's sister. (Bob had died five months earlier.) It also included GALA members Ginger Farley, David Elrod, and Jeff Hiles. Chaired by Lavanda Booth, the committee's report to the 1990 World Conference recommended that the church (1) become involved in ministry to AIDS patients,

[90] "January Retreat," *GALA-RLDS, Midwest Region, Newsletter,* February/March, 1988, 2.
[91] "GALA at World Conference," *GALA-RLDS Newsletter,* April 1988, 8.
[92] Allan F[iscus], "Hi, Everyone!" *GALA Newsletter,* August 1988, 1.
[93] World Conference Resolution 1201 (April 12, 1988), in Community of Christ, *World Conference Resolutions,* 2002 ed. (Independence: Herald Publishing House 2003), 78; see also *World Conference Bulletin, 1988,* 241-42, 327.

(2) encourage the expansion of sex education, (3) declare that the disease is not a judgment from God, (4) cooperate with organizations giving support to persons with AIDS or who are HIV-positive, (5) support the civil rights of infected persons, and (6) call upon governments to adequately fund research and treatment services.[94]

John Billings, a long-time church appointee minister, is one of the most active and outspoken advocates for including gays and lesbians in the church. (See his "A Story of Grace and Healing," chapter 1, this volume.) He was the planning coordinator for a GALA-related forum or worship service at every World Conference from 1990 through 2000, often sharing the planning and leadership with Ray Biller, who was GALA president during much of that time.

Early on, some members of the RLDS Council of Twelve took an interest in GALA. Apostle Joe A. Serig recalls a breakfast meeting with GALA people in Independence in 1987, which he and two other apostles, Phil Caswell and Kenneth Robinson, attended. Serig also attended a meeting between GALA leaders and most of the apostles during the 1988 World Conference.[95]

A significant number of past and present church officials have participated in GALA retreats and other activities. A partial list would include First Presidency members Grant McMurray, Kenneth Robinson, and Peter Judd, and Apostles Joe Serig, Phil Caswell, David Brock, Linda Booth, Ken McLaughlin, and Dale Luffman, Presiding Bishopric member Paul Davis, and Presiding Evangelist Everett Graffeo. Other highly placed church leaders include John Billings, J. W. ("Larry") Windland, Gary Beebe, Sue McLaughlin, Don Compier, Carolyn Brock, Dick and Barbara Howard, Matthew Naylor, Jack Ergo, Dick Hahn, Hal Davis, Scott Sinclair, Bruce Crockett, Eldred Spain, Mary Kellogg, Sue Sloan, Sandra Colyer, Dave Premoe, Bruce Crocket, and June and Ron Freeman.

The 1992 World Conference adopted World Conference Resolution 1226, which is the church's strongest statement on equal rights and opportunities, and is an affirmative statement regarding homosexuality. (See discussion earlier in this introduction). During the

[94] *World Conference Bulletin, 1990,* 264-65.
[95] Joe Serig, email to William D. Russell, September 21, 2000.

debate, Gail Biller, the mother of Ray Biller, gave the key speech in support of the resolution.

Both church and state in America have refused to recognize gay marriage, leading many gay and lesbian couples to seek some form of recognition of committed relationships in a religious setting. David Gilfillan, who had turned in his priesthood card when he came out, performed a union service for a gay couple during the week of the 1986 World Conference.[96] Gail Biller's husband, Ted, an evangelist in the church, officiated at an impromptu union blessing for Denise Hawley and Nancy Cecil from San Diego during the California Retreat in June 1992. Gail Biller, also an evangelist, officiated at a union ceremony in Clearwater, Florida, on February 17, 2001, for active GALA members Mark Dixon and Guillermo Salazar, both medical doctors.[97] Lauren Hall officiated at a union ceremony for Aaron Sherer and Paul Smith in Provincetown, Massachusetts, on June 1, 2002.[98] At least twenty Community of Christ couples have had "union services" or "commitment ceremonies" where family and friends gather for a ceremony resembling a wedding. When Lois and I attend commitment ceremonies, we recall how inspiring it was for us to have 175 loving family members and friends at our 1997 wedding in St. Louis. We can't help reflecting how sad it is that most gay and lesbian couples don't have the opportunity to receive this kind of public support.

The 1962 church policy had been somewhat liberalized in 1982 by allowing homosexuals to be priesthood members in good standing if they were not in committed relationships and were celibate. But some leaders have felt inspired to set this policy aside to respond to what they feel is God's calling of homosexuals to the priesthood. The winter 1991-92 newsletter reported that Ray Biller had been called to the office of elder (chapter 7), Herrick Carver as a priest, and Nilda

---

[96] Butler, telephone interview.

[97] "Union Ceremony February 17, 2001," *GalaNews,* Spring 2001, 3. See Mark's personal essay, chapter 21, this volume.

[98] "A New England Union Ceremony," *GalaNews,* Summer 2002, 4. Aaron Sherer grew up in Iowa, came out of the closet in 1996 as a senior at Graceland, and then lived in Boston. He and Paul now live in Oshkosh, Wisconsin.

Rodriguez and Dale Shaw as teachers. Ray Biller brought Nilda Rodriguez, who had been homeless for awhile, into the church. They were in the El Segundo (California) Congregation.[99] All four were gay and all lived in California.

In national politics no major party presidential candidate had ever dared to openly court the gay and lesbian vote until Arkansas Governor Bill Clinton did so in his 1992 campaign for U.S. president. The fall 1992 GALA newsletter, edited by Jim Barry and Reggie Jasper in Tulsa, urged readers to support Clinton, noting that never before has the gay and lesbian vote been so critical to a presidential election as in that election: "We are the main controversy over 'family values' and the future of our community depends upon this election's outcome. So, GET OUT THERE AND VOTE, and encourage others to do so."[100]

The next year (1993) Ray Biller went to the March on Washington where over 300,000 gays and their supporters assembled. "Since I have come out as a gay man, this has been the most profound moment of my life," wrote Biller, who was then president of GALA.[101]

At the 1994 World Conference, John Billings coordinated another AIDS Ministry Forum and Gail Biller had led another PFLAG meeting. These meetings were announced twice in the official conference daily bulletins, which meant a lot to GALA people. Grant McMurray, then a counselor in the First Presidency, helped facilitate this visibility with the cooperation of Sue Sloan, World Conference director. After that conference, Ray Biller wrote: "GALA seemed to gain a legitimacy within the RLDS institution which moves us onto another pla[ne.] We were very OUT and visible, and very well accepted. We were sharing our testimonies with many listening with receptive ears."[102] AIDS and PFLAG meetings at every subsequent World Conference have likewise been announced in the official conference bulletin.

---

[99] Beebe, telephone interview, December 22, 2004.

[100] Unsigned, untitled editorial, *GALA Newsletter,* Fall 1992, 2.

[101] Ray Biller, "President's Column," *GALA Newsletter,* Summer 1993, 1.

[102] Ray Biller, "President's Column," *GALA Newsletter,* May 1994, 1.

GALA attained another milestone at the 1996 World Conference when it received permission to share a booth with the Urban Ministries Group in the exhibits area on the lower level of the RLDS Auditorium, where the conferences are held. Here various organizations within the church pass out information and hold informal discussions with those who visit their booth. Thus, GALA was able to share information with conference delegates and visitors. At the next conference in 1998, GALA had its own booth in the Stone Church next to the John Whitmer Historical Association's booth. However, the Stone Church is a block away from the Auditorium and thus receives somewhat less traffic. GALA organizers were thrilled when, at the 2000 World Conference, its booth was located in the basement of the Auditorium next to the registration booth, a highly visible location. GALA members reported that the response from people was overwhelmingly positive; but one evening when the booth was left unattended, someone with a razor blade made about twenty slashes in the GALA poster. This anonymous attack reaffirmed the conviction of GALA's members that much work was still needed on assuring the affirmation and acceptance of homosexual Saints.

The 1998 World Conference was a breakthrough in another way. Grant McMurray had become church president at the previous World Conference in 1996. When he gave his traditional "World Conference sermon" on the first Sunday of conference, McMurray included a statement about homosexuality (quoted earlier in the section "Developments during the 1990s"), which confessed that the church lacked "ready answers" on the complex and troubling question of homosexuality but affirmed that there would be "no compromise" on the expectation "that every person who walks through our doors will be received with open arms."[103] At about the same time, Grant McMurray sent GALA officers a letter expressing his best wishes for the success of the forthcoming GALA retreat, scheduled for church-owned Camp Deerhaven in Florida in September 1998. GALA mem-

---

[103] W. Grant McMurray, "The Vision Transforms Us," 1998 World Conference Sermon, *Saints' Herald,* June 1998, 232. This statement on homosexuality was quoted in Helen T. Gray, Religion Editor, "A Call for Togetherness," *Kansas City Star,* April 30, 1998, excerpted in *galaNEWS,* Spring 998, 3.

bers appreciated every sign of understanding and acceptance from church leaders.

Another means of communication was created in the spring of 1997 when a GALA website was set up as an online brochure. It has since developed to include organizational information; local, regional, and international activities; answers to frequently asked questions; recommended readings on GLBT issues; and informative links to additional resources on gay issues, spirituality, and supportive Community of Christ congregations and mission centers. This website, under the direction of GALA webmaster Meredith Bischoff, provides online outreach to approximately 4,800 visitors.

The 1999 international retreat, held at Camp Doniphan near Kansas City, featured Presiding Evangelist Everett Graffeo and Apostle Linda Booth as guest ministers. Both demonstrated strong support for the goal of gay and lesbian acceptance. Graffeo stated his personal willingness as an evangelist to bless committed, monogamous, same-sex relationships in the same manner that he would bless a heterosexual couple's marriage. Graffeo also gave an evangelist's blessing to the entire group at the closing worship service. During the same retreat, Apostle Booth spoke at a special worship service held in the Community of Christ Temple sanctuary in Independence. Many GALA members deeply appreciated being allowed by the church leaders to hold a GALA worship service in the temple sanctuary. Kenneth Robinson, a counselor in the First Presidency, attended.

At the 2002 World Conference, First Presidency member Peter Judd attended the PFLAG service held Thursday afternoon. Perhaps the most dramatic incident to date in the development between the Community of Christ and its homosexual members occurred at the same conference during President Grant McMurray's 2002 World Conference sermon. Eloquently acknowledging that "our church stands in the midst of much ambiguity and inconsistency" on the issue of homosexuality, he confessed his personal conflict when he had been present at "conferences where persons I knew to be in long-term, committed homosexual relationships were approved for priesthood in jurisdictions where their lifestyle was known and their ministry was accepted." Should he behave as "lawgiver" or as "pastor"?

Should he "prevent the ordination of someone whose call to ministry I could not deny?" Compassionately and boldly, he stated: "This I could not do. This I will not do."[104]

The response among GALA members and supporters, myself included, was overwhelming. Probably not one of us had a dry eye as McMurray gave what I regard as an unquestionably prophetic statement on homosexuality. (See earlier discussion.) However, many conservatives in attendance were angry at this affirmative presidential statement. McMurray fielded many challenging questions in post-conference contacts.

In September 2002, President McMurray attended the annual GALA international retreat held at Camp Bountiful, near Jackson, Ohio. GALA people were very happy to have the president in attendance at a GALA retreat, and McMurray seemed comfortable and in good humor throughout the weekend. Some GALA people felt betrayed when, the next month, the World Church Leadership Council issued a statement reaffirming the 1982 Standing High Council policy: "As we continue this exploration we want the church to know that we will follow the provisions of the 1982 guidelines regarding calling and ordination." In essence, it restated that no new ordinations would be authorized for homosexuals who were not celibate. As a compromise, it indicated that current priesthood would be respected.[105]

It turned out that McMurray's April World Conference sermon had been a personal statement that he had not shared beyond his two counselors, Ken Robinson and Peter Judd, while the October statement was a joint statement by the First Presidency, the Council of Twelve, the Presiding Bishopric, the President of the Presidents of Seventy, the President of the High Priests' Quorum, and the World Church Secretary. It was thus impossible for GALA people to discern whether the backtracking represented McMurray's second thoughts or his yielding to pressure from the other leaders. Certainly McMur-

---

[104] W. Grant McMurray, "Called to Discipleship: Coming Home in Search of the Path,"2002 World Conference Address, *World Conference Bulletin, 2002,* 182.
[105] World Church Leadership Council, September 2002, "Community, Common Consent, and Homosexuality," *Herald,* November 2002, 28.

ray had received a lot of negative and often hostile criticism since
World Conference, much of it from the American South.

Over the protests of some church members, conference organizers
also gave GALA a booth at the 2004 World Conference, a heartening
sign. Whatever GALA people thought of the conservative step of reis-
suing the 1982 statement, most felt that they had lost a sympathetic
friend when McMurray unexpectedly resigned as church president
on November 29, 2004. The special World Conference held in June
2005 endorsed the Council of Twelve's recommendation that Apostle Steve Veazey, president of the Quorum of the Twelve, to be the
new prophet-president of the Community of Christ. Veazey is an un-
known quantity to GALA people generally, so it remains to be seen
if he will feel a need to mend fences with the conservative segment
of the church or whether he will continue McMurray's sympathetic
outreach that had moved the church in significant ways toward "gay
and lesbian acceptance," the goal of the GALA organization.

One important recent development from within GALA has been
a move toward involvement in the Welcoming Church Movement. In
April 2001, a small group gathered for a retreat at the Community of
Christ's Berkeley Peace Chapel. A key discussion at this retreat was
the Welcoming Church Movement, and participants were encouraged
by the possibility of starting a similar movement for the Community
of Christ. John Billings began to research and gather resources for the
project.

In January 2002, another group met for further discussion of the
matter. All were excited and hopeful about this possibility. Over several months, a number of meetings were held in Independence, Chicago, and Kansas City with different people attending from around
the country (members of GALA, parents, church leaders, pastors,
etc.). Gradually, a core group developed that took the lead in moving the Welcoming Program forward and developing what has now
become the Welcoming Community Network. John Billings and Arthur Butler, then GALA president, became co-coordinators. Susan
Cochran and Arthur Butler attended their first meeting with the National Welcoming Church Program Leaders and received a warm invitation to join with them. Billings reports that the relationship with

WCPL has been "an incredible blessing. The support they have given to our early beginnings enabled us to shape the Welcoming Community Network into a viable ministry."[106]

Many meetings and many document drafts followed in which purpose and mission statements developed, a process for becoming a Welcoming Church emerged, a brochure was created, and an information packet became available. In the summer of 2002, the first informational seminar was held at Graceland University during the Congregational Leaders Workshop. Committee members also shared information at the church's Appointee Field Leaders meetings, at meetings with the First Presidency, and at GALA retreats between 2002 and 2005. *galaNEWS* also carried extensive news and information about the development of the Welcoming Community Network. The WCN officially began in June 2003 at a World Church event called "Launch Out." John Billings and Arthur Butler held an informational workshop with about fifty enthusiastic people. Since June 2003, many people have been involved in meetings, fine-tuning information, attending training sessions, and working with congregations in the hope that they can make a different in helping Community of Christ congregations become open and welcoming to everyone, including persons of all sexual orientations and gender identities.

In the fall of 2002, GALA made a commitment to provide financial support for the work of developing the Welcoming Community Network. GALA has continued to offer this support to the present. In the fall of 2003, GALA hired Sharon Troyer to assist with program needs, and she became the key leader for the Welcoming Community Network. Sharon's leadership and the work of other GALA board members has been a key factor in establishing WCN as a ministry with potential and opportunities. In addition, under Sharon's leadership, they continued to be part of Welcoming Church Program Leaders and have been asked to be leaders with them in this national movement. Their relationship with the Lutheran "Reconciling in Christ" welcoming program has been particularly helpful to the WCN. "It is a wonderful gift to be involved with a national movement that is making a huge difference in creating a welcoming and open spirit in our

---

[106] John Billings, email to Bill Russell, July 26, 2006.

respective church communions," comments Billings.[107] Effective February 2006, the Welcoming Church Network became independent of GALA as a nonprofit organization.

At Graceland, 1995-Present

There have been other positive developments for gays in the Church. At the February 1996 Theology Colloquy, jointly sponsored by the Department of Religion at the Church-sponsored Graceland College (Graceland University since 2000) and the First Presidency, Aaron Sherer, a senior at Graceland, presented an eloquent paper on homosexuality that Herald House published in the colloquy's proceedings. Sherer discussed how difficult it had been "to face the realization than an aspect of my existence is cause for many to hate me." That fear extends to family, friends, and members of his faith community. He deplored the fact that the church "has adopted a position on homosexuality that would require me to practice life-defeating behavior to be 'accepted.'" As a result, "the church has identified the moral choice as a life without intimacy."[108] No student has ever "outed" himself in such a public way at Graceland to my knowledge. Sherer has been the editor of *galaNEWS* and GALA's secretary. He is one of the most articulate and outspoken advocates for gay rights and respect in the Community of Christ.

Several recent developments at Graceland College suggest that changes in attitude at the church's college have occurred. In the fall of 1995, C. Robert Mesle, professor of philosophy and religion, proposed a resolution which the faculty adopted by a large majority. It recommended the addition of "sexual orientation" to the list of categories of people that Graceland pledges not to discriminate against in its Affirmative Action Statement, published in its official catalog.[109]

---

[107] Ibid.

[108] Aaron Sherer, "The Redemption and Reconciliation of One Gay RLDS Member," in *Theology, Volume 4: Justice or Just Us?*, edited by Richard A. Brown (Independence: Graceland/Park Press, 1996), 96.

[109] Mesle's proposal would have added two words, "sexual orientation," to the catalog's Affirmative Action Statement: "It is the policy of Graceland College to extend equal opportunities to all applicants for employment, to all employees seeking ad-

The resolution was sent to the board of trustees. Disappointingly, the board adopted alternative language which merely added a general statement of nondiscrimination and did not include sexual orientation at all. Gay activist Michael Lewis, class of 1990 and a member of the Alumni Council, mobilized council members to ask the board of trustees to reconsider. Meanwhile, the board's legal counsel advised against including the general language because it could raise new problems. Two years passed before the trustees reconsidered the issue. A few days prior to the board meeting, the faculty again voted on the matter, asking the board to adopt the 1995 faculty resolution. This time the vote was counted, and the faculty approved the Mesle proposal by a vote of 48 to 8 (83%). Most of the eight negative votes came from faculty members who were either members of the LDS Church or of the various Restoration Branches—fundamentalist churches which have split from the Community of Christ since 1984.[110] A few days after the faculty meeting vote, the board adopted the Mesle proposal.

Another sign of change was the creation of a student organization on campus, the Gay/Straight Alliance. Begun in the 1997-98 school year by a Russian student, Andrei Dzhunkovsky (see chapter 19 by Hal McKain, "Graceland's Andrei"), this group met somewhat secretly for the first year. In its second year, the group met in a visible location in the Memorial Student Center on campus and often attracted twenty or more attendees at its regular Monday night meeting. About a hundred students, including some faculty and administrators, attended a midnight vigil in memory of Matthew Shepard shortly after he was fatally beaten and hung on a fence to die a slow

---

vancement, and to all students who apply for enrollment who meet the basic criteria established. It is further the policy of Graceland College not to discriminate against any employee, prospective employee, student, or prospective student, on the basis of race, color, religion, age, sex, national origin, sexual orientation, or disability." Graceland College Faculty Meeting Minutes, November 2, 1995. (The college's name was changed to Graceland University in June 2000.)

[110] At the time there were three LDS and five Restoration Branch faculty. Most of them were on record publicly in opposition to the proposal, but it is not necessarily true that these eight all voted in the negative.

death in the Laramie, Wyoming, countryside.[111] The group is well known and respected at Graceland, although there are occasional incidents of verbal harassment.

As of this writing, several lesbian couples have come out at Graceland, but gay men are more cautious. The men's dormitories are still not secure places for gay men. In the spring of 1999, a junior at Graceland, accompanied by five fellow students, painted several homophobic statements on campus. They named a particular student, calling him "gay" and "my bitch." If this graffiti had been the normal graffiti, like "BYU sucks," the penalties would have been light; however, Graceland's Council on Student Welfare took the strong position that this was a hate crime. The penalties were severe: a heavy fine, many hours of community service, being banned from all campus dormitories, and writing a letter of apology. The junior who had led the graffiti spree, who happened to be a Latter-day Saint, decided not to return to Graceland for his senior year.

Another controversy on campus over the gay rights issue occurred in 2001 when Mesle brought another motion to the faculty meeting, this one proposing a domestic partnership policy by which Graceland would give the same benefits, such as health insurance, to committed gay and lesbian couples that married couples receive. The Faculty Meeting on May 22, 2001, adopted his resolution, slightly amended. The motion as passed called for "an exploration of the adoption of a domestic partner policy which would grant committed, and properly registered, same-sex couples at Graceland, the same rights and privileges as married couples. This would include benefit packages for employees, and access to married student housing for students." The resolution also called for the administration "to work with the faculty and others during the upcoming academic year to create a community-wide time of education, dialogue, and exploration of the larger issues of human sexuality, human dignity, and mutual respect which must underlie any action like a domestic partner policy."[112]

---

[111] Steve Lopez, "To Be Young and Gay in Wyoming," *Time,* October 28, 1998, 38-40; Jon Barrett, "The Lost Brother," *The Advocate,* November 24, 1998, 27-30.

[112] Graceland University Faculty Meeting Minutes, May 22, 2001, 3.

The called-for dialogue was delayed for a year because of a transition of administrative leadership at Graceland; but in the 2002-03 academic year, a committee was created to plan a series of dialogues on campus. The first dialogue was to focus on scripture and occurred on October 24, 2002. Dr. Richard Draper from Brigham Young University, an expert in ancient Israelite law, was brought in to present the conservative view. He appeared with Dr. Howard Booth, retired religion professor at Graceland, whose interests are in contemporary theology rather than scripture. An interesting dialogue occurred with both men showing considerable respect for the other.

The second dialogue was held on November 21, 2002. It focused on the personal stories of four gay men. Two described how they had accepted their sexual orientation, and two reported that they had changed their orientation from homosexual to heterosexual through religious counseling, prayer, scripture study, and so forth. On the affirmative side was Rob Stephens, an art faculty member, who brought his partner, David Demelo, with him, and Tom and Vikki Morain, who read a letter from their son, Michael, who had come out as a gay man one year earlier, just before graduating from Graceland, where he was the student body president. The two conservative presenters were not Gracelanders. Chad Thompson was a media specialist from the Iowa Family Policy Center, and Jack Morlan was director of Exodus International and Freedom Ministries.

The third dialogue was to appraise the scientific evidence. Dr. Clive Davis, a Graceland alumni and retired Syracuse University professor of human sexuality, presented an overview of the scientific evidence on February 27, 2003. Dr. Paul Cameron from Colorado was to lecture a week later. When Davis arrived on campus, he was shocked when he learned of the invitation to Cameron. Davis said that there are lots of legitimate conservative scholars on the issue of homosexuality but that Cameron was not one. "He crosses the line into hate speech," said Davis. The committee sponsoring the debates respected Davis's opinion and withdrew the invitation to Cameron, later inviting Dr. A. Dean Byrd to give a conservative perspective on the scientific evidence. Byrd was adjunct faculty at the Department of Family and Preventive Medicine, the University of Utah School of

Medicine, and the former staff member with responsibility for homosexual issues in the LDS Church's Welfare Services Department. Like Draper earlier, Byrd's lecture seemed to be appreciated by people on both sides of the issue. Most gay supporters felt that Byrd's scholarship was reasonable, even though they disagreed with him on some issues.

Some of the anti-domestic policy faction were unhappy with the withdrawal of the invitation to Cameron, seeing it as a denial of free speech. As a result, local Baptists and Restoration Branch churches decided to invite him to Lamoni for a series of speeches. Cameron spoke at the Lamoni Community Center several times on Tuesday and Wednesday, April 22-23, 2003. His final speech was on Wednesday night at the First Baptist Church of Lamoni during the regular Wednesday evening worship hour. The Gay/Straight Alliance students decided to protest Cameron's appearance in Lamoni by picketing his evening lectures on Tuesday and Wednesday evening. The *Des Moines Register* published a news story on the controversy.[113] KCCI News, the CBS affiliate in Des Moines, ran two stories on the student protest. Its second story was a live broadcast from the Lamoni Community Center on the evening news.

Asked why he allowed Cameron to speak at his church, Pastor Scott Kallem told the *Des Moines Register,* "I feel we need to let Dr. Cameron come.... My concern is that they're not willing to sit and listen."[114] On both nights approximately sixty persons picketed Cameron's lecture, with about half of the Wednesday night crowd being new participants. More than a dozen students and some faculty also sat in on Cameron's lecture as well as picketing before and after the speech. The demonstrators were mostly students, but also included Barbara Higdon, Graceland's retired president; Orville Hiles, the former mayor of Lamoni; Bill Morain, a member of the Lamoni School Board member and a medical doctor; and sixteen faculty and staff from Graceland, including Dave Devonis, Priscilla Eppinger, Steve Glazer, Jo Logan, Susan Maroldo, Sherry Morain, Tom Morain, Lin-

---

[113] Madelaine Jerousek, "Psychologist to Talk in Lamoni after All," *Des Moines Register,* April 23, 2003, 1B.
[114] Ibid.

da Mountenay, Bill Norman, Bill Russell, Brian Smith, Rob Stephens, David Twomley, and Jon and Nancy Wallace. Also present was Rich Eichener, a prominent gay rights advocate from Des Moines.

The committee sponsoring the dialogues could not, of course, control what faculty members do in the classroom. One faculty member, who had recently served as an LDS bishop, Kimball Clark, invited Cameron to give a lecture on homosexuality in his Computer Applications class at Graceland. Since there was no relation between Cameron's homosexuality lecture and computer applications, many faculty and administrators believed this to be an improper use of classroom time.

The controversy stirred up a vigorous debate in the letters column of the local newspapers; the *Lamoni Chronicle* and the *Graceland Tower.* Students who wrote letters in the university newspaper were almost all supportive of the proposed domestic partner policy. Older letter writers usually published their letters in the local *Lamoni Chronicle.*[115] The *Chronicle* letters were about evenly split, with the dividing line being between conservative, fundamentalist church people (LDS, Restoration Branch saints, and Baptists), while Community of Christ members and those outside the Latter Day Saint tradition were almost entirely supportive.[116]

---

[115] *Lamoni Chronicle* published these letters: Graceland biology professor Gaylord Shaw wrote a strong criticism of the street protest, "Is This the Way We Do It Now?" May 1, p. 8. My letter, "The Public Needs to Be Aware" appeared on the same page. The following week's issue, May 8, pp. 6-7, carried four letters from local Restoration Branch members criticizing the street protest: Rob Rolfe, Decatur County magistrate, "It's a Strange World"; Mildred Smith, "Perturbed over Perception; John E. Colyer, "What Is the Truth?", another letter from Gaylord Shaw, "Points of Clarification," and one from Sandra Crandell, an elder in the Community of Christ. Two letters supported the protests (p. 6), one from Noah Lawrence, a social studies teacher at the Lamoni High School and one from Alicia Claypool, a Graceland student. The following issue, May 15, p. 6, included my "Response to Last Week's Letters," one from Unitarian David C. Devonis, a Graceland psychologist who had participated in the march; and two anti-demonstration letters, one from George Galusha, the most active anti-gay activist in Lamoni, "What It's All About," and another from John E. Colyer, "The Choice Is Yours to Make!"
[116] *The Tower,* Graceland University's weekly student paper, on May 2, published a front-page news story, "Speaker Protested in Lamoni," with a photo of ten faculty

The faculty had already approved the domestic partner policy on December 9, 2002, more than four months before this fuss occurred in April. At that meeting, the faculty discussed the proposal as a committee of the whole for one hour, before going into a legislative session on the issue. The most outspoken opponent of the proposal was a professor of finance, Yvonne Galusha, who gave an impassioned PowerPoint presentation to the faculty, setting forth the usual biblical passages used by anti-gay spokespersons. When the faculty went into legislative session, they voted down a motion to delay the vote until April, when the dialogue sessions would be over, and passed the domestic partner policy by an overwhelming margin. The anti-gay faction had been vocal on issues of homosexuality for several years, but it had not gained any new support. The faculty had heard enough and wanted to vote on it and be done with the matter. There was no call for a counted vote, but it appeared that only about ten voted in the negative—about 12 percent.

The faculty also voted on whether to include giving same-sex couples access to married student housing as part of their recommendation to the board. This recommendation was voted down 33-37.[117] Many supporters of the domestic partners' policy voted against applying it to married student housing so as not to muddy the waters at that time. The question was somewhat academic in any case: Graceland has only a handful of apartments for married students, and they are not very attractive.

---

members participating in the demonstration: Barbara Higdon (former university president, retired and teaching literature part-time), Brian Smith and David Devonis (psychology professors), Steve Glazer and Bill Russell (history), Priscilla Eppinger (religion professor and ordained American Baptist minister), Bill Norman and Nancy Wallace (sociology), Rob Stephens (art), and Susan Maroldo (speech). No letters were published opposing the demonstration but four supportive letters were included: Bill Russell, "Debating Paul Cameron," 2; Bill Norman, "Response to Paul Cameron," 2; and students Jeremiah Johnson, "Issues of Homosexuality," 2, and Karen Rohrer, "A Call to Human Beings," 3. The following week on May 9, p. 3, William A. King from Oklahoma, wrote "I'm Not Just Whistlin' Dixie!" protesting against the sign carried by Devonis, which read, "Take It Back to Dixie."

[117] Graceland University Faculty Meeting Minutes, December 9, 2002, 1.

The board of trustees, in considering the domestic partners' policy, decided to handle the issue quietly. Rather than pass a resolution approving the faculty's recommendation, the board simply clarified that domestic partnership rights for employees are clearly implied in the 1997 policy which forbids discrimination on the basis of sexual orientation. The board instructed Graceland President John Menzies to grant domestic partnership rights when an employee makes a legitimate claim to be in a committed monogamous relationship similar to that of heterosexual married couples.

Action by Individual Jurisdictions

On the matter of ordination, some officers in various jurisdictions of the Community of Christ have chosen not to follow the conservative 1982 policy. During the discussion at the 1996 Theology Colloquy prompted by Aaron Sherer's paper, John Billings, regional administrator for the East Central States Region, stated that as a matter of conscience he would engage in "ecclesiastical disobedience" and not enforce the church's policy of silencing gay priesthood.[118] At prayer and testimony service at the St. Louis Stake Reunion in June 1997, a few days after he had been set apart as the new stake president, Billings said that if there is not a place in the church for gays and lesbians, he would leave church appointment. The audience warmly applauded his testimony.[119] From anecdotal reports and personal conversations, it is quite clear that a number of other church administrators, like Billings, are not willing to silence gay priesthood members or eliminate them from consideration for ordination and service, simply for being in a committed same-sex relationship.

Several Church jurisdictions have knowingly ordained gays. The earliest case I know about of an openly gay person being approved for ordination was Ray Biller, ordained in Los Angeles Stake in 1990. (See chapter 7.) I also know about congregations in Michigan, New York, Minnesota, Missouri, Massachusetts, and California, where known gay men or women are actively involved in the priesthood,

---

[118] I was present when Billings made this statement.

[119] My wife, Lois, and I were both present on this occasion.

in some cases as the pastor or as a member of the congregation's pastorate. At this writing in the summer of 2006, I personally know of thirty committed same-sex relationships involving church members, and there are well over a dozen priesthood members who are in open, committed relationships. Many more out-of-the-closet homosexuals are in the priesthood but not in a relationship, which is acceptable under the 1982 policy.

Some congregations have officially shown openness and respect for homosexuals in other ways. In 1994 in Boise, Idaho, a local gay church—the Metropolitan Community Church—was having a difficult time securing a regular place of worship. It had rented several facilities, only to have leases cancelled or not renewed when pressure was brought to bear on the landlord. Even Boise State University, a state school, refused to let MCC rent the campus chapel. A common joke among the MCC members was that you had to be at church each Sunday to find out where to meet the next Sunday. When Community of Christ pastor Paul Davis read about this situation in the Boise paper, the *Idaho Statesman,* he arranged to have lunch with the MCC pastor to discuss renting the Community of Christ meetinghouse. They agreed upon satisfactory terms, and Davis took it to a branch business meeting for approval. After a spirited debate in which virtually everyone spoke, including several teenagers, Davis's resolution passed by seven votes, 31-24. One teenager stated, "We shouldn't keep our doors open if we can't let these people in." A few members were indignant at the decision and quit attending, but only one of them has not returned to church. The rental contract has been renewed every year since that time, and good relations have developed between the Community of Christ and MCC members, including some joint worship services on special occasions.[120]

Other congregations have gone further and officially decided to be a "welcoming congregation." On October 27, 1996, the congregation in St. Paul, Minnesota, passed a resolution declaring that they "welcome and encourage people of all sexual orientations to share in

_____

[120] Paul Davis, interviewed by Bill Russell, Lamoni, Iowa, August 2000. Also see his story, chapter 26. Davis was called to the Presiding Bishopric at the June 2005 special World Conference.

community life, worship, and sacraments, including leadership and ministry."[121] The choice of "ministry" was a cautious step back from "priesthood." Interestingly, this resolution originated in the teachers' group (in the Aaronic Priesthood) in the congregation. According to the Doctrine and Covenants, teachers are to be peacemakers. Stephanie Shaw was a teacher in the priesthood of that congregation but had not yet come out to anyone in the congregation; and another member of the teachers' group introduced the resolution. Shaw became GALA's president for 2000-02 and has been a member of the branch pastorate at the St. Paul congregation. Her partner has joined the church. Other "welcoming congregations" include the Basileia Congregation in Orange County, California, and the Peace Chapel in Kansas City, Missouri.[122] I know of other congregations where openly gay men and women are welcome and accepted, but statistics are not currently available.

A number of Community of Christ officials in California came out publicly, but as individuals rather than as church officials, against Proposition 22 in the March 2000 referendum in that state, which affirmed that California recognizes only heterosexual marriages. Scott Sinclair, then president of the Greater Los Angeles Stake, was one who signed a public declaration against the proposition. He recalls that several other Community of Christ pastors in the Los Angeles area also signed the declaration.[123]

As of this writing, Massachusetts alone among the fifty states in the United States formally recognizes same-sex marriage, with the State of Washington poised to follow suit. A goodly number of "union services" or "commitment ceremonies" have occurred in which gay or lesbian members of the Church have expressed their commitment to each other before God and their family and friends. The first union service for a gay couple of which I am aware was held in October 1986 in Independence, with a reception afterward at Arthur Butler's home. The *Salt Lake Tribune* ran a story in the summer of 1993 on

---

[121] Stephanie Shaw, "My Inclusive Congregation," *galaNEWS*, Fall 1998, 4-5.

[122] I have attended all three congregations, including a fourth at Berkeley, California (now defunct), and have preached at the two in California.

[123] Scott Sinclair, interviewed by Bill Russell, Lamoni, Iowa, August 2000.

the commitment ceremony of Elaine Hines and Dee Carver, held in Kansas City, Missouri, with 150 friends in attendance. Elaine's father, Elder David Hines, conducted the ceremony.[124] Although the Community of Christ does not officially recognize such services, they are becoming more common. Lois and I have received invitations to six such ceremonies since 1999. Some GALA members have been invited to many more than that.

At first I was surprised by the depth of appreciation in the gay and lesbian couples to whom I have expressed support for their relationship. But I suppose it is not surprising in light of the fact that most same-sex couples are denied opportunities to publicly express love and support in the same way that heterosexual couples enjoy when they publicly declare their love and lifelong commitment. Silence is often required instead. I often think of the contrast with my own marriage. Lois and I began our wedding by entering the church together and greeting with handshakes, hugs, and kisses the 175 relatives and friends assembled in the Unity Lutheran Church in St. Louis, Missouri. It was the best part of the wedding service for us, because the support of these dear ones is so important for us. We grieve for our gay friends who are denied a similar experience.

Conclusion

The conflict perspective, taught in social science courses, holds that dominant groups in society produce social mores and customs that reinforce their supremacy. Given the fact that religion is a powerful force in human society—witness the use that U.S. President George W. Bush has made of religion, for example—it appears to be no accident that for centuries women and gays have been shut out of the leadership of religious institutions. As a result, straight male dominance of society was not threatened by women and gays in powerful positions in the religious institutions of society. I strongly disagree on moral and ethical grounds with this exclusion of a group

---

[124] Susan Ager, Knight-Ridder News Service, "RLDS Elder Changes Views after Lesbian Ceremony," *Salt Lake Tribune,* July 3, 1993.

of people with valuable and much-needed abilities, who could make important contributions to society.

As this book goes to press, the Community of Christ continues to work on developing a new policy on homosexuality. For many of the pro-gay faction, no policy is the preferred option, as it allows the Church to be sensitive to the host culture in various parts of the world. In liberal jurisdictions the Community of Christ can ordain openly gay men and women to the priesthood, if they meet the same moral standards with regard to sexuality that is expected of heterosexuals—meaning monogamous relationships. In other places, where the culture is hostile to homosexuality, there will be no known gays in the priesthood, but an official liberal policy might very well alienate church members in those jurisdictions.

What follows are stories of men and women in the Community of Christ tradition who are gay or lesbian, or who are family and friends of gays, lesbians, and transgendered people. I believe that these stories will make the reader more informed about a difficult issue facing society today.

1

A STORY OF GRACE AND HEALING

John Billings

In 2006 John Billings retired after twenty-two years as an appointee minister with the Community of Christ. He served as pastor, administrator, peace and justice activist, and helped lead programs in urban ministry. John now continues his ministry with an emphasis on peace and justice and leadership development. He has taught classes on sexuality and has been active with GALA since 1986. John provided leadership in the development of the International Welcoming Community Network an organization working for the inclusive involvement of all people in the life of the church.

THE FOLLOWING STORY is a personal and life-changing experience that has given me "new seeing" for social action and justice—a "new seeing" for God's wonderful world.

At the 1986 World Conference Sherry (my partner, friend, and spouse) and I were invited by Larry Windland, a close friend, to attend a social gathering for GALA (Gay and Lesbian Acceptance). My personal reaction was immediate and strong. I had no desire to attend a potluck dinner with a group of gay people. Immediately I was confronted with all my homophobia. I could remember times in high school when friends and I would travel to a gay area of Houston to taunt and ridicule people we assumed were gay. We thought it was fun. Certainly, we thought it was the thing to do for normal red-blooded American boys. Sherry and I said no to the invitation. Yet Larry continued to encourage us to go. Finally, I relented and said, "Okay." Another friend, who conveniently had to leave early, was going to ride with us. This would be my excuse to escape early, too.

I can remember feeling so out of place, so uncomfortable, as if I might catch something by being around a group of gay and lesbian people. I remember standing in line at the food table actually contemplating if I wanted to eat food possibly prepared by a gay person. We spent a brief time eating and meeting a few people, with the time to go coming none too soon. What a relief it was to be away from that place.

Sherry and I dropped our friend off at his destination and headed to a local restaurant for some time to relax over coffee after this tense encounter. Again, just as if it were yesterday, I remember sitting there with Sherry, thinking about the experience, feeling relieved it was over, and suddenly realizing I had done something terribly wrong. I never know for sure how to explain encounters with God, but this was one of those times. A spirit of love and grace overwhelmed me. All of a sudden I was seeing and feeling things with new eyes.

Still caught up in the freshness of full-time ministry with the Community of Christ, I said to Sherry, "This is not right." I had made a commitment not too long before this to share in ministry wherever called, and yet the first time I was confronted with something difficult and new, I had turned my back and walked away. Actually, I had run as fast as possible. Then, as quickly as the Spirit came to us, I knew we must go back. Sherry and I left the restaurant and shortly found our way back to the place where the GALA group had gathered.

By the time we returned, others had left; and perhaps fifteen to twenty people were still there, getting ready to pull their chairs into a circle for a time of sharing. We were graciously invited to join them. The hour or so that followed was an incredible experience. Sherry and I listened to story after story, filled with struggles and pain, with confusion and discouragement, but also with joy and a love of life. Most importantly, those speaking shared a deep compassion for one another.

In these few moments, I came face to face with what I had feared and found only new friends who genuinely cared about Sherry and me—and in a way I had never experienced before. It was a healing experience. I encountered the love of God in a way that changed my life forever. I would never be the same again. This was definitely an experience of "new seeing." The people had not changed. There were no new sights. The sight was there, in a sense, just as it had always been. The difference was in my seeing. I saw people with joys and struggles just like me. And I saw God actively engaging these people in their joys and struggles. I even saw myself in new ways—as a person accepted in the most unconditional way I had ever experienced. My fear and repulsion were replaced with a wonderful spirit of love and acceptance.

My cup of life has been filled and is overflowing with the relationships that began that night at the GALA gathering. I will never turn away again.

2

ECSTASY AND AGONY:
Rozie's Legacy in the Gay Community

Hal McKain

In 1988 Hal McKain Jr. retired after twenty-two years as a teacher/coach at the University of Northern Colorado. For twelve years he was pastor for the Greeley, Colorado, Community of Christ. Since retirement he has lived in Lamoni, Iowa, where he has ministered to Graceland students and to the Gay/Straight Alliance on campus. He has had numerous articles in the church's Daily Bread. *Hal's wife, Martha, manages Liberty Hall, the Joseph Smith III home in Lamoni.*

1 March 2002 / One year after Rozie's death

ALL OF US have had life experiences that have created highs and lows that exalt and wrench our sensitive souls. How we respond and react to these pressures determine the type of character we become, ranging from strong to weak.

In memory of Rozie, my wife of forty-four years, I would like to share an experience in each category—one of ecstasy and one of agony. Both have to do with homosexuality, an issue that affected Rozie and me during our years together.

The Ecstasy: This experience occurred at her memorial service. Many members of the Graceland University family and I assembled in the Cheville Chapel to be a part of a very special memorial service, one that the students had requested.

The first person to share good memories of Rozie was a student who was out on the campus as a lesbian. She had been active in the Gay/Straight Alliance club on campus and had served one year as its president. She is Roman Catholic.

In addition to other comments, this student said, "Rozie taught me that Jesus loves me as much as a lesbian as if I were straight. And He is one in whom I can completely put my spiritual faith."

When I heard this beautiful statement, I thought, "This student could not pay Rozie any higher compliment." This student had been seeking some serious answers, and Rozie had helped her connect to the Almighty Holy Spirit that rules the universe with love.

I am so proud to have been Rozie's husband! She made my contribution much more effective!

The Agony: This occurred at the near-death of our son. Rozie was up early in the morning, the first one in the house awake, and found a suicide note left by our son, David. I can only imagine the wrenching of her heart at that moment, the panic, and the terror. Her only son, her first-born, her gift of life to the universe. Where was he?

Someone had been telling her son that he was made wrong, he wasn't needed, wasn't understood, and for sure was not believed when he asked in anguish, "Why can't you believe me when I say, as you do, I cannot help having the sexual orientation that God gave me?"

She ran out to the garage. It was filled with carbon monoxide, but David was not in the car. Thank God! She raced to his bedroom upstairs. Where was he? Was he still alive. She burst into his bedroom. Thank God, he was there, still breathing! She rushed into our bedroom, shook me awake, and poured out the situation. I will never forget the feelings of the next few minutes.

After some hours in an oxygen tent that would correct the carbon monoxide in his blood, our son recovered. As we waited in the emergency room, Rozie and I sobbed in each other's arms. The questions churned in our minds: "Why is this issue so life threatening? What has caused society to judge someone like David so harshly?"

Because we realized that we were part of a misinformed generation, Rozie and I strove to battle the ignorance endemic in the gay issue. I had had a significant spiritual experience when I once asked the Lord for enlightenment on David's homosexuality. In essence, the Holy Spirit said to me, "Your son David is different in the area of sexual orientation, and that is okay." That was the complete message. At the moment, I thought, "This is too simple." Then I realized that this was all I needed.

As the pastor in the Community of Christ in Greeley, Colorado, I had received other spiritual enlightenments, such as priesthood calls and prophetic messages to the congregation or individuals in the congregation. All of the spiritual experience came with the same forceful power and clarity. These messages came straight into my mind. I did not hear any sounds with my ears. The thoughts and words were distinct and clear. They never left any questions of accuracy in my mind. I was made to know that they were from the Holy Spirit. This message about David was exactly that kind of message.

When I shared this experience with Rozie, she finally understood the issue well enough to be able to tell a lesbian student at Graceland University: "Yes, Jesus loves you just the same. I know this as a fact. And the Holy Spirit is the source from which you can draw all your strength."

We continued to help Graceland University students, faculty, and staff at every opportunity. In fact, many times we were asked to give class lectures. We always said yes. Once in a while someone would just appear at our door, wanting to talk to us and hear our testimony. These heartfelt experiences were a blessing to all of us.

David graduated from the University of Northern Colorado and successfully completed five continuous years as part of the wardrobe department when the theater was producing *The Phantom of the Opera* in San Francisco. Despite the time that has elapsed since Rozie's death, I feel her humble spirit move within me to want to share with you this part of her testimony. So this then is a testament of a mother, wife, and friend who did, and always will, seek to spiritually spread justice for all of God's creation!

Yes there is some ecstasy and agony in our life and yet in all of this we can become healers of an otherwise paralyzing disease—ignorance.

3

Our Family Journey

Forrest and Donna Swall

Forrest and Donna Swall are both retired social workers. They were active members in RLDS congregations in Columbia and Independence, Missouri, and Lawrence, Kansas, and are now members of the Lawrence Unitarian Fellowship. They have been active members of GALA for more than ten years. Forrest served on the Human Sexuality Task Force for the Community of Christ from 1997 to 2001.

WE ARE PARENTS of three wonderful and loving children, a son, Ron, and two daughters, Tara and Maria. Shortly before her twenty-second birthday, following years of emotional turmoil, Tara, with the help of a skilled social worker-counselor and family friends, found the courage to come out to us as lesbian in her sexual orientation. She had known she was different as early as kindergarten but did not have a name for her difference. She knew that her difference was not okay and that she could not voice questions about her difference with friends or teachers. It was not okay to talk about it with us, her parents. It wasn't until just before she started Graceland College (now

Graceland University) at age eighteen that she was able to name her difference, and she was devastated.

Our hearts ached for our daughter when we became aware of the depth of her pain during her growing-up years. We felt the intensity of her struggle to move from self-hatred and shame to love and affirmation for who she was. Our pain grew out of the realization that Tara had felt she had to make that journey by herself. We weep at the realization of the loneliness she must have felt, believing she could not risk telling us for fear of losing our love and respect. Tara hated who she was; and she believed that, if we learned her secret, we would hate her, too.

As social workers, we had an academic knowledge of sexual orientation, but we had much to learn about what it means to have a family member who is sexually diverse. Paradoxically, getting to know Tara, as a woman who also happens to be lesbian, has been one of the most beautiful experiences of our lives. We had no way of knowing what a blessing Tara's sexuality would have for all of our family. As we came to terms with the startling information of her sexual orientation, we came to know the transforming power of love as we had never known it before.

Through our daughter, we came to know another remarkable facet of diversity in God's creation within our own family. Tara's willingness and ability to show us the way enabled us to affirm her sexuality. The revelation of who Tara was and is has moved us to another level of understanding the human dimensions of God's grace.

Tara was twenty-three when she met Kasey, a wonderful young woman who became Tara's beloved companion and our third daughter. Kasey and Tara have been together now for more than fifteen years. In August 1995, on the tenth anniversary of their private commitment to each other, we hosted their joyous public commitment ceremony. Approximately 200 guests and family members witnessed their mutual commitment of love and fidelity at the Unitarian Fellowship in Lawrence, Kansas.

Our family's journey speaks to the joy and freedom that parents experience when they accept and love their children unconditionally—when they find pleasure in their children for the people they are, including their sexuality. Paul, in his letter to the Galatians, captures the essence of our experience: "For ye are all children of God by faith in Jesus Christ. For as many of you have been baptized in Christ, have put on Christ. There is neither Jew nor Greek, there is neither bond nor free, there is neither male nor female; for ye are all one in Christ Jesus" (Gal. 3:26).

Our family journey became inextricably intertwined with Kasey's family journey, especially her parents, Pat and Read. Kasey's father, Read, initially had a difficult time accepting Kasey's relationship with Tara. We wrote to them, inviting them to stay with us during Tara and Kasey's commitment ceremony. Pat reported that he wadded up the letter, threw it on the floor, and declared that he had no intention of being in Lawrence, period! But eight months later he came to Lawrence with Pat, two of Kasey's four sisters, and a granddaughter. He also attended all of the activities surrounding the celebration, even the ceremony itself!

In the three years following the commitment ceremony, we became aware that Read's feelings gradually became more positive about Tara and Kasey's relationship. He had always been polite and kind, even though emotionally distant, through the previous ten years. Outwardly, he did not appear to be changing. However, Tara and Kasey became aware of a growing emotional closeness, including more frequent gestures of affection.

We believe that a large part of the gradual change grew out of the events leading up to Pat's death in March 1997. Tara and Kasey, with Read, formed the primary care team for Pat as she struggled against the cancer that took her life less than a year after its diagnosis. We were in regular email correspondence with Read. He told us he couldn't have provided the care required alone—that he had needed Tara and Kasey there with him. He spoke tenderly of their loving physical presence and emotional strength, consistently available whenever he needed them.

Shortly after Pat's death, Read sent Tara and Kasey an anniversary card for the first time since the commitment ceremony. He also invited them for coffee at Starbuck's where he hugged them and wished them a happy anniversary! The following spring, Read was diagnosed with a recurrence of laryngeal cancer and died several months later.

In the final days of Read's life, his emails spoke of how much he treasured both Kasey and Tara and how he valued their companionship. Read knew he could count on them to be there for him. As Read was taking his final breaths, he took Tara's hand and rested his head on her shoulder. Read's last email to us in late June 1998 spoke of his love for Tara, telling us he knew Tara loved him. He told us that we could not have given him a better gift than our daughter. Later, a mutual friend told us that Tara and Kasey had taught Pat and Read the true meaning of unconditional love.

We treasure the memories of our relationship with Kasey's parents. It is amazing what can happen when we allow ourselves to transcend barriers of homophobia, bigotry, intolerance, and rejection—when we embrace our loved ones and friends for who they are.

4

WE LOVE THEM, BUT . . .

Don Wiley

Donald J. Wiley of San Diego, California, has been in public service for over thirty-seven years and is closing his career of assisting America's workers as a District Director with the U. S. Department of Labor. He is active in the Community of Christ where he has served in almost every congregational position including eight years as pastor.

AT THE END of 1999, I attended a worship service at a very prosperous congregation. It was a lively yet warm service, and the pastor was sharing his concerns with the congregation about the approaching new millennium. He didn't like it that society had grown more liberal, which he saw as connected to the warnings in the scriptures about society's degeneration in the last days. The pastor then talked about the great value of the family unit and how the increasingly strong voice of the homosexual community was destroying family values. Quoting scriptures, he assured us that homosexuals were good people and affirmed, "We love them . . . but—" The rest of the message was that homosexual behavior was an abomination in God's eyes.

My thoughts went back about ten years to the family room of my own home. It was evening and I was watching TV with my two boys, ages eleven and thirteen. The program we were watching had some actors playing roles of homosexuals. I remembered saying the exact words that the pastor had just uttered. I worked with gay men and knew that they were good people. I actually told my boys: "Gays are good people, but homosexual behavior is an abomination to God. It says it right in the Old Testament." I didn't think I was being judgmental toward gays—truly, I did love them—but their behavior was "an abomination," according to scripture. I said it, thinking that what I was saying was true; but I did not realize that I was accusing my son of being an abomination to God.

My wife and I knew that our oldest son, Alan, was different. He had had a very difficult breach delivery and was literally pulled out of the womb feet first with the umbilical cord wrapped around his neck. For years I thought he was just a stubborn kid. Later I realized he was tenaciously fighting for his life.

In his early teens, he seemed quite rebellious and was difficult to live with. At times he seemed downright defiant. Again I thought his defiant rebelliousness just meant that he was an extremely stubborn boy. Later I learned that he was preparing himself for the ridicule and rejection he would face in the future, once again fighting for his life. As he went through school, he oscillated from being an excellent student at the top of his class to almost failing—the subject didn't seem to matter. It confirmed my feelings that he was stubborn, rebellious, and defiant. He seemed determined to mess up my life, not to mention his own.

In high school he would come into our room late at night bleeding from ripping out a toenail or something like that. We told him that he needed to stop doing such reckless things. Not knowing what the problem was but wanting to help him in any way we could, we finally convinced him to see a counselor. (As he remembers it, he went to therapy to avoid hospitalization. He knew what happened to kids who went to the hospital for being queer). Our constant praying for and talking with him didn't help.

With the third counselor, there seemed to be a change. On January 6, 1994, he asked us to come into the family room. There he sat, wearing his jacket. Unbeknownst to us, he also had a suitcase packed. He told us that he loved us, that we were wonderful parents, and that we didn't do anything to cause it, but that he was gay. He fully expected to be kicked out the house and disowned when he told us he was gay. That was what had happened to the brother of a friend when he came out to his parents.

Weeping, we embraced him and told him that we loved him. He quickly left to see a friend and we were alone, stunned, trying to assimilate the information and ponder the situation. That same day Alan told his older sister and younger brother that he was gay. Their response was less emotional than ours. According to them, they simply said "Oh," and told him that it didn't change anything: He was their brother, he was who he was, and they loved him. His sister was going to college at the time, so she was less impacted than his brother, who went to the same school and associated with many of the same friends. He had defended Alan to his friends before and continued to defend Alan whenever the issue was raised which, according to his memory, was not often.

Alan's mother initially grieved for the hardships that she anticipated he would experience, as well as the expectation that he would not bring any grandchildren into the family. She began crocheting afghans for each of the kids to keep "busy." Together we immersed ourselves in reading whatever articles and books we could find about homosexuality. We also talked to the parents and relatives of others whom we learned were gay. The more we learned and the more we discussed it, the more accepting we became and the more understanding we gained.

We found out other things. Alan had already tried to commit suicide three times. I had done an excellent job of letting him know that we "loved him but..." The message he got loud and clear was that his attraction toward boys rather than girls was an abomination to God. In his words, he felt that I loved who I thought he was; but if I knew who he "really" was, I would hate him. He didn't want to be an abomination to God. Wouldn't it be better to be dead? In counseling sessions he asked to be hypnotized, have regression therapy, or even have a lobotomy—anything that would change him and make him acceptable. He just wanted to be "fixed" (i.e., straight).

Once he came out to his classmates, his best friend of ten years stopped talking to him. Other close friends told him they were sorry that he was going to hell. He was spit on. Others threatened to beat him to a bloody pulp or kill him. He remained true to who he was and tried to help others who found themselves in a similar situation.

Alan states, "What I really wanted to do before I came out was inflict pain on myself in any way possible because I felt like I really deserved punishment for lying about myself so much and I wasn't getting it. That's why I stopped eating, started cutting myself, sewing up the bottoms of my feet, etc. Even through all of this, once I came out, these were some of the happiest days of my life. I finally felt free and didn't feel guilty. No matter what anyone said, I knew I was doing the right thing."

When he realized that we still loved and accepted him in our family, he changed. Prior to coming out, he would play the piano by pounding on the keys. The music was very loud and full of anger. Afterward he began to play with a much greater range of musical expression, in modes appropriate for the individual pieces. He generally had a more positive involvement with the family. Alan said, "For me this was the difference between night and day. Before, I left the house whenever I could, just to be away from the family. Afterwards, I actually enjoyed spending time at home."

The rest of that school year involved a lot of reading and a lot of growing on our part. I began to research more about sexual orientation, its cause, and the impact of negative social attitudes toward those identified as "homosexual." I was not surprised at what I found but was astounded at how blind I had been in the past. I was appalled at studies confirming what had become obvious to me: According to a U.S. Department of Health and Human Services Report on the Secretary's Task Force on Youth Suicide, homosexuals attempted suicide two to three times more frequently than heterosexuals. Studies done over the past twenty-five years in Canada (1997), Belgium (1998), Australia (1998), and throughout the USA (1978-98) all told the same chilling story. But even more profound was the finding that it didn't matter whether teenagers were actually homosexual or not. If others accused them of being homosexual, they were more likely to attempt suicide (1995 Seattle School Study).

Alan was eventually able to tell me that every time I made a statement like "I love them, but..." it felt like a direct physical attack on him. I thought I was doing what every good Christian should be doing—"judging righteously." Instead, I was pronouncing a death sentence on my own son. I thought I was recognizing homosexuals' need to change so they could be what God wanted. I didn't make the simple connection that, if they hadn't chosen their orientation, then God didn't want them different from the way they were. My assumption that they "had" to change was judgmental, a contradiction of the very love I said I had for them. How blind could I have been?

My son helped me to realize that he was who he was, and it didn't matter how he became that way, or that he never had sexual relations with a man or a woman. He was the way he was. He was totally repelled by the idea of making love heterosexually, just as I was repelled by the idea of making love homosexually. Even though he had been bombarded for years with heterosexual lovemaking displayed in the movies and on TV, it seemed totally unnatural and dishonest for him. Because of it, he felt judged by Christianity and society. He had tried to change. He had prayed about it. He had inflicted pain upon himself because he was "bad." He felt rejected and not welcomed in our home and community and church. He saw and still sees church people who would shun him.

5

LOVE YOUR CHILDREN

Lois Irby

Helen Lois (Moys) Irby graduated from Washington State College, married Raymond H. Irby a year later, and raised three children. She joined the Community of Christ in 1950. She has been active in the church. In 1969 she earned the MSW degree and has worked as a counselor for King County (Seattle) Juvenile Court and also as a counselor at Park College in Parkville, Missouri.

MY HUSBAND, RAY, and I have three children, and we love them all very much. Each is gifted in his or her own way. The middle child, Jeanne, came to us in 1971 when she was going through a divorce and told us that she was a lesbian. It was a shock, but we continued to love her and help her through a difficult time in her life.

Speaking as her mother, I think I struggled with this knowledge for several reasons. One was because my own mother was a devoted, conservative Christian, and I knew what her attitude would be. In addition, I had completed an MSW degree in 1969. My textbooks listed homosexuality as an illness. (In the mid-seventies, it was re-classified, as not an aberration, but as an alternative lifestyle.) I sat in

74

psychiatry classes and heard lectures and saw videos pointing to the relationship with the mother as the "cause" of children's problems, including homosexuality. As a result I felt a great deal of guilt. I asked myself over and over, "Where did I go wrong?" Guilt tends to place an invisible veil between people, and they are not as free and open with each other as they otherwise might be. This was the case with me and Jeanne for a short time.

It has also been said, "When the child comes out of the closet, the parents go in." There was certainly truth in that statement for us in our situation. However, we were very pleased with our daughter's choice of a companion. Diane is a kind, loving person, and we could see that they were happy together.

I continued to struggle with total acceptance of the situation. Then one day as I sat in church thinking of Jeanne's giftedness and wondering if she would ever be able to fully use her gifts in our homophobic society, words cut across my brain in italics: "It is not for you to judge. It is for you to love." It may sound like a reprimand, but it was really a reprieve. It was like a fresh breeze blowing away my doubts and fears. It totally freed me from guilt. I knew God was telling me that he unconditionally loves and accepts all people just as they are and that we are to accept and love each other.

My reaction was one of relief and joy. "Yes, I can do that. I do love her." If God loved her just as he created her, it was no longer a problem. I could also accept her just as she was and love her without any reservations. The veil was gone from our relationship. Ray and I have continued to love and support Jeanne and Diane for the thirty-three years they have been together.

Jeanne and Diane have helped each other in many ways. Each helped the other to further her education. Jeanne graduated from law school and has been an attorney for many years. Her companion owns and operates a small business. Because both women tried to conform to the cultural expectations of our society, they had been married. They have helped each other raise the three children those marriages produced. They are loving parents, and those children are now well-adjusted, responsible citizens, who are happily married and have established their own homes. They built strong family ties and celebrate holidays, birthdays, and special times together. Jeanne and Diane are devoted grandparents, and Ray and I have often remarked that we wish we had had grandparents like them. They have taken time off from work to babysit, take the children on trips, help with school work, and attend games, dance recitals, and swimming lessons. They also open their home and welcome many friends. They have a rich and fulfilling life.

When my husband and I retired in 1981 and accepted appointment as volunteer contractual assignees (that is, without salary) for the church, we encouraged Jeanne and Diane and their family to move into our house since we were moving to the Kansas City area. We lived in a "gathered community." There were nine Community of Christ families around the Crystal Springs Church and several more families within a few miles. Gradually, Jeanne, Diane, and their children were welcomed into the community and began going to church. In time they became active workers; and later (in the mid-nineties), Jeanne was called to the priesthood. She hesitated for a time to accept the call, knowing the attitude of some members, but finally accepted it. It was approved by the stake high council and World Church leaders and was to be presented to the stake conference the morning before the stake reunion began. Jeanne's photograph and statement of acceptance were in the conference bulletin. However, a decision was made late on the night before the conference to hold up the call. Everyone who had come in support of Jeanne's call to the office of elder was stunned, especially the members of the local congregation. Jeanne and Diane have chosen not to discuss publicly other details involving the political and personal reactions from members and church officers, and I am honoring their decision in this account as well.

My husband has always said that his biggest problem with Jeanne's lesbianism is because she has always been a very spiritual person, devoted to the Lord and to the church. This incident confirmed his fears that there would be no chance for her to use her giftedness within the Church. He says he feels cheated of the ministry she could bring, and so do I. This rejection, however, has brought our family closer, and Ray and I have definitely come out of the closet.

It has been our privilege to support other parents who are struggling to accept a situation that is not acceptable to many in our society, especially in our religious community. We have reached out in love to many parents and have formed warm and lasting friendships we cherish.

6

BLESSED BY A GAY SON

Gail Biller

Gail Biller and her husband, Ted, are retired educators. They joined GALA when their son came out and are still active in it. Gail has regularly planned PFLAG meetings at Community of Christ World Conferences. She serves on the Spirituality Committee for the World Church. Gail and Ted have both spoken on PFLAG panels at colleges for more than twenty years.

HOW GRATEFUL WE are that God gave us a wonderful son who is gay. Our lives have been changed and enriched by this journey we have been on.

After a long personal struggle, our twenty-seven-year-old son Ray came to us with a friend and shared that he was gay. Ted immediately went to him, hugged him, and told him that we loved him and always would. We all cried together.

There was, of course, a time of adjustment and letting go of our ideas and dreams. When a child comes out of the closet, often the parents go in. They have to begin sharing with the rest of the family and friends. Ray was wonderful. He shared openly with us and answered all of our million questions. We realized the tremendous hurt and struggle that Ray had gone through. It was very important to him to be open and honest with us about who he is. He introduced us to his friends, and they were great guys.

Ray received a call to become an elder. The Greater Los Angeles Stake High Council discussed it for over a year. They wanted to have complete agreement before it was approved. They had Ray, Ted, and me come in and talk to them, telling our stories. The council approved the call, and the recommendation was presented to the stake conference. Ray wanted it to be clear that he was gay and mentioned this fact in his acceptance talk. When his call was approved, the conference broke into applause. This was in 1991. As far as I know, this was the first approval of a clearly "out" gay man to the priesthood in the Community of Christ.

Ray wanted to have a GALA retreat at our second home. He asked Ted and me if we would come and cook for it. We went, thinking that was all we were going to do. Instead we were drawn into the most loving and hurting group of people we have ever known. Our hearts broke when we heard their stories of rejection. Three people talked openly about the fact that they had AIDS. But above all, we heard again and again how much they wanted to be accepted by the church, because they loved God. Never had we seen such open, raw honesty. I realized that I was hiding behind masks of my own and that I needed to be more honest myself.

The numbers of our "sons" and "daughters" started to grow. We had many GLBT (gay, lesbian, bisexual, or transgendered) people live with us for a time. Often they came because they didn't feel that they could be with their own parents. Often they said how afraid they were of their parents' reaction, were they to come out. We had an eighteen-year-old boy with us on his birthday, because his parents had kicked him out. We had a lesbian "daughter," whose background was so different from ours, share her enormous capacity for love and hugs. We had a young man, just out of college, come to live with us as he began his career. While he was there, strangers physically attacked him when they found out he is gay.

Our home changed. We began speaking out openly for GLBT people. We joined PFLAG (Parents, Family, and Friends of Lesbians and

Gays) and started speaking at colleges and university classes in hopes of creating more understanding.

We also became open advocates for greater understanding in the church. I stood up at the 1992 World Conference to speak for including homosexuality in the Human Diversity resolution, now World Conference Resolution 1226, that the delegates approved. I told the conference delegates that God had given us a gay son. I lobbied to have a PFLAG support group at the 1994 World Conference. At first, the First Presidency turned it down. I got in touch with Grant Mc-Murray, then a new member of the First Presidency and later church president. We received permission to meet at a congregation several miles from headquarters. That meeting was well attended, and we have had a PFLAG support group at each World Conference since then. I also taught a class at the Women's Peace Conference at the temple in 1993, entitled "Loving Someone Gay." So many people showed up that they had to turn some away. People with GLBT children or relatives have a strong need to say openly that they loved them and knew that God loved them, too. As women of the church held candles and encircled the temple, a young woman came to me and said, "I am a sister of your son." We hugged and cried together.

Today, our two daughters and their husbands, our four grandchildren, and Ray are very close. Our grandchildren were told about Uncle Ray as soon as they could understand. They say, "What's the big deal?" He is a fantastic uncle, and they love him. When my mother died recently, Ray came and stayed with her for several months. He gave her the highest gift—caring for her while she was dying. What greater love?

We certainly are grateful that God gave us our son Ray. He has been a blessing.

7

A JOURNEY OF NO CONSEQUENCE

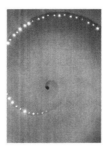

Ray V. Biller

Ray Biller is a former president of GALA and editor of the newsletter. He lives in San Diego and is no longer a member of the Community of Christ.

As a young child, I always knew I was different. I didn't know why. I just knew it. And yet, even though I was different, I also knew that I was special. It was a confusing message, and one I've had to examine from many angles throughout my life. The raucous roller-coaster that we call life has made me experience many emotional spirals. What still continues to amaze me to this day is that, no matter how different I realized I was, I wound up being even more amazed at how truly special I am. Here is my story.

I tried very hard to be the best little boy in the world. I wanted to do good for others, love all those I came in contact with, and be loved in return. I tried to always do right and serve my God and church wholeheartedly. But always overshadowing my need to be good was the realization that I was different. A dark cloud always seemed to keep me in check. No matter how good I tried to be, this enveloping blackness would come to haunt me. My mantra soon became, "If only they knew how different I was, then they'd never see me as special at all."

Many years passed; and much to my horror, one day I finally figured out how different I was. I remember going to the Graceland College library during my freshman year and looking up the word "homosexual" in the dictionary. My heart sank. Devastation engulfed me. I ran back to my room, tears running down my face. I screamed inwardly at God, "Why do I have to be different? Why can't I be special? Why? Why? Why" Searing pain flooded my body, my mind, and my soul. I melted into sobs. I cried all night.

Hard as I tried to keep up the façade of the "good little boy," my thoughts were overtaken by shame, fear, and disgust for the person I couldn't acknowledge that I was. I feared that I would lose the love of my family and my church. I lived in the shame that society would never be able to accept me. I loathed my very being; and no matter how hard I tried to do good, my self-hatred just pushed me further into the proverbial closet.

Despite all the suffering, a still, small voice within my soul kept whispering to me "You are special." Once again, the message was confusing; and because I had nothing else to believe in, I desperately clung to the hope that this voice was correct.

As one can imagine, I prayed and prayed to God to heal me, to make me feel normal. I promised my life to him. I swore that I would serve him for all time if only he would take this "sin" away from me. Yet the longer I chanted these prayers, the more I felt forsaken. Here I was doing my best to serve and honor God, yet I still had homosexual feelings.

Sometimes when we feel the farthest away from God, it's amazing how he can still direct our lives. I had decided that, to deal with these feelings, I needed to work for the church so that I could "work through" being gay. In May 1981 I applied for the church's contractual assignee program and was accepted. I thought, "Finally! I can turn my life over to God and he will heal me."

The contractual assignee program served many regions. I didn't care where God assigned me; I just knew that wherever he sent me, I was going to be healed,. So God, in his infinite wisdom and divine sense of humor sent me to San Francisco, the gay capital of the world. In August of that same year, I packed my bags and drove to the Bay area, where I began my service to the church. I threw myself into my work. I was very involved with two congregations and the stake's youth program. However, I didn't feel any better. My struggles became darker.

I remember one particular senior high camp in June 1982. We had a worship service on a ridge overlooking the Happy Valley Campgrounds in the Santa Cruz Mountains. We marched up a hill and were instructed to pick up a rock. At the top of the hill was a meadow, and in the meadow stood a cross. At one point in the service, we were asked to put our burdens in this rock and to lay it at the foot of the cross.

It was more than obvious to me which burden I wanted to put in that rock. As I knelt before that cross, reaching out to lay down what I considered my most horrific burden, something stopped my hand. Overcome with emotion I stood up, ran to the edge of the cliff, and heaved my rock into the valley below. I was flooded with tears. Many friends came up to express concern. Inconsolable, I realized I could never tell them why I threw this rock away.

One year later in September 1983, I finished my contractual assignment and headed back to my home in Southern California. I continued to throw myself into the work of the church, getting very involved with my congregation. I served on the worship commission and taught church school. I seized every invitation to sit on the rostrum. I delivered scripture, sang solos, served communion, and prayed that I would become whole.

My inner struggle became greater, and the conflict felt as if a war was raging inside my body. Finally, I stopped asking God to heal me and instead began praying for peace and wholeness. After spending the previous fourteen years of my life running away from my sexuality, I knew the time had come to face reality. After berating and degrading myself for all these years for having these feelings, I began to withdraw from my family and my church. I came to the conclusion that, no matter what the consequences were, I could no longer deny who I was: a gay man.

In December 1984, I packed up my things, said goodbye to my congregation, resigned all of my assignments, and moved to Long Beach, California, far from home, to face my demons. Alone and in deep despair, I made one last attempt to find acceptance. In January 1985, a dear friend who was aware of my struggles, put me in touch with Dave Premoe, a World Church appointee in the San Diego area. I wrote him this letter:

Dear Bro. Premoe:

For many months now I've been struggling to get this letter written to you. I don't know if you recall a conversation you had with Mary Kellogg this summer at the Singles Reunion, about a young man who was struggling with his sense of identity, his priesthood, and his feelings of homosexuality. You indicated to her that you'd be willing to talk and counsel with that person if he was so inclined. Well, I'm that young man and I'm asking for your help.

Let me be terribly honest, I'm scared to death about this letter and where it might take me. I'm afraid of many things in my life. I've struggled with who and what I am for a long fourteen years. I realize that I cannot become a "whole" person until I face this reality. But in doing that, there are many risks and sacrifices to make, and I'm afraid of where those may lead.

I really believe in the wholeness principle where all aspects of your life blend together and create who you are and allow you to function in the world you are living in. Unfortunately I just don't blend. My two worlds are so far apart, and I've allowed them to exist so separately. For years I've been able to suppress the dark side of me and allowed my public side to flourish. But as of late I've noticed a tremendous retreat and withdrawal from the happy-go-lucky public side of me. I'm beginning to dwell in and sort out this dark side; and it's nothing but frustration, disappointment, pain, sorrow, mystery, allurement, adventure, and extremely frightening. However, because my search has begun, I'm at a point where I can't go back to successfully suppressing my dark side, and yet I'm not sure I'm willing to give up everything I've known before that is dear to me.

I know that eventually I'll explode someday without some help and direction. I'm not looking for all the answers (but if you've got them, I'd sure take them). I'm looking for some guidance and someone who will hear me out and try to understand. Whether you can do this or not, I don't know. Whether or not you'd even like to try and help me is still an open question. If you do, then I would please ask for your silence regarding this letter and perhaps a recommendation of where I might be able to seek some help.

In many ways I wish I didn't have to write this letter to you. Please try hard to understand how hard it is for me to put this down on paper, and try even harder to imagine my embarrassment if this information went past you. If nothing else, it has been helpful just to write this problem out on paper and examine it further. I'm very anxious to hear from you.

Sincerely,
Ray Biller

Dave did agree to see me, and he successfully began to turn my fears of isolation and hatred into acceptance and normalcy. After our first visit, I drove to the beach, sat down on the sand, and cried hard for a very long time. I wasn't sure whether I was happy or sad. But what I do remember was that, for the very first time in my life, someone finally knew about my homosexuality and actually accepted me for who I was. My heart began to take flight, and the world was born new to me once more.

Mysteriously driven by the guidance of the divine, when I took that leap of faith and moved to Long Beach, I wound up moving smack dab into the middle of the gay neighborhood. I slowly began to integrate myself into the gay community and found a peace and wholeness which I never dreamed I could ever know.

Dave convinced me that God and the church still had an important place on my path to wholeness. He encouraged me to serve as a counselor at another senior high camp, which was tremendously healing for me. The kids in my cabin and I shared in some very moving and spiritual moments. The staff and I got along famously. The director of the camp came to me after the week was over. She said she was so excited about my ministry and participation with the kids that she could hardly wait to work with me again next year.

During this time, I was slowly beginning to come out to a few of my friends and family. The experience was daunting, yet rewarding, because of people's amazing ability to accept me for who I am. Rumors began to fly. I hadn't told my parents about my sexuality yet, but I knew that it was only a matter of time before they heard the news from someone. The church's rumor mills are notorious. I was going to have to share the news with them soon. Little did I know how soon "soon" was going to be.

The director of the senior high camp heard the rumor only four months after the end of camp, telephoned me out of the blue, and asked me if the rumors were true. I acknowledged that they were. She flatly stated that she never wanted to see me again and banned me from participating in any future camps. She also announced that she was going to call the parents of the teenagers I had become so close with during the camp to tell them I was a homosexual and instructed me to have no further contact with them. She then called my pastor and my stake president to tell them the news.

Her flat, cold voice in my ear shattered my world. Bigotry reached out and smashed everything important to me right before my very eyes.

I remember hanging up the phone at my office desk. I walked into my boss's office and said I needed to take the rest of the day off. It was only 10:00 a.m.

My boss stared at me and asked, "Ray, what's wrong? You're white as a ghost!"

I said, "I can't talk right now. I have to go. Please let me go." I ran outside and got in my car. Literally the next thing I remembered, it was 5:00 p.m., and I was sitting in the driveway of my cousin's house.

Obviously, my first task was to tell my family. They had to hear about my sexuality from me, not from rumors. While I knew I had a very loving and liberal family, the fear still existed deep within me that they would not understand my homosexuality and that they would turn their backs on me.

How fortunate I was to be able to walk into my parents' home, sit down with my mom and dad, tell them how much I loved them, and say that hard, hard sentence, "I'm gay." To my stunned amazement, my father walked right over to me, put his arms around me, and said,

"Ray, you are our son. We love you very much, no matter who you are. That will never change." That was the beginning of a long conversation that extended over many days. Their response and acceptance were immediate, but they themselves then had to go through the process of understanding what it meant to have a gay son.

It empowered me so much to have their acceptance that it was quite easy, by comparison, to tell the other members of my family and my friends. We struggled with how to tell my grandmother, who loved me dearly. My mother felt that my grandmother was of a generation who really wouldn't understand or be able to accept me. She knew how much my grandmother loved me and didn't want to see that love change. However, it got to the point where we were hurting my grandmother more by not telling her than by telling her. She knew something was up and was getting frustrated by everyone's silence.

When I shared the news with her, accompanied by my parents, Grandma said, "Ray, I don't understand this at all, but you are my grandson, and I love you so much, and that will never change."

Then my dad blew me away when he told her, "Margaret, the Ray that we've always known, whose dreams we had created for him, is now dead and gone from us. Fortunately for us, Ray is still here for us to love. It's just that we now have to learn to love him in a new light. We need to come up with different dreams and realities for him, and continue to love him in those new ways." It was a dream come true to bask in that love and acceptance as they so quickly came to terms with my sexuality.

My dear grandmother, while initially struggling with what this meant for me in my life, tried to find ways to come to terms with my news. One day, shortly after telling her, I received a concerned letter from her asking if I would take some different vitamins to see if that would help me. I cherish that letter to this day. It wasn't more than three months later, as I drove her home from my parents' vacation home one day, that she came right out and asked me questions about my sexuality. From that day forward, she was one of my staunchest supporters.

Within the next few months, I had many more opportunities to come out to friends and church friends. It was an exhilarating experience. The fears that had paralyzed me for so many years simply melted away. What amazed me most is that people kept saying, "Ray, we love you. It doesn't matter who you are. You're such a part of our lives that we don't want to give that up." What a relief it was to give up those fears.

Later on that year, I had the opportunity to go back to the Happy Valley Campgrounds. I challenged myself to go back to the cross in the meadow where the senior high worship service was held. As I climbed up the hill, I picked up a rock and took it with me. At the top of the hill in the overgrown meadow still stood the cross erected for that fateful service. I slowly approached that cross with my rock. Tears streamed down my face. As I knelt down and placed the rock at the foot of that cross, I realized for the first time in my life that my homosexuality was not the burden I thought it was. It was the gift that God had given to me to share with my world.

After all those years of fighting conflicting feelings, I realized that God loved me for who I am. My joy was overwhelming. I looked up and felt a presence, which I had never known. I felt that I was in the presence of God. He reached out his hand to me and said, "Accept this gift, my beloved. I have waited a long time for you to come to this place. Ready yourself, for I have a work for you to do."

A brand-new world opened up to me. For the first time in my life, I felt empowered, knowing that I indeed had a place at the table within the church. From that moment on, many wonderful doors have opened before me.

In June of 1987, I made contact with a group of Community of Christ gays and lesbians who were meeting in the Kansas City area. They called themselves Gay and Lesbian Acceptance (GALA). I learned that they were going to hold a retreat at Camp Manitou in southwest Michigan. A small group of twelve came together over the Labor Day weekend in September 1987 and a movement of transformation and healing began. We were bruised and brokenhearted as we shared our stories of hurt and alienation experienced within the so-called loving embrace of the church. I cried as they described the

88

destructive paths they had taken after they felt abandoned by this church they loved so much. I saw a group of people who were very fragile and who needed to rebuild from this pain. New appreciation for the worth of each person emerged. The group united in God's love, basking in the healing powers of redemption.

We yearned for our voices to be heard. What we had experienced that weekend was far too powerful for us to remain silent any longer. With this renewed sense of spirit, this small group incorporated GALA (Gay and Lesbian Acceptance) in September 1987. I remember flying home from that weekend emboldened and empowered. Much to my amazement, from the airplane window, I saw the most beautiful rainbow I had ever seen. Tears began to stream down my face. Right then I knew that we had a message for other Community of Christ gays and lesbians, their families, and most importantly, for the church.

During GALA's organizational meeting during that weekend, there was much discussion of how we should further our mission. We all wanted to continue holding retreats like this. We also talked about educating the church. There were even voices advocating protest and disruptive acts, in the style of the protest group Act Up. However, cooler heads prevailed, and we settled on a three-pronged platform: (1) to accept and affirm the worth of all persons without regard to sexual orientation, gender, race, or religious origins, (2) to offer spiritual ministry to other gays and lesbians through retreats and worship, and (3) to work with the church and help educate it to the awareness of the gay and lesbian members. This was part of GALA's original mission statement.

I was asked to be GALA's West Coast regional facilitator. I organized the next retreat in April 1988 in southern California. My parents had a small vacation home in the high desert and I asked them if we could meet there. They weren't quite sure what they were getting themselves into but willingly agreed to let us use the home. Then I asked if they would be cooks for the weekend. They agreed, but said they would only cook, not participate in the weekend's activities.

A group of fifteen came to this retreat and once again shared their stories. My parents had distanced themselves from the church because of their personal struggles with the Community of Christ. As they listened to these stories, their hearts began to break. Here is a passage from a letter my father wrote to the participants the night the retreat ended:

When our son, Ray, requested to use our little get away trailer home for a gathering of members of a group called GALA, I little realized that the experience would become one of the deepest of my life. I did not anticipate the experience would lead to new, rich friendships with men who have been outcast by family, church, and friends. I had no idea I would grow to understand more meaningfully what it means to be a homosexual in today's society. I could not realize there would be a manifestation of the Spirit of God that would reveal a true loving acceptance of men whom others had viciously denounced.

As Allan Fiscus spoke of his struggle with the church and being silenced from his priesthood office, and to think the only response the church, my church, could deem to take as action when he revealed he was gay was to take his priesthood away and sever him from ministerial function produced a special hurt. I was deeply moved when Bob Stoner shared his testimony about well-meaning members of the church, who made it clear that he had to mend his ways, and showed no attempt to understand him or accept him for what he is, but instead shunned him and told him he was no longer welcome in their midst. I learned how Tony Feliz and Alan Hose, both outstanding and talented persons and faithful ministers in the Latter Day Saint (Mormon) church, were excommunicated and cut off from the rich ministry that is such a great part of their lives.

I don't want to sound too prejudiced, but my son Ray, stood out quite special at this retreat. And, though I didn't think it possible, I came to love him more dearly than I already did. He brought a special ministry to this retreat that somehow touched us all. It is impossible to describe the height and depth of feeling he caused us all to feel and experience in the specially designed service on Sunday morning. Truly he opened a channel by which the spirit of God ministered to each of us that day.

I came out of this weekend experience with my friends from GALA with a clear new insight that God continues to work with and through them. Many of these young men were servants called and ordained of God prior to revealing they were homosexual. Though their church may have silenced or excommunicated them, I was made deeply aware that the love of God remained with them. I was forced to delve into my own conscience and ask the penetrating question "What makes them different from me and others `normal' like myself?" I could find no good answer to justify why they are so different, other than the blind force of prejudice. Like any other human bias, it is hardly a sound reason for cutting persons off from their church, family and friends.

Beyond what I have already said, I wish to make clear the confirming spirit of God that was present at our gathering. As I lay in bed tonight, following the GALA retreat, the spirit of God continues to manifest to me his deep love for, and acceptance of each of you who attended and shared in this retreat. This is my testimony and continued extension of my friendship to each of the friends I met and shared with at the GALA retreat.

Sincerely,
Ted Biller

Throughout the years, I have had the privilege of presiding over more than twenty GALA retreats. It was inspiring to witness the healing and spiritual renewal, which so many craved, and yet had felt was beyond their grasp. One young man, whose mother had convinced him to check out GALA, had his priesthood taken away. There was a lot of anger and hurt caused by the church, and he was very reluctant to participate. It was obviously a struggle for him to be at this retreat. During a service I had planned, I played a song by Don Francisco entitled "I'll Never Let Go of Your Hand." I prefaced the song by saying that we had all felt abandoned by our God and by our church but that the purpose of this weekend was to help us to reconnect with our spiritual journey. This young man, after hearing this song and feeling for the first time in many years the true love of God's amazing grace, sobbed in my arms and gratefully acknowledged the healing which he desperately desired.

At that initial retreat at Camp Manitou, June Freeman, an evangelist, was sent by Gary Beebe, the Michigan Region administrator, as an official Community of Christ representative. She openly proclaimed her love for us as gay persons and honestly wanted to share her ministry with us and the rest of the church. This had such tremendous and validating impact upon me that I wanted to have others within church leadership share this same experience and healing. Guest ministry at many of GALA's retreats included such individuals as Gary Beebe, John Billings, Dave Premoe, Apostle Dave Brock, Carolyn Brock, Dick Hahn, Scott Sinclair, Don Compier, Mary Kellogg, Apostle Joe Serig, and many others. But the healing didn't occur just for the gays and lesbians who attended. Mothers, fathers, and siblings, who feared that the church would shun their loved one, came away with a new hope of love and inclusion. Church leaders and congregants came to support their gay and lesbian friends and walked away with a new understanding of acceptance and love.

In addition to serving as GALA's West Coast regional facilitator for five years, I also began editing the GALA newsletter, which started out with a first mailing to twelve people and blossomed to well over five hundred within ten years. I was elected president of GALA in 1991 and served for five years in that capacity. We began to hold our annual GALA retreat over Labor Day weekend in September but have also held mini-retreats in various parts of the country. So far, we have met in Missouri, California, Texas, Oklahoma, Colorado, Michigan, Washington, and Ohio.

Our positive influence was well received by the leadership of the church. Our work was beginning to get noticed. I recall at the beginning of our GALA movement, many top church officials admitted that they were leery of us. They weren't quite sure what kind of group this was or what it would become. They wanted to see what developed before they would grant more official recognition to GALA. Despite their misgivings, they encouraged the group to continue its quest to make GALA a solid organization which would be trusted and respected.

I always felt our influence with the church had to come from a grass roots effort. John Billings, East Central States Region administrator and I, with GALA's support, took over the planning and presentation of the AIDS ministry forums at World Conference, beginning in April 1988. These sessions led to the establishment of the PFLAG (Parents and Friends of Lesbians and Gays) meetings also held in conjunction with World Conference, beginning in April 1992.

GALA had its first booth at World Conference in April 1996, reaching out to disenfranchised gay and lesbians within the church and helping to educate church members about the great love that God has for all of his children.

I want to share another significant story. A year after my hilltop experience. I began attending the El Segundo Congregation in the Los Angeles Stake. I felt very thrilled and excited to have the unqualified support of Pastor Steve Shields. At one point, he asked me to become his counselor to the pastor, and I was delighted to take on the task but felt the need to go before the congregation and share my story with them. I didn't want to take a leadership position without having their support. Steve and I put much planning and thought into how we would approach the congregation with the news of my sexuality. Gary Beebe, the stake president, was in attendance as well as my family. As I sat on the rostrum at the beginning of that service, my nerves began to fray at the thought of coming out to the congregation, I looked out into the congregation and realized that I knew every person there except for one older man whom neither Steve nor I had ever seen in the congregation before.

After I told my story, Gary got up and asked the congregation how they felt about hearing my story. The first person to speak up was the older stranger. He stood up and emotionally stated that it was high time we acknowledge gays and lesbians in our church. "If the church had done this fifty years ago when I was first coming out, it certainly would have made my life easier," he said. It was a warming moment. Everyone else who spoke agreed to accept my leadership as a counselor to the pastor.

Later on that year, unbeknownst to me, Steve recommended that I be ordained an elder. At this point, to my knowledge, no priesthood call for an openly gay individual had ever been processed. President Beebe instructed the high council (who goes through the process of approving all priesthood calls) that my call could be carried forward to the stake conference only if every single member of the high council supported it. This was new territory, and he felt that the call could not be processed without unanimous support from the high council.

The high council invited my parents and me to come and share our stories with them. Most of these people had known me since childhood; but after they heard my story, several of them said how moved they were by the honesty and depth of my desire to serve the church, despite feeling such alienation. My parents, who by now were very outspoken gay activists through PFLAG, admitted how scared and hurt they would feel if the church they loved and worshipped in, would reject the ministry of their beloved son outright. They knew what a bold and courageous step this would be and yet still feared rejection for their son. Now they felt encouraged by the challenge of this call for ordination which lay before the high council. After our meeting, the high council took another month for further discussion but eventually voted to accept the call unanimously.

The next hurdle was to present my priesthood call to the stake conference for approval. Everyone was nervous about the prospect, and discussion was intense. Friends came and provided me with lots of support. I was also keenly aware of whispering and sidelong stares of disapproval. President Beebe told me privately that I could accept the call without bringing up the gay issue and deal with the aftermath later. That didn't sit well with me. I spent a lot of time debating with myself about the right approach in accepting the call.

On conference day, Alex Khatava, the president of the Council of Twelve Apostles, was the guest minister. In his morning sermon, he spoke eloquently about how the church was in transition. He said "The church twenty years ago was a church that said, 'Come to us, accept our faith, and then we will minister to you.' However, today our church has matured and is beginning a new approach to outreach. Today the church says, 'Come to us as you are, and we will minister with you.' These were defining words to my ears. I made my decision.

During the business meeting that afternoon, where the entire stake votes on the worthiness of the ordinands, my call was the second to be presented. They called me before the congregation to make my statement affirming my call. I think you could have heard a pin drop as I walked to the podium. I stood before the congregation, filled with the assurance of the rightness of the call, and said, "As a gay man, I accept this call. I have struggled most of my life to be accepted for who I am. My struggling has stopped and I am ready to serve." I then shared my testimony about my hilltop experience. I described how deeply I had been moved by Apostle Khatava's sermon. I said simply that if the church was ready to minister with me, then I was ready to accept this call.

As I sat down and President Beebe called for the vote, I know that my heart stopped a moment. I'm pretty sure everyone on the platform was equally tense. But all over the hall, hands flew into the air, affirming my call. It was unanimous—not a single dissenting vote. Then to everyone's amazement, and mine, thunderous applause broke out and the congregation rose in a standing ovation. The first openly gay priesthood call was confirmed.

On February 23, 1992, I was ordained to the office of elder in the Masons Lodge in El Segundo, California. The El Segundo Community of Christ church house was not big enough to contain my very large family, dozens of friends, and the many well-wishers from the church family who wanted to attend the service. My dear friend and companion in creating and conducting many of the GALA activities Alan Cochran reported for the GALA newsletter in the 1992 spring quarterly edition:

> The spirit of the Lord touched a group of 100 people who gathered to celebrate the ordination of Ray Biller to the office of elder. The service was an expression of love from friends and family toward Ray. Affirmations of love and support were presented by four close friends from Ray's various walks of life: A GALA comrade, a chaplain from the Hospice where Ray began his life's work, a former pastor, and a family member.
>
> Ray was ordained by LA Stake President Gary Beebe and Elder Gene Painter. Gary's prayer reflected upon Ray's dedication to spiritual outreach, his personal growth, and a challenge for Ray to continue with the greatly needed leadership role he holds with GALA.
>
> We closed the service with a congregational response that brought us all together in one unified voice. "We support Ray in the response to his call. We affirm the worth of his personhood. We affirm the worth of our personhood. This challenge falls on each of us to love ourselves and

each other, as God loves us. Heavenly Parent, be with us as we carry out this commission."

I experienced much growth during this time of my life. I never dreamed I would become a religious gay activist, yet here I was providing a ministry which not even I could have anticipated only a few short years earlier. Doors continued to open, and I had the privilege of sharing my story with many in the Community of Christ. I was able to dialogue with church leadership on gay and lesbian issues. I provided seminars and educated church quorums on gay and lesbian issues.

In April 1996, I was asked to sit on the Human Sexuality Task Force formed by a resolution of the 1996 World Conference, which asked the First Presidency to create a committee to study the issues surrounding sexual orientation. The committee was comprised of many of the top theologians and church officials including J. C. Stuart, chair and former apostle; Joe Serig, former apostle; Sue McLaughlin, theologian; and Carolyn Brock, Ph.D. Among our number were a doctor, businessperson, teacher, administrator, and social worker.

From the grass roots of the church, the body was calling the church to task and asking them to respond. The Human Sexuality Task Force was ready and willing to accept the challenge. Throughout all of our early discussions, it became very evident that this was a group who wanted to do the right thing and create a new openness, which would profoundly affect the way the church reached out to the gay and lesbian community.

The First Presidency gave the committee a four-part assignment: (1) to provide a definition of human sexuality, (2) to report on the theology and scriptural implication of same-sex relationships, (3) to report on the topics involved with same-sex relationships (i.e., same-sex unions/marriages, priesthood calls, etc.) and (4) to provide an ongoing dialogue about how to educate the church regarding these issues.

I was very determined to see some positive growth come out of this task force experience. For ten long years, I had been working with the church to provide ministry to gays and lesbians and to offer education to the church's general membership and leadership. I had tried to be a good role model for all who were watching me. I felt that GALA and I had accomplished a great deal during that decade of preparation. Now was the time for strong language that would establish a policy of inclusiveness for gay and lesbian members. I was ready for engagement.

I felt that a new atmosphere of cooperation had been established in 1996 with the transition of the First Presidency to W. Grant Mc-Murray, and his counselors, Bud Sheehy and Ken Robinson. Most of our encouragement had come from the Quorum of Twelve Apostles, but now President McMurray actually spoke from the rostrum at the 1998 World Conference about accepting gays and lesbians and including them within the church structure. It felt like the right time to take bold action.

I discovered that our task force was not the first official consideration of homosexuality. Through our early discussion we learned that, in the early 1980s, a Sexuality Committee had been established; and even though the church never received its report and it was rejected by the leadership, it was decidedly inclusive and supportive. It sanctioned openly gay priesthood members and gay marriage.

The First Presidency, through the Standing High Council, adopted a policy that was only slightly better than the 1961 Standing High Council policy which stated that homosexuals could be accepted in the church and even hold priesthood office, as long as they were celibate. In 1995, a different Standing High Council reviewed this guideline but recommended that homosexuals should be allowed priesthood status and recognition of same-sex relationships. This report, we were told, was suppressed by the presidency and never released.

Initially, the Human Sexuality Task Force spoke with a united voice in stating that the church needed time to address human sexuality. The task force created a Temple School course and tried very hard to present it throughout the church to ask church members to address the humanness of sexuality. Some took the course; but by and large, the whole church did not really participate too much in this temple school course.

Next, I volunteered to formulate the follow-up Temple School class on homosexuality. In the spring of 1999, I once again turned to my friend John Billings and my cousin Glenn Johnson to assist me in creating an outline for this class. We spent a long Sunday afternoon debating the course for the class, and eventually came up with an outline that seemed informative, nurturing, and affirming.

As I was putting the final touches on the outline, I received a call from J. C. Stuart, the committee chair. He informed me that he was resigning as chair of the committee. J. C. was ready to fully retire from church work and felt the topic was too important to be chaired by anyone less than a member of the First Presidency. Ken Robinson became the next chair of the committee.

At first I thought this was a good move. It signaled the First Presidency's recognition of the importance of this committee. They wanted to oversee its work. Stuart also told me that the First Presidency felt that the conservative voice had not been heard enough on this committee, so they were adding conservative voices, which would provide a more balanced approach to the course work. I was even okay with that. Leery, but okay.

At our next committee meeting, in the fall of 1999, we were told that the First Presidency, wanted to shelve the outline and idea behind the Homosexuality Temple School course and postpone its release until after the World Conference of 2000, since that millennial year had been declared a year of jubilee by the prophet of the church. Brother Robinson told me point blank that the First Presidency didn't want any controversy at the 2000 World Conference. The time was not right to present this course to the church. Devastation engulfed me, and a hole began to form in my heart.

As a very young boy, I had felt called to serve the Community of Christ. When my cousin Mark and I were baptized into the church, at the age of eight, my Uncle Frank asked me what I wanted to do in the church. According to family folklore, I promptly answered, "I'm going to be president of the church, and Mark's going to be my apostle." Strong words from a young voice, yet one that spoke of a true calling to serve. During my dark days of struggling with my sexuality, I all but gave up that dream of working for the church, knowing that my sexual orientation would forever taint my ability to become a full-time minister.

And then I came out. My family accepted me, my congregation accepted me, and I was ordained into the priesthood as an openly gay man. The ministry with GALA flourished, and for ten years I reached out to my community, reconciling lost souls with their spiritual journey and their church. This is the work of the Seventy in the Community of Christ. I was performing all the duties, but without the official ordination. I was walking the walk and talking the talk. Then things changed, people changed, and I changed.

I went back to my home in Seattle from the task force meeting that weekend and stared blankly at the outline for the Temple School class on homosexuality. A sense of desolation and emptiness swept over me. I had certainly felt this feeling before, but this time the meaning was different. This time, a more honest reality was staring back at me. This church, which I had devoted my life to, was not going to affirm me as a full person of worth. I felt betrayed. They placed conditions on my acceptance. They placed conditions on their love. I would always be a partial person in this church. It finally dawned on me that I needed more.

I sat down at my computer on the evening of December 27, 1999, and wrote the most difficult letter I have ever composed:

> To the President of the Community of Christ World Church:
>
> The following is my resignation letter from the Community of Christ Church, as well as the Human Sexuality Task Force.
>
> This decision comes at a time in my life when I feel it is time to begin some new chapters regarding my spiritual growth. It is a decision based on my personal journey. It is a decision based upon my need for full acceptance and for who I am as a person of worth in this universe. This decision is not based on malice, frustration, or alienation.
>
> While the Community of Christ church will always be looked upon as a cornerstone in my personal development, I have come to realize that it is an institution I have outgrown. I am extremely grateful for all of the life lessons I have received from this institution. Without the assistance of some amazing mentors who have shared their deep, abiding faith with me, I know that I would never have become the person I am today.
>
> And though I've had some extremely powerful, uplifting, emotional moments within this institution, I have also experienced some profound

lows. There is nothing more demoralizing to an individual than when a person, institution, or community says to them, "We will accept you, as long as you don't exhibit the behaviors of being gay." "We will work with you, but don't ask us to affirm your sexuality." "We will ordain you for the gifts you have to offer us, but will take it away from you if you get involved with a committed love relationship." These are rules I can no longer live by, nor should any valued human being of God's great creation.

From the moment I was born and blessed by the Community of Christ Church, I have had a mad, passionate love affair with it. I always dreamed that one day I would work for the church. Even during the emotionally trying days of my coming out process, this church played a foundational role in my coming to terms with my own acceptance of who I was as a gay man.

I am proud of the accomplishments I have achieved with this institution: being ordained a priest and then an elder, working with the youth and camping programs, serving as a counselor to the Pastor at the El Segundo, Ca. Congregation, helping to establish (with many others) the GALA organization, organizing and facilitating many GALA Retreats (which helped to bring much healing and hope to gay and lesbian Community of Christ members and their families), being an advocate, educator, and voice for the gay and lesbian communities to the church, participating in the sacraments of the church, organizing the AIDS Ministry services at four World Conferences, and serving on the Human Sexuality Task Force Committee.

But now my spiritual journey calls me on to new horizons. And this cannot be fully realized within the framework of the Community of Christ Church. I leave with a twinge of sadness for dreams not fully realized. I leave with a heart full of pride for the work that has been established on behalf of my gay brothers and lesbian sisters, and their families who still wish to participate fully within the bounds of the church.

My one big disappointment is that I must leave part of my work unfinished with the Human Sexuality Task Force. The more I have tried to put together the Homosexuality Temple School course, the more I realize how far away I have moved from the Community of Christ Church. This is an important piece of work and my heart is not in it.

For my colleagues whom I have worked with on the Task Force, I hope that you continue with the work that is at hand. It has been a true joy serving with you all. I shall miss our conversations and discourse. I still believe very strongly in educating the Community of Christ constituency and highly favor the path that we have begun.

I ask that you remove my name from your membership rolls, disavow my priesthood status, and accept my resignation from the Human Sexuality Task Force.

I thank you for the firm foundation, which you have granted me. I encourage you to continue the work to truly accept all persons as people of worth, unconditionally. I ask that you bless and release me in my journey, as I shall do the same for you.

In God's Warmest Wishes,
Ray V. Biller

In my life, I have indeed felt very different, yet very special. My story is no different than any of the others you may have heard. But what is unique about my story is that, with lots of hard work, the rethinking of my ways, a spiritually inspired belief in my self, and lots of faith in God's plan, I have come to a much greater acceptance of myself as an individual of worth. I'm not finished with my growing, and I'm not finished with my learning, but at least I have an assurance that I do have a seat at God's table and that his love for me is unending.

The church has a long way to go in understanding differences of all kinds. I think Marjorie Williams states it best in her brilliant story of *The Velveteen Rabbit*:

> The Skin Horse had lived longer in the nursery than any of the others. He was so old that his brown coat was bald in patches and showed the seams underneath, and most of the hairs in his tail had been pulled out to string bead necklaces. He was wise, for he had seen a long succession of mechanical toys arrive to boast and swagger, and by-and-by break their mainsprings and pass away, and he knew that they were only toys, and would never turn into anything else. For nursery magic is very strange and wonderful, and only those playthings that are old and wise and experienced like the Skin Horse understand all about it.
>
> "What is Real?" asked the Rabbit one day, when they were lying side by side near the nursery fender, before Nana came to tidy the room.

"Does it mean having things that buzz inside you and a stick out handle?"

"Real isn't how you are made," said the Skin Horse. "It's a thing that happens to you. When a child loves you for a long, long time not just to play with, but REALLY loves you, then you become REAL."

"Does it hurt?" asked the Rabbit.

"Sometimes," said the Skin Horse, for he was always truthful. "When you are Real you don't mind being hurt."

"Does it happen all at once, like being wound up." he asked, "or bit by bit?"

"It doesn't happen all at once," said the Skin Horse. "You become. It takes a long time. That's why it doesn't often happen to people who break easily, or who have sharp edges, or who have to be carefully kept. Generally, by the time you are Real, most of your hair has been loved off, and your eyes drop out, and you get loose in the joints and very shabby. But those things don't matter at all, because once you are Real you can't be ugly, except to people who don't understand." (pp. 3-5)

8

MY BROTHER'S KEEPER

Merlene Swoffer Brush

Merlene Swoffer Brush graduated from Lamoni (Iowa) High School and earned a B.A. in physical education from Graceland in 1969. She taught in several schools in the Kansas City area and received a master's degree in counseling at the University of Missouri-Kansas City. She is a Licensed Professional Counselor and is currently a Psychological Examiner for the Kansas City School District.

ONE OF MY earliest memories is of being carried into a room in my father's arms and looking down into a bassinet to see a small, squirming baby. "This is your brother," my father said.

I was almost three years older than Bob, so from the beginning he was destined to have two "mothers." I remember a photograph taken at my Uncle Merle's house in which my cousins, Bonnie, Terry, Marie, Bob, and I were all standing in a row. Bob was just beginning to walk and was being held up not so comfortably by his ever-helpful big sister. The look on his face was rather pained, but I was determined to keep him standing with us.

Our childhood was spent on the shores of Lake Huron in Michigan surrounded by family and friends. We lived much of the time in a duplex with my mother's parents. Bob and I were so tied to my maternal grandmother that I can remember, when I was about eight years old, crying to go home from reunion in Sanford, Michigan, because we missed her so much.

My mother's sister's family lived next door to us, and Bob and their youngest son, Rick, spent much time together. For my part, I spent a lot of time with Rick's older sister, Sandi. We kept trying to "escape" from our two little brothers, whom we had now decided were pests. We did make use of them as our "customers," though, when we played restaurant. Sandi commented later in life about how quiet, peaceful, and "good" Bob was as a child. She remembers his dazzling ability with his Etch-a-Sketch. He knew early in his life that he wanted to be an architect, and he accomplished that goal.

We moved to Lamoni, Iowa, when Bob was in the fourth grade, and he fit easily into the new situation, as he always did. We continued to go back and forth to Michigan in the summers, so we retained our connections with Michigan while developing new roots in Iowa. Bob had started piano lessons, as I had, in Michigan, and we both continued them in Lamoni. His greatest piano achievement was mastering "Glissando Mazurka," which I had played in a recital in Michigan. It's quite difficult and spoke well of his intent to keep up with his big sister.

Bob always had an interest in athletics but never was really big enough to play football. He did play end on the Lamoni High School team one year and even caught a touchdown pass. Unfortunately, the referee ruled it incomplete because his foot was out of bounds. In later years, he pitched for and coached a softball team in a Kansas City gay league. He was student council president his senior year at Lamoni High and active in music and drama.

Bob went to Graceland College in Lamoni following his high school graduation in 1967. He was a member of Cheville House (a dormitory unit) and was involved in college activities. He transferred to the University of Kansas in Lawrence and obtained his B.A. in architecture and urban design in 1972. He was called and ordained

a priest in the Community of Christ while he was in Lawrence. Former Apostle Arthur Oakman, giving him his patriarchal blessing on
May 6, 1971, told him, "You have a rich heritage in the Church of
Jesus Christ, for not only your immediate forbearers but those who
have gone on before [and], in the distant past, have looked down the
stream of time and seen this day and prayed for you; and because
of this heritage, because of their concern, you have been preserved
in many ways from many of the evils which come upon others of
like-mindedness in this generation. Therefore, dear brother, you have
great cause to rejoice for you have been selected by him to be one of
his servants and to walk in the pathway he would have you go."

Bob joined VISTA International after his graduation from Kansas University and spent two years helping to build houses in Salt
Lake City. He joined the Peace Corps in 1974 and went to Guatemala
to help build schools. He was in Guatemala City in 1976 when the
earthquake hit. He told us later that he was sleeping on a waterbed
and had quite a "ride." He had planned to leave the very day of the
earthquake, to travel by himself through Guatemala and Mexico. He
was fluent in Spanish by this time. Not knowing the extent of the
damage, he embarked on his trip without letting us know that he was
all right.

Communications between the United States and Guatemala were
difficult, to say the least, but after several attempts I managed to get
through to the U.S. Embassy in Guatemala City. A person who only
spoke Spanish answered the phone but seemed to understand my
faulty attempts to remember what I had learned in college. He answered, "Si" when I asked, "Es Roberto okay?" It was still a long
week, however, until we got a phone call from Belize saying he was
fine and on his way home as he had originally planned.

After returning to the United States, Bob decided it was time
he put effort into his chosen career of architecture. He worked for
several different firms, moving as opportunities for advancement occurred. Abend-Singleton gave him the opportunity to be involved in
designing and drawing the Clay County Detention Center in Liberty
and the United Missouri Bank in downtown Kansas City. Devine Ar-

105

chitects, his last employer, was very supportive during his fatal illness in 1986.

Bob most probably contracted the HIV virus during some visits he made to San Francisco in the late 1970s. I learned about his illness in July 1985 when he was hospitalized with pneumocystis pneumonia, one of the diseases that can develop as a result of an HIV-weakened immune system. I was then a student at the University of Missouri, Kansas City, working on my master's degree in counseling. A close friend gently suggested that I might want to look up the connection between HIV/AIDS and pneumocystis.

Bob had not come out to our family, but my dad and I had already suspected he was gay, even though we never talked about it. I had begun wondering when he had a close woman friend whom he, at one point, seemed interested in marrying. That didn't happen, and she had suggested to me that Bob had some things he needed to "talk to the family about."

I'll never forget the summer afternoon that I walked out of the UMKC library after reading an article about HIV/AIDS. My worst fears were confirmed. My brother had the most dreaded disease on the planet. Being the proactive person that I am, I called his doctors at St. Luke's to make sure they were aware of the possibility. They were, of course; but later when they told Bob I had called them, he vehemently chastised me for overstepping my bounds but acknowledged that he was, in fact, gay.

Bob recovered from that illness but spent the next year in declining health. He even made a trip to Mexico to obtain some drugs which were illegal to the United States but which he thought might be helpful. He spent time in denial and in all the other stages of loss, including preparation for his death. We spent a lot of time talking on the phone. One of my four children commented that I was "talking to Uncle Bob a lot." I only wish I could have talked to him more.

I'll also never forget the day that he came out to our parents. It was a Sunday afternoon, just the four of us at my parents' house. He told them he had something very important to talk with them about. It was a triple whammy—first, that he was gay, and then that he was HIV-positive and had AIDS.

106

My mother didn't say a lot, but my father said, "Bob, you are our son. We love you and we're proud of you. We're sorry this has happened to you, but we will be with you through it and pray for God's presence and healing spirit." Then we all stood in a group hug and prayed fervently that God would help us make it through this experience together. It was one of the defining moments of my life: a family facing a formidable foe, but facing it together in love.

Bob belonged to Affirmation (a coalition of Mormons and Community of Christ members), helped found GALA (Gay and Lesbian Acceptance), and became associated with the Good Samaritan Project (an organization to help victims of HIV/AIDS). When he died, our family gave some of his furniture to the group. I remember Bob telling me that he had gone to some classes where they encouraged the participants to visualize their own deathbed scene. Bob shared his thoughts with me about that and, in fact, when the real thing happened, it was much as he imagined it. He didn't want to be in a hospital but at home with family and friends, and he was. He did, however, believe during his last months that he would be cured. I share some of his own thoughts that I discovered after his death in a letter he had written to a friend. He wanted so badly to have a testimony of healing:

> In July 1985, I was diagnosed with Acquired Immune Deficiency Syndrome (AIDS). I developed several symptoms gradually over a couple of months but ignored the signs and pressed on with work and regular activities. I knew about this dreaded disease from articles I had read in the gay news media, but I never thought it could happen to me. I was a good person. And although I had been sexually active as a homosexual for eight years, I knew many others who I thought would certainly get it before I would.
>
> I got pneumocystis pneumonia, was in the hospital two weeks and recovered quickly. I was never angry or bitter, but felt God would guide me to whatever outcome.
>
> I was administered to by the elders and felt the assurance of God's love. I had much hope and faith—not for a healing—but that God would guide. I went back to work in August 1985, three weeks after entering the hospital. I sailed along from then to February 1986. I gained back twenty of the thirty pounds I had lost, and felt good, but in February

1986, I developed CMV (Cyta Megalo Virus) in my colon. It was a very painful, constant abdomen ache which made eating difficult. I lost 40 pounds! There was no certain treatment for CMV, and I began to plan my funeral.

A member of our Affirmation group started talking to me about a possible healing. I had never really thought about it. My feeling had been that whatever happened, if I could witness of God's love, even in dying, I would be blessed. I knew the statistics—no one survived! He kept prompting me, and I guess I started to think and wonder about the possibility of a healing. I had to admit that if all I professed to believe about God and church, and so forth, was true, then the God that worked miracles of former times could work them today. But I felt so unworthy. Why would an all powerful God do this for me? I soon came to admit that it was possible, but still doubted it would happen. I accepted my pending death. I prayed for God's will, not mine.

Our local Affirmation group knew everything about my condition and was very supportive. They began to pray more fervently and to fast for me. Several of them began to discuss healing and they decided to hold a special worship service at my apartment, centered around administration. This was during World Conference 1986, and I was in bad shape. I was down to 112 pounds.

Before the service, the fellow who first suggested to me the possibility of a healing came early and said he had prayed and fasted all day, and the Lord had revealed to him that it was not his will that I should die. But that in exchange for a healing, God wanted a covenant from me. God wanted me to turn away from promiscuity. This was not pleasing to him! And he wanted me to be valiant in my testimony of all that God had done for me. Both of these seemed logical to me, and I thanked the man for sharing that with me.

During the service, but before the actual administration and laying on of hands, I shared with the group that I had come to believe a healing was possible, but that I still left it up to God. During the laying on of hands, I prayed. I told God that I would covenant with him as he revealed to me through my friend—to not be promiscuous and to be valiant in my testimony. I felt the Holy Spirit in my body. I knew I was being blessed. I cried. I believed I was being healed. Afterwards I shared that with the group.

I have faith that I am being healed. It will take a while for all the evidence to surface so that I can say I know. The pain in my abdomen

108

is much less and therefore my appetite is better. The doctors gave me no medicine for the CMV because they had none, so I really believe the improvement there is due to the Holy Spirit and God's blessing. I am still very weak, and I know it will take awhile, maybe several months, to gain back the lost weight.

I am so joyful about what I believe God is doing for me. It has certainly increased my faith. Time will tell the whole story, but I think I already know the final chapter.

Oh yes, there was a confirming experience. The same week we had the laying on of hands service, my father was awakened in the night and the Spirit told him to pray for Bob. My father is very religious. He is a pastor. He has had numerous experiences with the Holy Spirit. As he prayed (several hours), he remembered an experience he had when I was eight years old and baptized and confirmed a member of the Community of Christ. My father and another elder confirmed me; and during that service, twenty-eight years ago, the Holy Spirit told him that if I were faithful, I would some day serve in the same priesthood office as he and his father before him. Both my father and grandfather were elders. Keep in mind that I am a priest and about to die and my father prays and remembers a promise that I would be an elder (if faithful) and so my father basically claims the fulfillment of that experience twenty-eight years ago. And the Holy Spirit spoke to him and said okay, [but] only if I repent. Now my father knew nothing of our group experience. This was entirely separate, yet they both happened the same week, the week of April 6. This was enough confirmation for me.

So, this is my testimony. It is still coming to pass. I still need your prayers as the road ahead is long, but as I said, I believe I know the destination for me is spiritual and physical healing.

After being diagnosed with HIV/AIDS in 1985, Bob lived alone in his large apartment on Central Street in Kansas City, Missouri, for all but the last one and one-half weeks of his life. He, in fact, bought the building and a brand new silver Mazda RX-7 shortly before his death. He liked to entertain and had a large group of friends and supporters from both the gay and straight communities.

In mid-August 1986, it became apparent that Bob could no longer live alone. My parents and I moved in with him and took care of him night and day until finally, a few days before he died, we found a night nurse to give us some relief. I had a family of four kids that I checked in on every afternoon, making sure they and my husband had what they needed for the next twenty-four hours before returning to Bob's apartment.

I took the children to see him once during that week and a half, and he assured them that God would heal him. My two youngest, ages six and seven, didn't really know what their Uncle Bob was up against, but they knew it was serious. My intention was to tell them the truth when they were older, but I waited too long to do that. My youngest daughter learned that he died from HIV/AIDS from her best friend, whose mother was one of my best friends. She was pretty upset with me for not telling her the truth, and I regret not doing that in a timely manner.

On the day of my brother's death, Wednesday, 20 August 1986, we went through our usual routine of trying to feed and care for his physical needs, as he had become completely bedridden. He was pretty incoherent a lot of the time but had moments of lucidity. His last earthly smile was bestowed on a young man who came to help us care for him and whom he met for the first time that morning. None of us will forget the warmth of his personality and the love of his heart.

I had left the apartment in the afternoon, as usual, to go home to check on my family. I was physically, emotionally, and spiritually exhausted and decided to call the Sante Fe Stake offices and ask for administration for myself. They had elders there who were willing to do that, so I went by on my way back to the apartment. They asked for no explanation, but I told them I was helping care for my brother who was terminally ill, and I needed help beyond myself.

Almost immediately, I felt the warmth of the Holy Spirit descending through my aching body, starting from the top of my head where the elders' hands were resting. The warmth spread downward; and as it reached my legs, the ache and tiredness that had been there when I arrived left. I went out from that experience renewed. I needed that renewal as I was soon to discover that my brother was leaving this realm.

When I walked into his apartment, several persons were holding vigil, praying in his living room. My mother, my father, and another elder were in his bedroom with him. Bob appeared to be unconscious. His eyes were rolled back, and his breathing was labored, but he was not struggling or gasping. Dad and the other elder laid their hands on his head; and in the course of the prayer, my brother simply drew his last earthly breath. It was a peaceful, spiritual moment that has become another defining experience in my life. I have since felt privileged and blessed to be part of my brother's departure from this realm. It was an extremely traumatic moment, as I loved my brother deeply and I didn't want him to leave. I felt disappointed that his vision of physical healing did not occur, but I felt assured that he was "safe in the arms of Jesus."

One of my most difficult personal losses was the fact that the desire of Bob's heart was to be involved in building the Temple in Independence. That process was beginning in 1986, just when he died. Sometime within the next year or so, though, I was at a retreat at Lake Doniphan during which J. C. Stuart, a former apostle (1972-82) spoke about the process of planning the Temple. As J. C. was speaking, I was impressed that my brother was in fact involved in some way on the other side. This was a great comfort to me.

Are we our brother's keeper? The dictionary defines a "keeper" as a "protector, warden, or custodian—any of various devices to keep something in position." I wanted to "keep" my brother in this realm of existence, but his calling was to move to another. At one point, after he died and we were waiting for the ambulance to come get his body, I was alone in the room with him. I put my hand in the small of his back where I could still feel his warmth. I said out loud, "Well, Bob, we gave it our best shot." But I had to let that little baby I saw just after he was born thirty-seven years before move on to the next world. Hard as I tried, I could not keep him here with me.

I have missed him tremendously since he left, but I have also been excited for him. I thank God for the time he was with us here and look forward to seeing him again when Christ comes in his glory. There is no doubt in my mind that Bob will be there then, praising God and singing with the other hosts of heaven. I am excited for the opportunity which he has had to be involved in the life beyond this world and thankful to have been a part of his life here. I know he's been busy there as he was here, even though his part in building the kingdom of God on earth changed focus that August day.

I have continued to pray for him. I feel his support in my life. I believe love transcends this earth and breaks the bonds of time as we know it. I am not his "keeper" but rather one of his "soul mates" who is honored and privileged to be his "big sister."

9

A LETTER TO A MARRIED GAY MORMON FRIEND

Bob Swoffer

NOTE: Bob Swoffer, Merlene Brush's brother, wrote this letter dated Sunday, 27 November 1983, to a friend who had written to the Affirmation group in Kansas City for information and support regarding dealing with being gay and being Christian. At the time he wrote this letter, the church had not yet changed its name to Community of Christ, but that term is used here for consistency with the rest of the volume. Bob graduated from Lamoni (Iowa) High School where he was student council president. He attended Graceland for two years and went on to graduate from Kansas University in environmental design. He spent two years in VISTA (Volunteers in Service to America) and two years in the Peace Corps. He worked for several architects in the Kansas City Area. Bob was the catalyst in the creation of GALA. He died in August 1986. This book is dedicated to him.

Dear Friend,

We're thankful for your courageous letter and pray that the Lord Jesus Christ will grant to you and your family a special portion of love and understanding.

Your letter brought tears to my eyes as I read it and remembered not so long ago how I struggled with my religion Community of Christ and my sexuality.

I was raised by loving parents who provided a Christian/Zionic home environment for me and my sister. When I was eight years old, my family moved from Michigan to Lamoni, Iowa, where my father began teaching at Graceland College. We lived in Lamoni for ten years and were very much a part of the church family there. I was active in Scouting (which was sponsored by the church) and Zion's League. I was both president and worship chairman of Zion's League. Lamoni was a quaint little town with a large percentage (more than 50 percent) of Community of Christ families. Most of our lives as a family were centered around church activity. My father served as an associate pastor.

In 1968 when I was in college, my parents moved to Independence, Missouri. After graduating from college in 1972, I spent four years in two government programs, first, VISTA (Volunteers in Service to America), and then the Peace Corps. I began to grapple with who I really was. It was not easy for me, largely due to my conservative Christian upbringing. As a child growing up, I had taken seriously all of the church innuendos about sexual activity being "sort of dirty." In looking back now, perhaps I misread the real attitude of the church toward sex—but somehow, through church and/or family, I believed it was wrong for a young man or woman to acknowledge sex as a natural physical/emotional drive. I diligently repressed all sexual desires and, as a result, grew up very naive sexually.

Years later, when I found myself away from the watchful eye of church and family, I began to think about my sexual feelings. My journal from my Peace Corps days reports a classic struggle between what I thought God required of me and what my newly discovered inner feelings wanted to express. I prayed continually that God would grant me the strength to overcome what I thought were sexual temptations. Somehow, and I thank my Heavenly Father for it now, I knew I was basically a good person. I knew I was caring and loving and tried to practice such Christian attitudes in my daily actions. I knew God loved me, and I believed there was some yet to be fully realized purpose he had for me. I wasn't certain, but little by little I began to feel that his purpose for me might include my feelings of sexuality. After much careful soul searching, I therefore began to take specific steps to experience what I

114

felt, for me, could be a natural and loving sexual experience/relation with another man.

I won't elaborate now, except to say that it was very difficult for me; and without God's continued watchful care, I most likely never would have survived. "Coming out" for an honest gay Christian can be the most devastating experience of a lifetime. It is usually not a single event but a continued process of self-revelation which can dominate one's life for several years with much pain and grief. However, at the same time, it can be the liberating experience necessary for one's continued spiritual growth.

In regard to your specific questions, I am happy to be able to give you good news! The Community of Christ leadership at the headquarters level has been studying homosexuality for some years, with apparent desire to find enlightened contemporary answers. Please read the subcommittee report on homosexuality first. It will warm your heart. Even though it is only a subcommittee report and was not fully accepted by the Standing High Council, it represents the most "enlightened" Christian perspective I have yet to read on the subject. I feel it is one that we as a group should slowly and carefully promote throughout the church. The concept of "responsible homosexual expression" is a true gem of contemporary understanding and warrants continued study and refinement.

The official position is reflected in the "Standing High Council Statement on Homosexuality," adopted 18 March 1982. Although not as accepting as the subcommittee report, it does reflect some very advanced thinking. You will note that the church chooses to distinguish between "homosexual orientation" and "homosexual activity." In your particular situation, based on information in your letter, this is quite significant. As a "non-practicing" or "virgin" homosexual (see #1, 3, 5 in the Standing High Council guidelines), you would undoubtedly have "legal" basis for continuing in your priesthood! This, of course, would become an issue only if you decided to tell your pastor or district president. Under no situation is excommunication ever mentioned.

I also am a priest in the Community of Christ. I am active in my congregation but have told no one in the church of my homosexual orientation and behavior. I am searching for the "responsible homosexual behavior" experience referred to by the subcommittee. In gay lingo, I am looking for a "lover" with whom I can develop an honest, trusting, lifetime relationship. I know such relations are possible. My uncle, now deceased, lived faithfully with his lover for forty years!

So much of the gay community today centers around the social bar life that it is difficult for those of us who want to experience more than one-night stands to meet others with similar desires. It is one of our hopes that Affirmation will help provide an alternative to the bars for meeting others. Thus we get together twice a month for some kind of activity. We have ten or twelve members in the Kansas City group ranging from ages twenty-one to forty. We are a new group, having been together only ten months. We are mostly Community of Christ (eight) with four LDS. I personally know about a dozen more local gay Community of Christ members who are not yet interested in our Affirmation chapter. So there is good potential for us to do some missionary work!

I never married, so I cannot exactly say that I understand your situation entirely, but I know of several others who have dealt with similar situations. If you intend to eventually act on your gay feelings, you may feel as though you should share your inner self with your wife. This may be quite traumatic. If you decide to do so, I would, at the least, do some reading to prepare yourself and possibly enlist the aid of a sensitive counselor.

There seems to be no universal route for gay men who are married. Most eventually either choose to express their sexuality and leave their wives, or end up frustrated by repressing their deep sexual feelings. There is much that has been written about how gay men can come through this experience. Many gay men are able to maintain loving relations with children and ex-wives. It is, however, likely that you will have to pass through a period of hurt either way.

Well, I wish I could say more to assure you that confronting one's true feelings is the only way to progress. My experience has taught me that, when the truth hurts, don't lie, just say it carefully. I hope some of this speaks to your needs at this time. Please feel free to correspond as you wish with us. I can send you more pamphlets and general information as you desire. We are here to help you—not to push you one way or the other. Take your own time and work it out for yourself, considering all the ramifications of church and family. Don't forget to include your Heavenly Father in all your decisions. He knows all and knows you better than you do.

God loves you as the person you are and gave you the wonderful ability to love both men and women. Many never can admit this, due to years of societal teaching to the contrary. For some reason, however, some of us figure it out.

God Bless You,
Peace,
Bob

10

A Family Rearranged But Not Broken

Fran Zimmerman

Fran Zimmerman has been a member of GALA since 1997 and was its treasurer for four years. She lives in Lee's Summit, Missouri, and is an accountant and a priest in the Raytown Community of Christ. Fran was married to Alan Zimmerman for thirty years. They still maintain a close relationship.

My JOURNEY BEGAN in the spring of 1996 when my husband, Alan, came out to me shortly before our twenty-fifth anniversary. I had wanted to take a vacation to celebrate our years together; but Alan, who loves to travel, seemed very unenthusiastic about going. In frustration, I finally confronted him and demanded why he did not want to go anywhere. He evaded my questions and stalled until the following evening when he suggested we go for a ride and "talk."

We went to a lake near our house where he finally told me in as loving and nonthreatening a way as he knew how that he was attracted to men. He didn't use the terms "gay" or "homosexual," which at that point would have been frightening words for both of us. I was upset, but not totally shocked. I had begun to suspect that something was wrong and had even wondered about the possibility of homosexuality being an issue. He was politically liberal; but even so, his interest in gay issues and books seemed unusually intense. Whenever such a thought crossed my mind, I brushed it away, thinking I must be imagining things. That sort of thing happened in made-for-TV movies, not in my world.

He assured me that he had never done anything that would jeopardize his health or my own, that he had not acted upon his feelings, and that he didn't want a divorce. He confessed that he had not wanted to take a trip because he knew I would see it as an opportunity for a romantic second honeymoon and the hypocrisy of hiding his feelings was getting harder and harder to deal with.

Alan and I decided to visit Michigan's upper peninsula for a week, saw some beautiful scenery, and spent a lot of time talking and sharing in a way we had never been able to before. When someone is hiding such a vital part of himself, it affects communication in many other ways as well. It was a relief to have everything out in the open and be able to talk.

When we returned, the hard work of adjusting to this new reality began. On the night that Alan told me, he also "outed" himself to a minister in the Community of Christ, so that I could have immediate support. Phyllis was not only gay friendly but also someone with whom I could feel comfortable discussing the situation. That really helped. I needed someone other than Alan to talk to, to share my concerns and fears. She gave me books and articles to read and a shoulder on which to cry. She also gave me some priceless words of wisdom. She told me that there were "no roadmaps" for the journey that Alan and I were taking, that we would have to find our own path. There was no right or wrong way, only what was best for both of us.

Since we were planning to stay married, we decided not to say anything to our two children or any other family members at that point. Our son was twenty and living on his own, and our sixteen-year-old daughter was a sophomore in high school. Alan and I both needed time to work through our feelings individually and with each other, without worrying about dealing with others' feelings. I needed Alan's support focused on me.

The next eighteen months became a time of learning and adjusting. Alan developed some gay friendships and attended some gay group functions. I read everything I could get my hands on. Three books were especially helpful. Mel White's *Stranger at the Gate: To Be Gay and Christian in America* (New York: Penguin Books, 1994) helped me understand the struggle that Alan was going through. This man's deep love for his wife was evident as he struggled to come to terms with his sexual identity. *When Husbands Come out of the Closet* (New York: Harrington Park Press, 1989) by Jean Schaar Gochros, and *The Other Side of the Closet: The Coming Out Crisis for Straight Spouses and Families,* rev. and expanded (New York: John Wiley & Sons, 1994) by Amity Buxton were full of helpful information for straight spouses and let me know that I was not the only one going through this same struggle. That information was vital for me.

With illness, death, job losses, divorce, etc., you can usually turn to family, friends, and church for support. Because of the moral and emotional issues surrounding homosexuality, that support is often not seen as an option, and feelings of isolation can become very strong. I also began seeing a therapist to help me deal with my feelings and fears. I began meeting with a straight spouse support group, and it became a lifeline. The women in that group understood my feelings because they were going through the same thing. We shared stories and tears, hugs and laughter. We shared ways of coping and feelings of despair and anger.

PFLAG (Parents and Friends of Lesbians and Gays) is a wonderful group for parents and family members, but it doesn't always provide what straight spouses need. Our needs are very different from a parent's needs. As a woman, there were many times when I wished that it had been one of my children who was gay instead of my husband. As a mother, I was glad that it wasn't. I don't mean to downplay the struggles and adjustments of parents of gay children, but theirs are different—and from my perspective, easier—struggles.

I also prayed. By the summer of 1997, I felt trapped in a maze. Others have described it as wandering in the wilderness. Alan and I loved each other, but how did that fact mesh with the other fact: that he was gay while I was straight? One night before going to bed I prayed from the depths of my heart, asking God what He had in mind for us. I desperately wanted to stay married, but I wanted it to be a healthy relationship. I was convinced that, with God's help, there had to be a way to reach that goal. I prayed for guidance, a way out of the maze.

I woke up in the middle of the night hearing these words very plainly in my mind: "Love him."

My response was immediate and joyful. "Yes, I can do that!" I felt a peaceful warmth spread from my head downward to my feet. I had never experienced anything like it before, nor have I since. I was convinced that our marriage would work, but I still didn't know the way out of the maze.

A couple of weeks later, I again prayed for guidance before going to bed. Again, in the middle of the night, I woke up with the words in my mind: "Love him." This time I protested. Didn't God understand? I did love Alan! That was the problem! Then came these thoughts: "All I am asking of you is that you love him. Let Me take care of all the details." Again I felt at peace and was convinced that our marriage would last. Somehow God would find a way to work it out.

I had never thought that God was going to somehow "make" Alan straight, nor did I interpret these experiences that way. I fully believed that He had created Alan as a gay person and loved him as he was, just as he loved me as He had created me. I just had faith that God had an answer to our dilemma.

I began to attend GALA (Gay and Lesbian Acceptance), an organization for education, fellowship, and support affiliated with the Community of Christ, with which Alan had become involved. It began as a way for me to share in that part of Alan's life, to lessen the feelings of exclusion I was beginning to experience as he developed more gay friendships. I went to some of the monthly social activities and then attended the international GALA retreat over Labor Day weekend in 1997 in Michigan and felt loved and accepted by the group. I met many wonderful people who became, and still are, a tremendous source of supportive friendship for me. They included me in their circle in spite of my being straight. We laughed together and cried together. Their stories of struggle broke my heart and they, in turn, cared deeply about my struggles.

Late in September 1997, the bottom fell out of my world. Alan admitted to me that he did not think it would work for us to stay married. As he became more comfortable with himself as a gay man, he wanted to explore the possibility of developing deeper gay relationships. I was devastated. I was terrified of divorce. I couldn't even say the word. I wanted Alan to be able to accept himself as a gay man, but I wanted him to choose to stay with me. My feelings were perhaps naive, but I still felt that there must be a way to work things out.

On top of that, our son was to be married in a couple of weeks, and I did not know how I could possibly face celebrating the beginning of his new life while my own marriage was collapsing. Alan had not planned to say anything to me until after the wedding; but in one of our long talks, the subject came up and the truth came out. I spent many hours with my therapist during that time, working on ways to cope with the wedding without letting on that anything was wrong. We had told our daughter earlier that summer that Alan was gay but had said nothing, as yet, to our son. We had decided to wait until after the wedding to tell him because we didn't want anything to cloud this time for him. With a lot of prayer I not only coped, but also was able to find some enjoyment in our son's special day as we welcomed a wonderful daughter-in-law into our family.

Alan and I did not separate immediately after the wedding. In fact, because of other issues, we ended up staying together another two years, until the late fall of 1999. During these months, I slowly adjusted to the change in our lives, accepting it gradually, and coming to terms emotionally with it. As strange as it seems, we went apartment hunting together and shopped together for bargains to furnish it.

At the same time, it was still hard for me to face the reality that Alan would be moving out. Hadn't God assured me that things would work out? When moving day came, I helped him, even as my tears flowed freely. I was terrified of living by myself. I had gone from my parents' home to college to marriage. I had never lived on my own. I honestly didn't know if I could.

But a strange thing happened. Once Alan moved out, I found that being on my own wasn't nearly as bad as I had dreaded. Alan and I still had a close, supportive relationship, and he was only a phone call away if I needed anything. We still saw each other frequently and talked on the phone almost every day. I didn't feel abandoned.

Over the next several months, I even discovered some benefits. There were new freedoms. I had control of the TV remote! If I wanted to clean house at eleven o'clock at night or read while I ate, no one complained. It became a time for me to explore who I was and what made me happy. I had always been a daughter, a wife, and/or a mother. I had loved these roles, and I adored being "Grandma" when our first grandchild was born. But who was I as an individual? What was my purpose in life? What opportunities were out there waiting for me? It has been an adventure to begin to discover some of the answers.

About a year after Alan moved out, he found someone with whom to share a committed relationship. Because Alan and I had taken time for our relationship to evolve from marriage into friendship, I was honestly happy for him. I feel fortunate that Richard is someone whom I can respect and admire, someone I have become very fond of. I know that he cares about me as well. He, too, was married at one time and has remained close to his family. He understands the importance of family and is not threatened by Alan's relationship with me and the children. He has become an accepted and valued part of our family. We have even spent holidays together. On Christmas morning, everyone comes to my house for our traditional breakfast and gift exchange before we all go to Alan's parents' house for the extended family gathering.

Alan left the decision about divorce up to me, whenever I felt I was ready. That time came in the summer of 2001, after we had been separated almost two years. I realized that if I was to have a chance to find the happiness that he had found, I had to make that final break. I also realized that while our marriage needed to end, our relationship would not. In January 2002, after thirty years of marriage, I was a single person again.

Our family is somewhat unusual, but it is healthy and strong. Alan and I remain close friends who love and support each other. Our children know that even though we don't live together anymore, we both still love and support them. We all enjoy spending time together. Our family has not been broken, just rearranged. Someday, when the time is right, I hope to meet someone special with whom to share my life. But I am in no rush. This is my time for me.

I realize that God did answer my prayers. The answer is not what I expected or thought I wanted, but so much more than I could envision at the time.

11

WHERE WILL YOU PUT YOUR TRUST?

Carol Cavin

Carol Cavin recently retired from the Community of Christ headquarters staff. She was a member of the 2004-06 Human Sexuality Committee for the church and is active in the Walnut Gardens Congregation in Independence. She was married for thirty-five years to Larry Cavin before he came out in 2000. They raised two children: son Chris and daughter Kelley, who died in 1990. Carol has been editor of the Compassionate Friends Kansas City regional newsletter since 1991, and for the past three years she has edited the GALA newsletter.

W HERE WILL YOU put your trust? We all begin life as infants relying on the big people around us, sometimes with tragic results, but what other choice do we have? People whose trust has been broken violently and repeatedly as children, or even as adults, may think with good reason that no one is trustworthy. However, while some persons give up hope, others in similar circumstances continue to live in hope. Why? Perhaps trust and hope come to us as gifts from God, or through the loving, trustworthy people around us.

The choice is ours to either accept or reject such gifts. Any time we choose to trust in this imperfect world, we also risk being disappointed. No matter how honorable people may try to be, they are still human beings capable of making mistakes.

I have always trusted that God is guiding me—when I pay attention! One of the most memorable events of my life occurred at the 1960 World Conference when I decided to go back to Graceland College as the result of a message delivered by Dr. Roy Cheville, longtime religion professor at Graceland who had recently (1958) become the Presiding Patriarch of the Church. My husband Larry was persuaded to do the same thing at the same time, and I have believed for the past forty-plus years that we were pointed in each other's direction. I still do, even though in March 2000 he told me he is gay, and moved out to live with his new partner in April 2001.

How did this happen? Larry was operating out of the cultural standards of the 1950s and 1960s. He thought that getting married was the appropriate thing for him to do as a gay man trying to live straight. For thirty-five years, we had what I consider to be an excellent partnership and friendship. We worked hard together, raised two children to the best of our abilities, struggled to survive the death of one, and were privileged to share in the lives of seven exchange students. We both grew a lot through the years, to the point that Larry was finally able to openly acknowledge his sexual orientation and move on independently.

Does that mean our life together was one big mistake? I don't think so. I have always trusted Larry completely. I believe him to be one of the most gentle, nurturing, honest people I have ever known. I suppose you could say that trusting him has led to the pain I experience, even as I celebrate his freedom to live openly as the person he has always been. But I trust that God will continue to support us as we learn to live with the results of Larry's choices and mine.

We continue to be close friends and members of a newly defined and evolving family. Our son Chris and I helped Larry move into the apartment he shared with his partner, Bobby. We trade recipes, dishes, cooking equipment, furniture, photographs, and numerous other things accumulated during our thirty-five years of marriage. Larry and I were honored to be present last fall when Chris proposed to Shannon and she accepted. We were all together at Larry and Bobby's apartment, along with members of Bobby's family, for dinner on that first Christmas Eve. We opened gifts on Christmas morning after our traditional Christmas breakfast at the family home where I still lived. That afternoon we all had Christmas dinner at the home of Bobby's aunt and uncle. Larry, Bobby, and I shared in Chris and Shannon's wedding celebration. Chris, Shannon, and I were present during Larry and Bobby's commitment ceremony.

Such activities can be painful and may seem strange, but continuing to love and honor each other is the only choice we want to make. Estrangement, anger, judgment, and isolation bring nothing but pain to all the parties involved. The people in my congregation have prided ourselves on welcoming gays into our church family, but we have never talked much about what that means. We try to be loving and accepting, but it's sometimes tempting to keep our distance from things we don't understand or that make us uncomfortable. And sometimes a spirit of cautious acceptance comes across as disapproval or even rejection. I hope that, as individuals and as a community, we can seek opportunities to dialogue. How do we reach out to each other, even while we are coming from very different places?

President Grant McMurray, in his sermon on the first Sunday of the 2002 World Conference, offered some very helpful insights: "We must not succumb to our fears nor fail to respect those who disagree with us. We must instead be voices of reconciliation and ministers of healing.... Gay and lesbian brothers and sisters are walking with us on the path of the disciple. They have chosen to be there because they feel God's call to them....Ministry is not just about calling. It is also about acceptance of that calling by those who will receive the ministry."

Grant then quoted Henri J. M. Nouwen: "We are not the healers, we are not the reconcilers, we are not the givers of life. We are sinful, broken, vulnerable people who need as much care as anyone we care for. The mystery of ministry is that we have been chosen to make our own limited and very conditional love the gateway for the unlimited and unconditional love of God." (*In the Name of Jesus: Reflections on Christian Leadership* [New York: Crossroad Publishing, 1989], 43-44.)

12

A JOURNEY OF CRYING OUT
TO OTHERS

Larry Cavin

Larry Cavin lives in Kansas City, Missouri, with his partner where he is a docent for the Kansas City Zoo and a volunteer for Youthfriends. He was married for thirty-five years to Carol Cavin prior to coming out in 2000. He retired in 2002 as the manager of the regulatory program for the U.S. Army Corps of Engineers after a thirty-year career. He was formerly active in the Walnut Gardens Community of Christ but is no longer active in the church. This essay is a testimony shared at Walnut Gardens Community of Christ, Independence, Missouri, March 17, 2002.

HE WAS ONLY in grade school but somehow he knew that he saw the world differently than others. He had feelings that he couldn't understand and they made him strangely uncomfortable. He sensed that he shouldn't feel the way he did, but he didn't understand that either. He didn't know what to do or whom to ask. He really didn't know that he needed to cry out.

As a young teenager, he began understanding who he was. He understood that it was unacceptable for boys to have feelings for other boys, but he knew that he did and he knew there was a name for it. It was not who he wanted to be, but it seemed to be true anyway, and he was afraid to cry out. So as the years passed, he learned to excel in music, art, schoolwork, leadership, and church work. He learned to exercise great control over his life, being very careful what he said and did, and very measured in showing emotions and affection so that he would always be protected from disclosure. Above all, he learned how to achieve approval and recognition from respected adults. If he could not be accepted for who he really was, he would become the best of someone else.

Thus, he began living his lie. It was hard and he felt guilty. And what he loved most in the whole world then—the Community of Christ—told him he was an unacceptable person; but he committed his life to the church anyway, rarely missing an opportunity to serve or to participate. It only complicated his life. He cried out to God in anguish to make it "right." Surely God could fix what he had created. Surely God loved him and wanted him to be healed. Why would God force him to live a life of fear, deception and guilt? For reasons that seemed unclear and unfair, God seemed not to hear his cries.

The isolation was ever present. It existed because he knew he was different and could never talk about it, could never ask questions about it, could never seek forgiveness for being someone he was not allowed to be. The fear of discovery was frightening. What would it do to his life? How could people continue to like and accept him if they knew?

Finally, he tried to cry out. During a time of turmoil and self-doubt, he sought counsel from a college psychology professor who would surely understand and help. The professor reassured him, "Don't worry. You are okay. You are not one of 'those.' You are having normal feelings and they will pass." Either the professor wasn't listening, or he didn't want to hear what the young man had to say. He vowed never to cry out again.

So he did what many closeted gay men of that day did. He denied the gender orientation essential to his selfhood and chose to be someone else. He dated. He married. And it was a good marriage; in many ways, it was almost an ideal marriage. For over thirty years he shared in building a family, in a community that was loving and accepting. But would they—could they—love and accept him if they really knew the truth? Would life really be the same? How could he know?

He lived with the conflict of loving someone but not being in love. He lived with guilt and isolation. He lived with the fear of discovery. And most of all he lived with the yearning for the freedom to be the person he knew he was but was afraid to become. He couldn't take the risk. Crying out didn't seem an option—or was he crying out when he didn't even know it?

One day, bursting into his life with judgment and pain, came the realization that he could no longer deny being the person he was created to be. He wrote in his journal: "I think I can no longer escape who I am." He knew who he was, even though he desperately wanted to be someone else. One Sunday in church, he was so moved by a worship service on diversity, which spoke of the need for acceptance, that the tears welled up in his eyes. He wanted to jump up and tell his story—to finally share his secret truth, to finally be cleansed. And yet, he still did not know how to cry out. He got up in tears and silently left the service.

When it seemed that his life would soon unravel and he was convinced that he had no future as a gay married man or as a gay single man, he finally found the strength to cry out in desperation and despair. A wise and loving counselor helped him pick up the pieces and begin to reconstruct a life that might yet be lived in honesty and openness. It required that he learn to be honest, first with himself and then with others. It meant that out of fairness, respect, and love he would end his marriage to a loving and compassionate woman who was willing to understand and support him in his efforts to be the person he was created to be, even when it meant sadness and uncertainty for her.

This is my story, but it is also the story of many others just like me. I am rebuilding. Life for me is uncertain, just as it is for all of us, but life for me now is authentic. Joseph Campbell said: "The greatest privilege in life is to be exactly what you were meant to be."

Even though my story is that of a gay man needing help and acceptance, there are many kinds of stories. I hope we all learn to listen to the variety of pleas for help—which may not all be spoken pleas. I have shared my story because I hope it will reinforce how important it is to listen with our hearts and not just with our ears. People do not always know how to cry out, or they are afraid to cry out, or they refuse to cry out. I think we need to work hard to develop the kinds of relationships and live the kinds of lives that will help us to be sensitive to the needs of others and to be loving reconcilers.

One of the things I have learned over the years is that being right or wrong is not always what is most important. We have values. We have laws. We have scriptures. We have expectations. And the list goes on. All of these provide assistance in living our lives. But the overriding need is for reconciling love and acceptance of each other as we are and as we hope to become. The cries of others may be loud and clear, and may even come crashing into our lives. Or they may be voices speaking so softly, so tentatively, that we need to listen with our hearts and reach out with healing hands and words.

I have shared this very personal experience with my community—a community of people who have shared my marriage, the births of my children, the death of my daughter, and many other events over the last thirty years, and now this new challenge of learning to be the person I was created to be. I have done it in the hope that it will help each of you to be who you are called to be and to listen for the cries of others who are seeking their own way to wholeness.

13

SILENCED AFTER A LIFE OF SERVICE

Rogene Smith McKiernan

JOURNEYS ARE INTERESTING things. You may not be sure how they started or when they will end. You cannot say for sure what would have happened if you had not taken the turn you did. Sometimes you move on because you choose to. At other times, you are presented with circumstances that force you to leave behind what you know and have been. Reflections on our lives help illuminate what the journey is all about. This story is my attempt to do just that—to recount the ups and downs, joys and sadness, pain and pleasure, my self discovery. I cannot reflect on who I have become without exploring the role of the Community of Christ in my life, because it has touched me with both beauty and ugliness.

I grew up a devout Community of Christ member with the proud history of three generations before me who believed in the church as deeply as any I have met. They were honest, hardworking, loving, Word-of-Wisdom-obeying Christians. I was raised to be an example to those around me of the goodness of God and the rightness of my church. I was supported, nourished, challenged, and taught to judge the world from our understanding of the scriptures.

Nauvoo was a great place to grow up, surrounded by the Mississippi River, church history, and an extended family. Through our home passed a constant stream of church officials, missionaries, and members from around the world. Those moments provided me a sense of wonder and appreciation of how much the faith meant in people's lives. Those visitors were revered, interesting, and important because they interpreted and lived the message of the gospel, and validated who we were. Leaving my childhood and teen years behind could have been a traumatic change. Instead, it was a wonderful next step.

Graceland College (now Graceland University) was a grand experience where I was surrounded by many members of the faith, I no longer felt that I stood alone. I soaked it up like a sponge, and I stayed to graduate from the newly instituted religion major in 1961. The mental and spiritual stimulation was wonderful. My worldview expanded mightily. I suppose I must have heard the term homosexual; but even if I had, I don't think I would have applied it to myself. After all, I was following the tradition of my family which included marriage and a family. That, too, came to pass; and I immersed myself in the task of being a wife and mother. I have no regrets about marriage and family except that, unknowingly, I was unable to give my all to the marriage relationship.

As a wife and mother, I followed in the footsteps of those who had gone before me. Like them, my husband and I made the church the center of our lives. I developed women's retreats and classes, directed camps, served as a conference delegate, taught at reunions, and in my local congregation did everything I could and, as far as I know, did it well. During my thirties, my cousin was ordained a patriarch. During his ordination, I received the knowledge that I was called to receive priesthood. I was stunned by the thought, fully aware that it was impossible in a church that saw a woman's highest calling as a member. For the first time I began searching outside the church for that which was denied me in the church.

I began to teach at a Catholic girls' boarding school. Working with the nuns and the Catholic church destroyed many negative stereotypes I was raised with. Again my worldview broadened. It set the stage for discovering homosexuality and confronting what that might mean in my life.

In the meantime, my husband became ill with Amleotrofic Lateral Sclerosis (ALS). Our local congregation and district were our main support and comfort. During those five years, Larry was dealing with the process of dying, and I was dealing with the process of surviving. We were both desirous of retaining dignity and love. We both wanted our three sons to remember the good times, and we struggled to remain faithful and positive about life. Writing was part of my way of coping. I found myself trying to understand what was happening to Larry, to me, and to put into perspective that part of my journey.

I HAVE KNOWN ALS

Inside I have known
for so long
the feelings of hopelessness,
despair,
ultimate death
and yet
no one has said
a word.

I know there will be struggles
greater than I have met before.
Tears well up so easily
almost as a daily part of life.
Some are for me
some for Larry
some for our sons
who must now face
some of life's most difficult moments.

We are so unprepared.
How does one start?

135

They say all this makes us stronger!
But I must admit
I would rather remain weak!
Commanded to give thanks in all things.
Is it possible?
I guess I don't know how.
My thanks are so short lived
like a sparrow flitting from one bush to another.

PERSPECTIVE

Across eons of time
pain of such duration is nothing
and yet
for the moment it is all there is.

We have stood in God's presence
for so long,
almost half of my life.
and I must watch him leave
haltingly
stumbling
and the Lord says Peace.
I make a mockery of that word
when my thoughts run rampant through my head.

To survive I must learn to accept that
Peace without mockery.
Lord, help me beyond myself.

After Larry's death in April 1985, I continued to teach until my sons were out of high school, but I became involved with Outward Bound during the summers. Outward Bound is a wilderness adventure-based program. It utilizes experiential education as it challenges people to "do more that we think we can do and recognize that we need each other." Nowhere had I been more affirmed as an individual. The other staff did not put me in the pigeonhole of a "productive" Community of Christ member but simply challenged me to grow as myself. As I became certain that I was a lesbian, they accepted that, too. Their desire to help people come to know themselves supported my journey of self discovery. Again my worldview grew by leaps and bounds. Working with Outward Bound as an instructor from about 1987 to the present has been a marvelous, freeing experience, reflected in a poem I wrote in the spring of 1989:

RELEASE

I've watched a large pool of water
trapped by a dam of ice
And wondered how long it would take
before it was released to go on its way.

Each day as I walked past, the pool became deeper
and flooded a larger area,
I sensed the pressure pushing against
one small outlet, frozen for months.

Then one day two young boys
with crowbar in hand
Began to chip away with boyish glee
until a trickle oozed forth.

It only took one small crack
to allow the water its chance to be free
Slowly but ever increasingly
the water broke free—shouting its joy.

It roared down the creek
filled with debris
Muddy and brown tearing away at the soil
bouncing over rock and slipping over logs.

I thought, how like me with
part of me dammed up behind
Blockades placed there many years ago
because of what I thought should be.

Then into my life came a friend
crowbar in hand!
Sensing the pressure closed up inside of me
began to chip away at that which held me bound.

A trickle of thought began to grow
and force its way through my barriers.
That which was released was muddy with confusion
and tore away at the restrictions in my life.

My new self is unsure of the path to travel
and bounces around.
Rebounding off those around me
carrying off the debris of my soul.

I sense that one day my new self
will become more ordered and purposeful
Sustaining new growth and opportunities
now hidden from my view.

But I hope never to lose the fantastic
sense of freedom and joy
Of bursting forth to a newness and oneness
tumbling joyfully over rocks, gurgling a song of gladness.

In the fall of 1988, I went back to school and entered Western Illinois University's Department of Recreation Administration for a master's degree. I also began to study Christianity's treatment of women in general and lesbians in particular. The more I studied, the more concerned I became that the Community of Christ had taken a wrong turn. Of all things, during that questioning period I was called to the office of elder in the spring of 1992. (The first Community of Christ women were ordained on November 17, 1985.) I thought long and hard about accepting the call. I did so knowing that the calling was from God and feeling that somehow I might be a witness to the rightness of women's place in the priesthood. I had not shared my sexuality with those in the Nauvoo area as I felt no one would understand, and so I began my journey as a priesthood member while still

developing as a lesbian. It was a time of emotional turmoil which I
again tried to express in an untitled poem:

> I feel like I'm going so far, far away,
> away from all that I've learned,
> away from loved ones
> away from the faith that has sustained my life.
>
> Will my journey bring me full circle?
> back to where I started while the rest have gone on,
> back to loved ones enriched or starved,
> Back with a faith deepened or lost?
>
> Will I find a greater depth and breadth—
> in myself and the gifts God invested in me,
> in my loved ones and their uniqueness,
> in the essence of life all around me?
>
> Dreams I had as a child I leave behind.
> Some have been fulfilled.
> Some no longer hold interest for me.
> Some have been broken.
>
> Now I must redefine my life,
>
> and so a new journey begins,
> a journey seeking greater understanding
> a journey seeking new life in old familiar paths
> a journey into myself.
>
> Do I only feel like it's so far, far away,
> is it really just the next step? or
> is there a giant chasm between where I am
> and where I will be?
>
> If I jump, can I jump back, or must I leave—
> those I love so very much,
> the comfort of my faith,

the peaceful loving life I've known?

If it is but a step, why am I so fearful at times?
for my life has been a series of steps
each bringing its own joys and growth
and I understand how to walk.

It is a path I have not walked before.
Are there signposts along the way?
Are there friends who've traveled before me?
Will I become lost or find a greater life?

My hope is that my life will be a spiral,
touching new boundaries pushing me upward,
touching loved ones with new understanding,
touching myself and infinity.

I finished my master's degree in 1989 and stayed on in Macomb
to teach at Western Illinois's Department of Recreation Administration. I developed a relationship with Carol there. We decided that our
life as a lesbian couple was to be open, not closeted. I had lived in an
open relationship as a heterosexual and refused to do otherwise as a
lesbian. It was only a matter of time until a letter arrived from my
pastor. In July 1995, she wrote:

> Having known you and your family all your life, I find it quite difficult
> to write this letter to you. In accordance with the policies of the church,
> it is my duty as Pastor of your home congregation to inform you that
> effective immediately you are placed under ministerial silence. As such,
> you will not be permitted to serve or function in the priesthood of the
> church. Please surrender your priesthood card immediately, so that it
> can be transmitted to the office of the First President.
>
> The silence imposed upon you comes about because of your choice
> to lead an active homosexual lifestyle, which is not acceptable to priest-
> hood ministry, by church standards. This silence is an administrative
> procedure, and no church court is involved .... Because this is an ad-
> ministrative procedure, you may not use non-members to formally as-
> sist you as counsel. Civil courts do not have jurisdiction over this mat-
> ter. You have the right to appeal this action, if you believe a substantial

error has been committed . . . . You have sixty days from the time this notice is received to appeal this action. Your appeal should be to the next highest administrative officer, who is the Nauvoo District President.

To be denied the right to function as a minister means that a priesthood member has committed a serious immoral or criminal act. In effect it prevented me from functioning in my office and calling because I was found immoral. When that happens, the member can appeal the decision of the church through the administrative levels. I naturally felt I had not committed any immoral acts and should not be restrained from ministering because of my sexual orientation.

Carol was as supportive as she could be. Not being an active member of any religion, she found the church proceedings hypocritical. She sensed my pain but could not fully understand it.

Church administrative procedures were not familiar territory for me, so I naively believed that, since I had been an accepted, loved, valued, productive church member all of my life, I would be dealt with fairly. Little did I realize that the church lived by the "letter of the law" as set by the church with no consideration for the expertise of those outside the church.

The district president warned me that making the "administrative appeal" would not change the verdict, even though I had the right to appeal. Stubbornly I thought that maybe my appeal would help someone who came after me. Perhaps some good could come from this. I had not concealed my relationship with Carol and had no intention of becoming celibate.

I thought hard about who should represent me and chose a cousin who had known me all my life. I was comfortable with him and had always felt supported by him. The first appeal session was rather simple. We met in one of the classrooms of the Keokuk, Iowa, church. Present were the district president, two of his counselors, my cousin, and I. The district president asked if I was a practicing homosexual. (I was tempted to say I was no longer "practicing," but refrained.) I said yes. He asked why I was appealing the silencing. I answered that I felt I was doing nothing wrong and that I wanted the church to reconsider its position.

During the discussion, the district president stated that he knew I wasn't the only gay priesthood member in the district. He was sure someone else was gay, but "we haven't caught him yet." That was the last straw! I was so horrified that they were out to get a homosexual priesthood member that I knew I would never again fully trust the church. I certainly had no desire to try.

The district president asked my cousin if he had anything to say and he said something to the effect that he felt he must abide by the church's decision that I be silenced. I was taken aback! Horrified! Betrayed! He was supposed to be on my side! As I look back on it, that should not have been a surprise considering that I had required years to assimilate who I was and he had had only several months. I think there was a prayer asking for guidance and support, which seemed unmeaningful to me. I was told I could appeal to the next level if I chose, then the meeting was over.

I did appeal and the result of the appeal at that level was to uphold the silencing. I came away from the meeting quite shaken and was not surprised when I received a confirming letter from the Nauvoo District president in December 1995:

> The Reorganized Church of Jesus Christ of Latter Day Saints policy states that "if a member of the priesthood admits to, or is found to be engaged in homosexual behavior, the administrative office having jurisdiction should institute procedures for silencing according to church law." In view of your admission to being an active homosexual, in accordance with the policy of the church towards homosexuality, I have no alternative than to uphold the silencing action taken .... You have sixty days from the time of this notice [to appeal] .... Your appeal should be to the next highest administrative office, who is [the] North Central Region President.

I was determined to carry my case to the next level. In February 1996, I again made an appeal to the North Central Region president. Again we met in the same Keokuk church. I asked a good friend, Ken Duke, to accompany me this time. He had been a member of both the RLDS and the LDS churches and had gone through appeals concerning his membership in both churches. He was very supportive of me. He was able to ask questions of the administrative officers that I wouldn't have thought of and, in a very respectful manner, point out the inconsistencies of their Christian response.

I came away from the second procedure very much aware that nothing was going to change their view. Sure enough, the North Central Region president replied in March 1996:

> After hearing your appeal of silencing taken with regard to your priesthood on July 14, 1995 . . . and the subsequent upholding of that action following your appeal hearing with High Priest . . . I have made the following decision.
>
> I have chosen to uphold the original silencing action . . . based on your statement that you are living in a homosexual relationship . . . . Further, you indicated that no substantial error has been committed in the procedure related to your ministerial silence.
>
> You now have sixty (60) days from the date this letter is received to appeal this action. Your appeal should be to the next highest administrative office who is: Apostle Phillip Caswell.

The third administrative appeal wasn't really a hearing—just a reaffirmation from the apostle that the decisions of the last two appeals was upheld. It left me with the cold realization that I was definitely in no position to help create change. Yes, he said I was welcome and accepted as a member. How hollow that sounded and felt.

It was very clear to me that unless I did something, no one in the congregations or in my district would ever know what was happening. So in February 1996, I wrote a letter—one that took every bit of courage I had—to inform those I loved and had served with for decades through camps, retreats, and other ministries even before being in the priesthood. I wanted them to know my position and that of the church. I sent a copy of that letter to the district president, to every pastor of the fifteen congregations in my district, and to approximately two dozen friends:

> This is not an easy letter to write, so I am sure it will not be an easy letter to read. Most of you I have known much of my life. We have worshipped, worked, and played side by side over the years. Part of my story you do not know, so let me attempt to share it with you.
>
> After my husband Larry's death in 1985, my second adulthood began. During my life to that point, I had lived as I was "supposed to"—I

was educated as a school teacher, married a good man, raised a family in the church, and invested all my talents and energies in my family, the church and related activities .... It took many years for me to become comfortable with, let alone celebrate, the knowledge that I am a homosexual ....

That does not mean that I did not enjoy being a mother, did not love Larry, or did not believe in the church work, because all of those brought me great joy. It simply means that I now face the future with greater integrity and more freedom to choose what I will do and what I will believe .... Three years ago I began a relationship which has brought me love and life again. We both agreed that we would prefer to be open about who we are. That has been a wonderful experience ....

As some of you know, I am an ordained Elder. Because I have not tried to hide who I am, the church officials have followed procedures and silenced me. I have appealed and will continue to appeal that silencing, as I believe the basis for the church legislation was based on information which needs to be reviewed and understood in light of ongoing research and scriptural interpretations.

I am writing to ask you to express your concerns to our delegates to World Conference who will be voting on G-3 Sexual Orientation Consideration from the Denver Stake. I, of course, would like to see our delegates vote positively on the legislation, but most importantly, I would like to open dialogue on the subject to reach a greater understanding and acceptance on this matter.

Except for my home congregation of Nauvoo, there was no response. Not even one phone call. Not even one letter. It was as if they, too, had been silenced. I am sure that is what happened—that they were told to disregard the letter and not bring it to anyone's attention.

My home congregation, Nauvoo, was the only exception. During the years that followed my silencing, a few people wanted me to come talk with them and help them understand. I will always regret that I did not do that, but I was too drained. All I wanted to do was to get away from all who were connected to that betrayal. I felt very alone. My parents were dead. My sons distanced themselves from me. My siblings were supportive but confused.

144

I was fifty-seven years old. After more than four decades of service and three years in the priesthood, I closed that chapter and left my home in Nauvoo, my place of history, my space, and all that had defined who I was.

> I sit here
> listening to the rain
> feeling sadly content.
> Decisions were made, bridges crossed
> and I cannot go back.
>
> My soul is enlarged
> by the conflict and
> the knowledge that this is
>
> no longer my place.
> There is a quietness inside,
> waiting for the new tasks.
>
> Fall is not the time for new growth,
> but I've always been just a little off!
> So as the leaves rustle to the ground,
> I push up new shoots
> starting the cycle over again.
>
> The pain has passed
> and the grieving is over,
> but real they were.
> At the moment both heart and head say,
> I won't return.
>
> I leave behind a
> special place,
> special time,
> special friends
> and I take away only me.

I think with affection about all those who touched me throughout my childhood, youth, and adulthood in the church. I often wonder how the church is doing. But I have no desire to be betrayed again. The hardest part was leaving behind my community. I had allowed my spiritual self to be so intertwined with the church that it was difficult for a while to find a spiritual self separate from the church.

Those events were eight years ago from the time I'm writing this reminiscence. I have found wonderful people from all walks of life who feed my soul.

Carol and I are no longer together. There were simply too many stresses during that time. Into my life has come a wonderful woman, Kathleen; and together we have created a loving, supportive relationship. Our home is a place where others come from many walks of life. They validate who we are and enrich our lives. My sons and their families bring warmth and understanding, making my sense of family complete. They have also added a grandson and granddaughter to my circle of love. My world is no longer centered on the church but on life with all its wonderful complexities. From time to time, I long for the rush of the Holy Spirit during conference or corporate worship, but I have replaced it wonderfully by experiencing the good earth and the people upon it. I find that rush now in everyday life.

THE STAR AND I

It was a quiet sky-clear blue
scattered, wispy clouds frozen for a moment
the earth silently bidding farewell to another day.

The sun shed forth its light,
a soft glow over all

with one concentrated shaft reaching high into
the heavens, calling my attention by its singleness.

As the sun sank behind the bluffs,
it became a soft, pink-orange globe,
banded by clouds of soft gray

as if preparing it for another land.

Scattered clouds, edges gilded with gold.
became for a moment delicately special,
each changing to its own hue of pink,
as the sun caressed it in a farewell embrace.

The sun, no longer visible, still energized the shaft of light
with the same quiet intensity,
infusing a puff of clouds in its path
sharing for a moment the same time and space in oneness.

Fading, as had the sun, the singleness of light
blended into an afterglow of blue
marked by clouds of varying hues of gray
blended to the earth by a hazy rose band.

Only then did my gaze pick up a sliver of light
peeking around a cloud—
At first only a gentle reflection
that began to glow more brightly in the darkened sky,
a perfect crescent sharing the sky with
one bright star and me.

My journey continues outside the church. Right now, I distrust all religious institutions. Perhaps at some point that too will pass. It has been good to reflect upon my journey, as it has helped clarify the effects of those events. I can better define who I am and how I have grown. I can accept both appreciation for and anger against the church. I am thankful for my life experiences. I like who I have become.

14

WHEN MY MENTAL SUITCASE POPPED OPEN

Stephanie Shaw

Stephanie Shaw of Hudson, Wisconsin, is a lifetime member of the Community of Christ, having been baptized and confirmed in 1967. In 1988 she was ordained a teacher in the Community of Christ. Stephanie is a former president (2000-02) of GALA.

IT WAS A difficult thing to look back on my entire life and try to pinpoint the exact moment when I became certain about my sexual orientation. I guess it was the day that my suitcase popped open. Ever since I was about six, I knew that I felt more comfortable around girls, but it wasn't until I was thirty-five years old that I finally figured out why.

A number of years ago, I found myself feeling very attracted to a woman whom I had only known for a short time. I experienced very strong feelings for her that I didn't quite understand. I became confused and frightened. "Why am I feeling this way? What does this mean? I can't possibly be the 'G' word, can I? No way! But what is happening to me?"

After a few days of feeling painfully confused, something drastic happened. The mental suitcase that I had been stuffing for years popped open. Since childhood, I recognized that I was attracted to girls, then to women. When these feelings surfaced, I promptly got rid of them by stuffing them out of sight. It was hard enough going through those awkward growing-up years without having to deal with the fact that my sexuality seemed different from that of my friends. I didn't want this "thing" that those around me said was such a horrible sin to be seen in the light of day and to become the subject of ridicule and scorn. So I hid that part of me, even from myself.

Shoving my "difference" away seemed safe at the time, but I paid a price for such "safety." I frequently became withdrawn and depressed—not quite able to put my finger on why this was happening to me. And I continued to stow away my feelings into an increasingly crowded space. But finally, those cramped items in my suitcase burst loose and flew up in my face for me to see—one by one—to remember, to acknowledge, and finally to put on and wear. It would have been impossible to cram one more article into that suitcase. I would never again be able to hide this part of me from myself. I was finally free.

However, those first few months of self-exploration were scary. I didn't know any gay people very well, certainly not well enough to seek out someone for a meaningful conversation. I felt very isolated, confused, and frightened. The only one I could talk to was God. Never once during my coming out process did I separate myself from God. In fact, I grew closer to my Creator. Even though it was very confusing, this was also a very affirming period of my life; I knew that God had to be at the center of it.

Prayer was an integral part of my day, every day, during that fall of 1994. When I started to listen to some of the unkind and condemning societal and biblical words used against homosexuality and homosexuals, I sometimes began to doubt that I was the good person I'd always thought I was. It was only when I approached my Creator in prayer that I was calmed and comforted. With each prayer I received a blessing, and I was impressed with the knowledge that God loves me just the way I am. I also felt that I was being guided to search the scriptures more deeply for the truths contained within them and to search within myself for the good within me. The more I searched, the more I saw and felt the love that the Creator has for me. I knew that I, and others like me, were not condemned sinners but cherished children of God.

With that knowledge, I was able to slowly move forward in faith and come out to my friends, my family, and my church. I was scared to death to tell my family, especially my parents, that I was lesbian. It was a golden opportunity to find out whether all of the tender love and care that I received throughout my life was conditional or un-conditional. Although it was the most difficult thing that I have ever done, in June of 1995 I finally found the courage to reveal my sexual orientation to my parents. When I did, I received a blessing. My parents, and the rest of my family, have shown me nothing but total ac-ceptance, love, and caring concern both before and after I came out to them. And my good friends treat me no differently now than they did before I told them that I was gay.

During this period of self-exploration, I was very active in my home Community of Christ congregation in St. Paul, Minnesota, as I am now. In fact, seven years before my coming out, I had been or-dained a teacher. During those first weeks in the winter of 1995, when I finally acknowledged to myself that I was gay, my congre-gation was in the midst of having priesthood meetings. The people in the different priesthood offices were holding separate meetings to figure out ways to effectively serve in their specific offices.

In our teachers' group, someone (not me) suggested that we do something to affirm the worth of gays and lesbians. We all agreed that it sounded like a way in which we could serve as peacemakers in our church. So we drafted some legislation proclaiming ourselves as a "welcoming congregation." During the numerous sessions in which we carefully crafted our resolution, I came out to my fellow teachers. They were all very loving and supportive. Their love helped give me the courage to proceed with the resolution and to come out to even more members of the congregation.

Although we needed several discussion sessions to adequately prepare ourselves, my home congregation unanimously voted in favor of the resolution. St. Paul Congregation now officially "welcomes and encourages people of all sexual orientations to share in community life, worship, and sacraments, including leadership and ministry." I felt blanketed with the love of my family, my friends, my church, and my Creator.

In the midst of all of this self-exploration and coming out, in January 1995 I found the love of my life. Her name is Barb. Before I met her and when I was still under the mistaken impression that I was a heterosexual, I always felt awkward with the "significant others" in my life. Something always felt not quite right—not natural. I was never able to experience true spiritual or emotional intimacy. Then Barb came into my life, bringing her four adult children and her—our—two grandchildren. Now I have the intimacy that I craved all those years. I also have a loving, trusting partner who listens to me, takes care of me, comforts me, laughs with me, cries with me, argues with me, and lets me argue with her (in a healthy way).

After we had been together two years, we had a commitment ceremony. It was a very beautiful and spiritual experience for us and for the people who attended. Although we knew that this ceremony would not be recognized legally nor by the institutional church, we still wanted to share this celebration of our love for each other with the people who are closest to us. We wanted to honor our families, our friends, and those who have supported us throughout our relationship by including them in this special moment in our lives.

Although Barb was not active in any organized religion and had developed a personal spirituality that helped her through some very rough patches in her life, she started coming to church with me almost from the start of our relationship. She wanted us to be there together as a couple. She knew how important my church was to me, and she wanted to be a part of that piece of my life. The members of my congregation have been super! They love Barb and miss her when she isn't there on a Sunday. She is very aware of the love that they extend to her, and she gives it right back to them. I'm proud of them all.

Barb surprised me. In September 1999, we had attended a GALA retreat in the Kansas City area. GALA (Gay and Lesbian Acceptance) is a group of (mostly) gay Community of Christ members, their families, and their friends. The service in the temple during our retreat was a special one for all of us. But it affected Barb with particular intensity. She was aware of and touched by a beautiful spirit in a church setting for the first time in many, many years. The presence of that spirit, combined with the tender love and care shown to her by our many church friends, helped Barb make an important decision. She came to me shortly after that retreat and told me that she wanted to be baptized.

I was speechless. Never once had I even suggested to Barb that she think about joining the church. She was influenced by that tender spirit that loves us and is with us. And she was touched by the people—God's loving children—in her life. She was baptized in March 2000. I couldn't be happier than I am now!

It is my prayer that each of us will open up to that spirit, so that we can listen and learn about what it means to be a child of God and what it means to live among all of God's children in love and peace.

15

THIS IS MY CHURCH.
YOU'RE STUCK WITH ME!

Allan Fiscus

Allan Fiscus has been a member of GALA since 1986 and was its first president. He has been a leading GALA activist ever since. A nurse by profession, Allan is an elder in the Lansing, Michigan, congregation of the Community of Christ.

FROM MY EARLIEST recollections, I've been active in the RLDS faith: attending church with my family in our home congregation or in the congregations of my grandparents. Living in a community where we were the only RLDS family was difficult. My peers didn't understand why we were driving twenty miles or more to attend church, bypassing the local Catholic or Methodist church. Kids can be cruel and prejudiced when faced with differences. But attending Zioneers, Zion's League, singing in youth choirs, attending reunions, and participating in retreats were a great joy in my life and a safe place. I learned about community and the love of Christ through the fellowship of the Saints.

Looking back, my first awareness of my homosexuality (though I didn't know the terminology then) was at about age six or seven. Somehow I knew that I was different. As I continued to mature, I didn't have the same feelings I was hearing the other guys talk about.

My junior high and high school years were a terror for me. I didn't fit into the cliques. I didn't join the sexual games or activities that were occurring in the gym showers or bathrooms. Sure, I was excited about what I was seeing, yet it wasn't right. That isn't what being gay is all about.

I was "the queer." I was the guy who received the gay slurs. The other students ripped my clothes, defaced my books. They shoved me into lockers and slammed the doors on me. Once, I had to go to the emergency room to have a partially severed ear reattached. When I told the principal what happened, his response was, "You'll just have to deal with it." A teacher whom I later learned was a lesbian tried to give me hope. She encouraged me "hang in there," promising that it would get better. It never did. I hated school, and my grades showed it.

My only solace was attending church and being with the youth and Saints I could trust. But other church families were twelve or more miles away, so daily contact was impossible.

I prayed for God to "fix me," to make me normal. The sense that I had a work to do in the "gay world" was always present. When I talked to my pastor about my gay thoughts and ideas, his response was, "It's a phase. You'll get over it." As a freshman in high school, I was given to know that I had a calling to the priesthood. As I continued in earnest to pray about that calling, again the sense of having a special work to do filled me.

At age seventeen, I received my patriarchal blessing. It reinforced my calling and that there was future work for me to do. As the years have gone by, I have seen many things stated in my blessing come to pass. I was ordained later that year in September 1972 by my grandfather and my pastor.

In my senior year, knowing my grades were not good enough for college, I joined the Navy, using the delayed enlistment program. After graduating, I started to have doubts about this choice. Seeking clearer guidance, I prayed for answers to five questions, feeling that unless I could have these answers, I could not join the the Navy. I received the answers during a reunion two weeks before my enlistment date. God does answer prayers! I went to my enlistment with great reassurance.

I have to laugh about the government's "Don't ask, don't tell" policy. I had never seen so many gay and lesbian people in my life. I learned more about the gay life and came out in the Navy. I also had my first boyfriend. We dated for two years, until I left the Navy.

For some reason, I seemed to be a person other gay people could talk to. My home was filled with gay and lesbian military who needed a safe place to be themselves. I listened to others struggling with their orientation, their fear of the Navy's "witch hunts" (investigations to rout out gays), and tried to provide stability for those dwelling on suicide.

While I was stationed on Okinawa, I wrote to the First Presidency, asking for guidance regarding homosexuality and the church. I stated that, if being gay was incompatible with my priesthood, then I would surrender my priesthood card. I received a response generally stating that I should continue to do the work I had been called to do.

In 1980, I left the Navy, returned to Michigan, and decided to enter nursing school. I love the medical/nursing field and figured that church reunions and retreats are always looking for nurses. This way I could attend church camps, which I dearly loved, and provide a service, too.

While attending Nazareth College, I had confided to a Community of Christ woman that I was homosexual. She responded supportively, stating that she still cared about me. But a few weeks later, I learned that she had gone to my pastor (the same man who had called me to the priesthood) and told him. He came to my apartment and asked me if it were true. I said it was. He then told me that I was being silenced. When I asked why, he said, "Because you are a homosexual, you can't control your sexual urges and will abuse children." I was shocked by his ignorance of homosexuality and the breadth of his assumptions. Never in my life have I been interested in children, only in men my age or older—in fact, ironically, in men of his age.

I told him about my letter to the First Presidency and asked him if he had consulted the First Presidency. He said that the letter didn't matter. He was handling this situation locally.

The next day, the district president telephoned to say that I would no longer be needed at the camps and reunions where I was scheduled to work. He would notify the camps. I was not to attend any church function without a family escort. I could no longer play the piano or organ for church services. I could no longer clean the church or mow the lawns. I could attend church services, but only with my family. The congregation was not to be informed.

I was devastated. It seemed as if my whole world was gone. My family was just as shocked as I was.

Then a couple of weeks later, we found out that my stepfather, a teacher in the Aaronic Order, was having an affair. When my devastated mother and I went to this same pastor and told him about the affair, his response was that the needs of real men are greater than a woman's needs. Mom should increase her activity with the Women's Department and other church activities. Not long afterward, my stepfather was called to a higher priesthood office. This really rocked my faith in the church. A man having an affair with a married woman not only keeps his office but is called to another, while I can't sweep the chapel floor because of the pastor's homophobia? It was unreal.

I tried to attend church; but when there was a need for a pianist and I wouldn't play, the Saints would hassle me for not helping out. Or when the communion emblems were not ready and the service should be starting, I would get pointed questions: "Why aren't you doing your job?" Other comments followed: "Allan, the lawn looks terrible. The church is dirty." I had a choice between accepting the injustice silently or disobeying the pastor and explaining the situation. People were mad at me. It was impossible to be part of the congregation under these circumstances. The final straw was that the district president didn't tell reunion and camp directors that I wouldn't be coming, so they were mad at me too.

When we visited my grandparents, Grandpa had always had me sit on the rostrum with him. Now I had to lie and make up excuses to leave before church time, so I wouldn't have to explain my silencing to the man that ordained me. My family was now lying to cover for me, too. I could no longer handle the anger and disappointment of the Saints. I stopped attending church. At this time, I was twenty-four years old.

To fill the void and emptiness, I started hanging out with friends, going to gay bars, and attending parties. Eventually I got mixed up with drugs and alcohol. For years I tried to cover the loneliness and pain with parties and drugs. I was a heavy user, a fifth of alcohol a day, two or three joints a day. I dropped out of nursing school, lost my home and car, and eventually filed for bankruptcy.

Finally, I realized that this was not the world I wanted to live in. My church life had been taken away from me. The drugs and alcohol were separating me from my family and my God. So I decided I wanted out of this world. One Saturday, I made plans for committing suicide. That afternoon, my mother showed up at the door, her mom-telepathy telling her I might not be alive tomorrow. We talked.

She understood my despair, and she really couldn't give me a reason to go on. She admitted, "Your church has let you down. We have let you down. Your gay friends have let you down. Your dreams to be a camp nurse are gone." She pleaded, "Allan, before you do anything, go to your God. The one person in your life that hasn't let you down has been God. Remember the times in your life when you were healed when the doctors said you would be blind, or that one leg would be shorter than the other? He's answered your prayers clearly when you've gone to him. Go to him before you do anything." We said goodbye.

I spent the rest of the afternoon and evening on the living room floor with a butcher knife in front of me, praying: "God, help me find a way back to the church and to a productive way to live, or help me leave this world." In the very early hours of the morning, I felt surrounded by a warm presence and heard a calming voice saying that I was loved, that the things I desired in my life would come to pass if I healed myself of the drugs and alcohol, that I should prepare myself to do the things I have always known I would be doing in this church.

The following morning I went to church and sat down next to Mom. I was twenty-eight and had been driven away from the church four years earlier. That day I stopped the alcohol and drug use. I terminated the negative friendships. I started to rebuild my life. I started being active in the church as I felt led.

Over the next few months, I spent a great deal of time in prayer while going through self detox. Part of my prayer focus was "God, help me find other gay Saints." One evening, while working as an orderly at a local medical center, I happened to be doing CPR on a patient when a phone number came into my mind. The number had the 816 area code, which includes Independence, site of RLDS world headquarters. For days that number stayed in my mind. Finally I dialed it.

When a man answered, I said, "My name is Allan. I'm a member of the Community of Christ, I'm gay, and looking for anyone who knows of any possible Community of Christ gay support system." He asked how I got his number. I told him.

He said okay. He then told me that he, too, was Community of Christ and gay. In fact, at that very moment, he was meeting with a group of GALA (Gay and Lesbian Acceptance)[1] members in his home in Kansas City. I then shared my story with him.

Eventually I met the members of the GALA group. A GALA non-gay support person asked me, "Why were you silenced? If you did nothing wrong, what were the charges that created the silencing?" I had not been violating any policy, so I should not have been silenced. This person encouraged me to write to World Church and ask for an explanation. I did. The response was that I was silenced because I couldn't handle being gay, that I had voluntarily surrendered my priesthood—this was a surprise!—and that I should contact my local leaders if I had any more questions.

---

[1] GALA (Gay and Lesbian Acceptance) was formed in 1984 by a group of Community of Christ members, to offer support and education to our faith movement's gay, lesbian, family, friends, and congregations. See www.galaweb.org.

When I went to the pastor—by now a different man—I shared my story with him. I asked if he could find out what really happened. He checked with all the congregational priesthood present at the time of my silencing. None of them had supported the pastor's action, although nobody had spoken to me about it. My new pastor started proceedings to reinstate my priesthood. A year later, the paperwork was complete and my priesthood restored. That was in 1988—eighteen years ago; and despite my joy, it has only been within the last twelve years that I have stopped fearing another silencing and felt safe within my church community.

The things I knew as a child have started to come to pass.

I finished my associate nursing degree in 1994. That same year, I was camp nurse for a reunion at the grounds where I had my first reunion experience at age five. It was the fulfillment of a dream.

In 1998, I was called to the office of elder. I'm now the pastor of a mission group in Lansing, Michigan.

In the Michigan Region in 2000, I was asked to be the program director for Gay and Lesbian Ministries, the first such assignment in the Community of Christ. I worked with regional Church leadership, other Saints, and GALA members to develop a workshop on "Homosexuality in Our Faith." It's been presented to all districts in the Michigan Region, and now is being presented in other jurisdictions.

GALA helped build support systems I could trust again. I became GALA's first elected president. Since 1987, I've been working with GALA and the leaders of the Community of Christ to build trust and openness about homosexuality so that the church can minister to the gay members of this faith and their family, friends, and congregations. It has been a challenging and exciting journey. It's also a bumpy road, but one worth traveling because I'm not alone.

In June 2002, I was one of the guest ministers at a church reunion in Ohio. After I shared my story, someone asked, "Allan, after all the hassles you've been through and the hassles people give you at the workshops and in general, why do you stay with this church?"

I didn't hesitate in answering the person, using the same words I told President Grant McMurray, whom I am proud to call my friend: "This is my church. My faith community. Wherever I have been in my travels around the world, I have found family and friends by simply walking in the door. Each of us is called to ministry. Some paths are different from others. This is my calling—my path to reach out to those who are questioning, searching, and struggling to understand a volatile subject. To be an ensign of peace. This is my church, and you are stuck with me."

16

(ALMOST) PASSING 3RD GRADE
A Poem in Five Acts with Epilogue

Jesse Davis

Jesse Davis currently lives in Eugene, Oregon, with his cat, Thaniel. Thaniel was originally Jesse's old roommate Tracy's cat, and Tracy named him Nathaniel, but at his first vet visit the doctor said she was really a girl, so Tracy "femmed up" her name to Thaniel.

ACT I: THE ACT

Industrial carpet,
collapsible orange
panel walls.
The year is 1978.
The teacher hollers,
"Line up!
Boys on the right,
girls on the left;
The quicker you are
the more recess you'll get."
Every face new to me

except one,
I jimmy my way into
a spot across from
cousin Billy.
Cousin Billy says,
"Hey, Cork, come
stand with me."
I say, "I can't."
Cousin Billy says,
"Why not? Roger
don't mind.
Do ya, Roger?"
at the kid behind him.

Roger glances at me
in the girls' line,
shrugs, and looks away.
I whisper, "I can't."
Cousin Billy says,
"Why not?
Nobody cares."
"But the teacher said. . . "

I say.
"Aw," says cousin Billy,
"Ms. Bown don't care.
C'mon!"
I glance at the girl behind me.
She glares and hisses,
"You're in the wrong line.
Go on. We'll never
get to play."
And so I sidestep
two short feet
to my right into the
slot Billy's left for me
and he's right:
Ms. Bown don't mind.
It's easy as sin
just a walk down the hall
with the girls on my left
and out the doors to play.
Except
if Ms. Bown don't mind
me breaking the rules,
why's she have 'em
for everyone else?

ACT II: THE TRAP

A noisy schoolyard.
Single lines form for a turn
at the swings,
on the slide.
Kids hop scotching,
jump roping,
tetherballing, and
full-voice miming:
"Y-M-C-A!
da-da-da-da-da-da-da
Y-M-C-AAAAAAAAY!"
The recess bell rings
and we run to the door
where Ms. Bown's shouting,
"Line up! Line up!
Two rows:
boys on the right,
girls on the left!
Hustle! Hustle! Hustle!"
I gravitate to the left,
but Billy catches my glance
and draws me to him with just
raised eyebrows and
a jerk of his chin.
Marching up the hall,
easy as sin,
feeling included
with family near.
We stop,
two turns shy
of the classroom
as Teacher says,
"Bathroom break!
Everybody go now 'cause

I don't let anyone
out of class."
I freeze next to the teacher,
emphatically
shaking my head
at cousin Billy
who's waving me into the john.
His john.
Watching the girl
with the glare
go in the other side.
It occurs to me
maybe I'd been hasty
blending in with the boys.
I suddenly know
this is the biggest rule
I've ever broken
and No One
will find this amusing.
I was somehow stuck
in boyhood
in thirst
in bladder pain
and I cringe
as Ms. Bown says,
"You sure? Last chance.
No special breaks
in my class.
Better go now.
Hurry, everyone else
is almost done."
I don't recall
voluntarily speaking
the rest of the year.

ACT III: BENDING THE RULES

A quiet classroom
all heads bent
in concentration
save one squirmy kid.
The words swim before me.
Sharp ache in my bladder.
Even as I decide against it,
my hand rises,
slow as a flag.
Ms. Bown'd been
watching me fidget
and snaps, "Corky?"
before my hand
gets all the way up.
I snatch it down
like I'd been stealing air
and have to raise my voice
above the heads
of the other kids
to squeak, "Bathroom?"
"I told you the rules,
Corky. No breaks during class."
Ashamed, I stare at my desk.
"Is it an emergency?" she says,
more concerned.
Emergency? I think.
911?
Fire trucks,
Police officers,
Ambulance?
Confused I mutter, "No,"
and hold my crotch,
cross my knees,
cross my ankles,

163

balance myself
on the outside edge
of my chair
and try not to squirm.
Ms. Bown watches.
Finally she says,
"Do you have to go badly?"
"Yes," I whisper.
"Well, that's what
emergency means."
I just stare.
"You can go this once."
And I'm in such a hurry
I almost don't hear her say,
"Just be aware you should
go when everyone else does
from now on."
In the extra-wide main hall
I manage to wait
just long enough to make sure
no one will see me-the-boy
go into the "wrong" bathroom
and then I peeeeeeeee
and peeeeeee
and peeeeeeeeee
and pee
and peee
and pee
and pee
and pee
and pee.
I decide
I'll have to give up
all things liquid
for school.

ACT IV: THE OUTING

Early May.
The trees have budded,
the sky has cleared,
and coats are forgotten
on chairs and hooks,
in cubbies and on playgrounds,
only to be sorely missed
in the morning.
The class has come back
from a double-row trip
to the library and I
can't get comfortable.
My stomach hurts something
    awful
and my mom always says,
"Lie on it. It'll feel better."
So I pick a spot
near the teacher's desk
and read and doze
read and doze only
to snap awake
just in time
to puke.
A surprise attack,
I don't even have a chance
to turn my head
and spare my book.
Wave after wave after wave
in front of everyone.
I finally stop,
sneak a shame-faced look
at Ms. Bown who says,
in the gentlest voice,
"Are you done?"

164

I nod but start to cry:
"The book, the book
I've ruined the book."
But Ms. Bown says,
"Never mind, it's okay."
"But it's a book
and it's not mine
and I've ruined it."
I can't stop crying.
"It's okay," she's saying.
"There are more important
      things
like, do you remember where
the nurse's office is?"
I shake my head,
wipe my chin on my sleeve,
and follow the teacher's pet
down the extra-wide main hall
to my fate.
Lying on a cot
in a white-bright room
I struggle to stay awake
while the nurse calls my mom.
The nurse's calm, friendly voice
gradually stretches
in confusion and surprise.
"Mrs. Davis?
This is Nurse Sweet
from William Yates Elementary
      calling.
Sorry to disturb you
but we have your son here
and he's pretty sick.
Are you able to come pick him
      up?
You are Mrs. Davis?

Mrs. Hal Davis?
Excuse me; Sally Davis?
Yes, Corky, he's right here. . .
well, he . . .
He's really sick and we think
it'd be best if he just went . . .
she went home?
Corky?
He is?
She is. . .
I'm very sorry,
we've been under the impres-
      sion. . .
Well maybe you should just
      come get her;
we can talk about this later."
Much, much too frightened to
      sleep now,
afraid of what I might wake to,
I could not stay awake.

ACT V: CONSEQUENCES

Monday morning,
10:00 a.m.
A teacher's voice rings out,
"Line up, everyone.
The quicker you are,
the more recess you'll get.
Girls on the left,
boys on the right."
After an extended weekend
hashing and rehashing
right from wrong,
truth from lies,

I stand behind
the other kids
between the rows.
Cousin Billy says,
"C'mon, Cork,
you'll make us lose time."
Ms. Bown was waiting.
I duck my head,
edge to the right.
Ready for it,
hoping for it,
Ms. Bown grabs my shoulder,
declares loudly,
"Girls on the left."
Angry that I would dare,
jubilant that I had tried.
"Corky, you are a girl
and will behave as such
while in my class."
Her class
turns to stare
and Ms. Bown
waits calmly
for the snickers and snorts
poking and pointing
to die down
before marching us
funeral-slow
down the hall.
Once over the threshold
I break free,
run to the far end
of the schoolyard
to hide in the bushes.
I listen to the other classes
demand of my classmates,

"What took you guys?"
I keep my head down,
try to avoid the girls
in the bathroom
but it's not much of a challenge.
It seems I stepped into
a four foot bubble when
I stepped into the girls' line.
From that day on
I'm followed home,
followed to piano lessons
by sixth-grade boys
who giggle and push each other
as they yell,
"Hey!
Hey, kid!
You!
I know you hear us!
You think it's deaf?
Naw, it's just scared.
You scared?
Hey you!
Hey!
Kid!
Hey! what are you?
Yeah! are you
a boy
or a girl
or what?
Hey you!
Are you a what?
Hey kid!
We know you can hear us.
Hey!
Hey, lift up your shirt!
Yeah, show us your chest!

C'mon; you afraid?
It's afraid!
It won't show us
it must be a girl.
Hey you!
Are you a girl?
Are you a sissy?
Are you a faggot?
Yeah, what are you?
Hey!"
But I take it
because it's only
a fifteen-minute walk
and I have to deal
every other minute
with my family
who had made it clear
exactly how mortified
I'd caused them to be,
and they would absolutely flip
if I flashed my
eight-year-old chest
made of ribs.
Needless to say,
I'm not disappointed
when they announce
we'll be moving again
this summer.

EPILOGUE: THE PUNISHMENT

One week before
being thrown into
a new sea of faces,
cicadas moaning in the
      oppressive

Arizona sun,
a listless yet emotional
battle is being waged.
"No; no dress.
I won't."
"It's only
for two weeks."
"Two weeks?!
Moooooooommmmmmmmm!"
"Oh, honey,
you're such a
pretty girl.
I just want
everyone to know it."
"But I can be a
pretty girl
in jeans!"
"Corky, this is not
a discussion.
Two weeks."
"No way!
I'm not going then.
You can't make me."
But she could.
And she did.
And the fight dragged on.
"How was school?
Did you make any
new friends?"
"How can I?
I'm the only freak
in a dress!
Everyone else
wears shorts
or jeans
except JerriLynn

167

and it's her religion or some-
  thing!"
"They just don't
know you yet."
"And who'd want to?
I don't even talk to
girls in dresses."
"Well, maybe you should."
"Mooooooommmm!
I can't ride my bike to school!
I can't climb the jungle gym.
I can't skin the cat!
I can't jump rope.
I can't run.
I can't even sit
on the sidewalk
to play jacks
with the girls!
Pleeeeeaaaaaase,
can I wear jeans tomorrow?"
"You know the deal.
Two weeks."
"Two weeks?!?
Moooommmm!
They hate me!"

"They don't hate you."
"I can't do anything!"
"Oh, come on now."
"It's unfair."
"Life is unfair."
And so it drags on
day after day after
day after day after
day after day after
day (including the
dress-to-church war).
Sunday evening Mom started
  to cave
and said at last,
"Maybe one week
is long enough."
And I think I've won.
Think I've won until
it occurs to me
years later
my sister,
the girl,
never had to wear
a dress to school.

17

GRACELAND'S ANDREI

Hal McKain

Andrei Dzhunkovsky graduated from Graceland University in 2001 and has returned to his native Russia where he is getting established as a film and TV director. He was the prime mover in getting the Gay/Straight Alliance started at Graceland, which has been an active group on campus for the past decade. For Hal McKain's story, see chapter 2.

Iɴ ᴛʜᴇ ғᴀʟʟ of 1997 someone put a note in the Graceland College (Graceland University since June 2000) newspaper, *The Tower,* asking if there was an interest in beginning a Gay/Straight Alliance on campus. I quickly sent a positive reply to the mailbox listed in the announcement.

A few days later as I was sitting at the checker's desk by the door of the McDowell Commons (the student cafeteria), a smiling young man approached the desk. I was glad that there was no one else around. He said, "I got your reply about the Gay/Straight Alliance and want to get acquainted with you." It was a great start for our friendship.

I felt that it would be appropriate and very helpful if, in the privacy of this moment, I knew his sexual orientation. Rather than wait for a possible disclosure later, I asked him, "Are you gay?" He quickly said, "Yes." I was proud of him for coming out to me so freely.

Andrei was a student from Russia. A year in Iowa as an exchange student had helped him develop nearly perfect English. His family in Russia was not aware of his sexual orientation because in Russia the subject is not openly discussed. He also asked me if he could quote my statements in *The Tower*. I agreed, since I was anxious to take an active part in establishing a Gay/Straight Alliance at Graceland.

Andrei Dzhunkovsky, with the assistance of Professor Bob Mesle in the Humanities Division, took the leadership in establishing the Gay/Straight Alliance at Graceland. Andrei became the first president of this college-sanctioned club and did a fantastic job of setting up meetings, leading discussion groups, scheduling topics for discussion, and openly representing the club on campus.

Bill Russell, Bob Mesle, and I enjoyed being part of the group as faculty and staff. The meetings and activities, advertised in *The Tower* and on campus bulletin boards, were fun and significant. Many students received support and encouragement. They are great people! My gay son David would have really appreciated this friendly club had it existed when he was a student here in 1977-78. I believe he would have wanted to continue at Graceland until he graduated.

Andrei majored in theater and psychology. He was very involved in all phases of the campus dramatic productions—directing, performing, scene design, and so forth. He was very competent and conscientious in both his work and studies.

Andrei attended the GALA international retreat in Excelsior Springs, Missouri, in 1999. He said that he wanted to meet some of the people who had been writing for *galaNEWS*, such as Alan Cochran, a past president of GALA. A nice contingent from Graceland attended this retreat.

It is amazing to me how much difference one person like Andrei can make. The timing of his attendance at Graceland (whether accidental or spiritually guided) was perfect. In the fall of 1997, the board of trustees adopted a policy of nondiscrimination on the basis of sexual orientation, and I am sure everyone on campus knows it. It was one of the main reasons that one gay person, Rob Stevens, applied for and got a faculty position at Graceland. He had seen it on the Graceland website; if he had not known about the nondiscrimination policy, he probably would not have applied for the job.

It is a tremendous feeling to realize that Graceland can provide a safe place for such an important growing experience. Graceland and its sponsoring church, the Community of Christ, really needed the catalyst provided by Andrei's organizing a Gay/Straight Alliance on campus. It helped us understand the validity of diversity in sexual orientation.

Andrei will always have many good friends. He will consistently be ready to stand up for what is right and fair. That is what he did at Graceland. He graduated in the class of 2001. I proudly watched him as he stood up in front of the graduation crowd with a small group of students being honored for their perfect A (4.00) grade point averages.

I am already looking forward to his visits for Homecoming reunions. I know that, as an alumnus, he will continue to support Graceland's good causes. He indeed is a special person whose proud, perfectionist, caring legacy is forever stamped on the "hill" that we call Graceland—the hill that many of us consider sacred.

18

God Accepts Me as a Gay Man

Kip Dawson

Kip Dawson graduated from Graceland in 1979 and for twenty-six years has been a teacher in Wichita, Kansas. He is a member of GALA and still is involved in the Community of Christ. He gives his time and talents to worthwhile community projects, loves to travel, and is still in search of a life partner.

I KNEW THERE was something strange about the way I felt. But me? Gay? No way!

As I grew up, I would hear about "fags" and "queers" and how I had to be a "man." I loved to cook and clean house. Oh, no! That's a woman's job! But I could also assemble things and even fix a swimming pool pump. Where did I fit into all of this mess?

All through high school I lied about where I had been or whom I was with. "He" became "she" or "they." I learned to cover my tracks, and I tried to be happy while doing it.

Growing up in a Christian family, I heard repeatedly that God does not love those who deviate from the norm, whatever that was. I was not sure where to turn for help. I felt lost. I sought counseling but they had no idea what to do with me either. Again I felt lost.

During my years at Graceland, I was seeking an education but also soul-searching, trying to figure out who I was. After counseling, I was referred to a psychiatrist in Des Moines, Iowa. The physician decided my difficulties were a result of a chemical imbalance in my brain and prescribed three different medications to take daily. These medications made me lethargic. My outgoing personality became so dampened that my friends were making comments to me about my behavior. After six months of growing dependency on the medications, I decided to stop taking them and also dump the psychiatrist. These medications did not alter my gay feelings. They only suppressed them.

After graduating from Graceland, I moved back to Wichita, Kansas, still very confused, and began teaching at age twenty-eight. After taking a weekend trip to Tulsa, Oklahoma, I needed to find a way back to Wichita. My pastor in Wichita, John Billings, happened to be going back and offered me a lift home. I thought he was really cool. We talked for the first hundred miles about the weather, school, and other superficial topics. Around the 101-mile marker, I blurted out that I was gay, was having an affair with a man, and needed to talk about it with someone. I was desperate and decided it was time to get some "real" help.

I had no idea he had never counseled anyone on this topic before. I must say, he handled it beautifully! I talked. He listened and never expressed any negative feelings about what I was saying. Being young, I thought he would have all the answers to the questions I was bombarding him with. I am sure he was glad when I left the car, to give him time to process everything I had said.

I suppressed my feelings once again and decided to marry because that was what I was supposed to do. We divorced because we both wanted it. We figured out that we were both gay. However, I had not resolved the question of who I was and what I wanted out of life.

I had been teaching school in LaCygne, Kansas, but in 1982, I moved back to Wichita again and renewed my friendship with Larry, another member of the Community of Christ. In September he told me about GALA, a group of gay people raised within the church. He

173

said that they were going to have a retreat in Oklahoma and invited me to go with him. I went with much reluctance and hesitation.

That retreat changed my life. I found other people who were having the same problems I had been having. They all seemed to be searching for something just like me. Some were further along toward finding it, others were just beginning, and some were caring parents just wanting to support gay people and help them on their journey.

On the second day, we came together in a group to share our personal stories. At first, I thought I would not be able to say anything. But as I listened, I heard experiences I could identify with. All my life I was taught to hide everything, talk superficially, and admit to nothing. In this group, I felt safe, so I opened up and told my story. It felt so good to finally share my secret feelings out loud.

It was Monday, the last day of the retreat. The entire group came together to celebrate communion under a tree, to break bread, and drink from the cup. Music was playing, and a nice breeze was blowing across the water. There was a great spirit there—one I had never felt before. The Holy Spirit came over me, and tears began to roll down my cheeks. I knew at that point that God loved me and accepted me as a gay man.

As I cried, an arm came around my shoulders and someone pulled me close. I looked up to see my former pastor, the one I had come out to four years earlier. The very man I had opened up to was holding me with an understanding of the pain I had been through.

That was twenty-two years ago. Now I am an openly gay man living in Kansas. I don't hide my sexuality any more. My family members know about my gay lifestyle; and although most of them aren't comfortable talking openly, I know they would be there for me should I have a need. My mother has become an advocate for gay rights and supports me in every way. More importantly, I have accepted myself and find that others can respect me when I respect myself.

19

ON BEING GAY AT GRACELAND, 1968-72

Michael Crownover

At a PFLAG conference, Brian McNaught challenged the gay, lesbian, and bisexual participants to write a letter to an educator in their past and tell their story of what it was like to be closeted while attending the institution that brought them together. Michael Crownover sent the following letter to J. C. Stuart, who had been the campus minister when he was a freshman at Graceland. Michael now lives in Glendale, Colorado, and is employed at Wild Oats Marketplace. He continues to paint both in oils and watercolors, executes scientific illustrations and pursues his deep interest in paleontology. He will soon have some illustrations published in a book on Colorado fossils being prepared by the state of Colorado.

IN 1996, I attended an educational conference, "Building Bridges of Understanding," sponsored by Denver PFLAG (Parents, Family, and Friends of Lesbians and Gays). Brian McNaught, author, lecturer, and creator of the PBS videos *Growing Up Gay* and *Homophobia in the Workplace,* was one of the featured speakers. He said that in his twenty-plus years as a sex educator, the single most effective thing he does is to tell his own story. And he challenged the gay, lesbian, and bisexual participants in the audience—as a means of "building a bridge"—to contact or write a principal, counselor, or teacher from our past and to tell our own story.

So I wrote to J. C. Stuart, who was campus minister at Graceland College (1965-69) when I was a freshman in 1968. This essay is adapted from that letter. While I was a student, due to severe depression I had sought counseling with him on at least two occasions. Having this connection and hearing that J. C. was chairing the church's Task Force on Human Sexuality in the mid-1990s motivated me to contact him. This letter was the first time I'd ever really "outed" myself to anyone beyond my circle of trusted friends or known sympathizers, such as the PFLAG membership. His response heartened me and promoted my further growth and healing. Since then, coming out has become easier, and I truly see the value of sharing.

To tell my story is to bear witness and by doing so hopefully ease the way for those of my brothers and sisters who follow. But mostly, I realize my story is a means of standing up for myself, affirming that I AM HERE, that I count—something that I was unable to do throughout my education and beyond.

It would be impossible to isolate what happened at Graceland from what preceded it, so my tale also involves incidents from my pre-Graceland years. I do not wish to be maudlin about my time in college or start pointing fingers, even at myself. After all, how can I blame anyone for my situation? Where could I possibly start? Culturally, we are all caught up in homophobia. Even though I am gay, I am also homophobic. I can't take responsibility for a social pattern that is bigger than all of us or how it plays out in others' lives, but I can be responsible, now that I know better, for myself and my own interactions with others. Healing the shame must start with myself. I am convinced that sharing is the best path.

For me it was a shattering conflict—the reality of being both homosexual and homophobic—that brought about my suffering and consequent illness, my self-hatred and alienation. This unfaceable, embraced duality resulted in a denial, a self-deception, self-censorship, and self-control so tight that it took over and ruled my life. I gave away my free will and ability to act to a power whose sole purpose was to divert me from any self-awareness, crippling me at the core. I knew there was something different about me—something that was wrong—and that if I looked too closely, my world would be turned inside out. I sensed that I would find myself condemned. This vague fear never left me, sitting in the pit of my stomach like an undigested meal.

So I instinctively buried this unwanted dimension and simultaneously began keeping everyone away just in case someone would see what was chewing at me, recognize its nature, and then point it out to me. I jailed myself and swallowed the key, placed blinders on, stopped up my ears, put on a straitjacket and gloves, and braced myself for punishment from a source I couldn't know and refused to guess. I had, before my childhood was over, completely and unconsciously internalized social attitudes toward homosexuals. I no longer needed a father, church member, teacher, or friend to put me down. I'd taken over that role.

My time at Graceland somehow strengthened this pattern of avoidance, deception, and self-loathing. For me Graceland was a very threatening place where I was bereft of my former support system and vulnerable to a vague but ever-present threat of being judged and found wanting. I didn't trust others to care about me because I could not love or respect myself. I was alone. I could count only on myself to get through. In preemptive moves, I prevented contact as often as possible. I avoided making friends. I ignored or turned aside overtures, especially from the "smart" people, the ones I really admired and longed to know. I was sure that they would see through me and find out that I didn't measure up. Even here I refused to see the outlines of what I really feared. It wasn't incompetence.

Some friendships were inevitable, however, despite myself. But I am ashamed to admit—and I was consciously aware of it then—that I permitted relationships primarily with people who somehow didn't threaten me or with people I felt sorry for. In other words, with other oddballs and outcasts like myself. Often, I later learned to respect them and enjoy their companionship. But I never lost the sense that these relationships were tainted, soiled by my inability to truly give of myself. In all of my blindness, I hypocritically took the position that "they need someone" and that I should step up and fill that need. I never admitted that I needed to be needed, that I needed to be wanted. In my conviction that I was unworthy and unlovable, I never allowed myself any true closeness.

Friendships weren't the only arena where I seemed adrift. I simply didn't fit in at Graceland, and I didn't want to fit in. But finding my niche in any situation had always been a problem, no matter where I'd been. It was such a pervasive feature of my life that I just surrendered to it as unchangeable fact. I had first noticed this dislocation when I entered kindergarten. I didn't have a name for it then; but by the time I was eight, I was blaming it on my "difference." In third grade I'd discovered that I was gifted in art, and I eagerly embraced the conclusion that my "difference" was my ability to empathize (granted, at a distance) and my artistic sensitivity, both of which seemed so often lacking in my classmates. Art became my excuse for not fitting in, empathy my reason for not getting too close. Already being an open sore, I could absorb only so much additional pain. I can look back now and see that my very eagerness to accept this explanation for my withdrawal and avoidance indicated a deeper problem.

So girded with my excuses, I stopped trying to fit in and accepted my feelings of separation and of loss. At Graceland, where my parents could not "guilt" me into unwanted participation, I brought my avoidance into full flower. About the only extracurricular events I can remember attending were the movies and other similar entertainments. And they weren't really activities. They were escapes where I dissolved and reality could be replaced for a moment. Small comfort, but it's all I allowed.

I determinedly avoided all sports events, not only because it would have brought me into contact with other students but also because sports had other disquieting dimensions. My biggest excuse was entangled with my dad. He had been an All-American football hero type, and was bound and determined that I should follow in his footsteps. When I was young, he pushed and pushed; but between his demand for excellence and my lack of coordination and poor eyesight, I never felt that I could ever satisfy him.

His frustration was sometimes tinged with a bit of anger, or so I believed. Eventually I spiraled down into resignation, shame, and a pervasive sense of failure. I believe he had no idea how his disappointment affected me. He would occasionally call me "sissy boy" when I failed to catch a ball or refused to punch my younger brother. (We were wearing boxing gloves.) I suppose it was his way of trying to challenge me, but it only magnified my humiliation. I was too quick to agree. What else could I feel? He was my father, and I accepted his verdict. We began to grow apart, and then he stopped trying and left me alone. That was worse. It took half my lifetime before I was able to deal with my blind anger, accept him, and forgive him.

So I had my excuse: I hated sports because of my dad and I wouldn't attend or participate. Granted, sports were a reminder of athletic failure, but the real truth was more horrifying. It brought me too close to that secret I couldn't bring to consciousness, couldn't acknowledge. Every required gym class I took left me in a quiet panic. Regardless of the sport or degree of activity, my heart raced and I couldn't focus. Nausea was a constant companion, particularly when it came time to shower. This should have put me wise, but I had a will to look in any direction but the truth. Physical movement made me aware of my classmates' bodies and, on some suppressed level, my attraction, and I couldn't face it.

Years later, after a slow and silent groping toward resigned acceptance, when I finally vocalized that I was gay, my homosexuality became suddenly and surprisingly, almost magically, concrete. Over the next few days, my life seemed to pass before my eyes. Every aspect, every episode, every interaction took on a different meaning. It was like rewriting history except that I wasn't changing content. I was seeing things from the correct angle, how they had really been, seeing the undeniable truth behind every disguised evasion.

What surprised me was how young I'd been when I must have subconsciously realized I had socially unacceptable feelings. The behaviors to hide my feelings were already in place when I started school.

I remember feeling vaguely uncomfortable when anyone touched me, particularly men. I remember trying to walk to school with my arms held rigid at my sides; swinging them was too expressive and made me disquietingly aware of my body. I remember avoiding watching other boys at play. I remember avoiding their company. I remember trying to vanish, so that my feelings wouldn't be noticed—so that I could avoid any awareness of what truly drove me.

By the time I got to Graceland I was a real mess. I was almost phobic about being touched. You can imagine what it was like when I finally tried to date and encountered that expected ritual of holding hands or, worse, kissing. My body-image was so poor (and threatening) that I tried to cover up every inch possible. I never wore shorts or T-shirts. In fact, in my subconscious effort to disappear, I wore the plainest slacks and long-sleeved shirts, remarkably stupid in the heat and humidity of southern Iowa. It seemed natural. My excuse was that I was "modest." But deep within, I knew better. My body rebelled and betrayed me once during my junior year. My physicality needed recognition, needed release. I'd finally got up the nerve to pursue a secretly cherished dream. I can now laugh about the "Levi incident," but at the time I was horribly embarrassed. It was my first pair, and as soon as I slipped them on I got an erection. I couldn't come out of the changing room. I finally realized I'd need to remove them if I had any hope of getting back to campus. It took me a month before I could wear them publicly.

To say the least, I needed to accept my body and its attendant feelings and responses, but it was so very difficult. Repression of my physicality and need to touch and be touched led me to an odd but profound habit. Occasionally, usually in the dead of night, when I seemed to feel a hopeless desperation kindled by loneliness and longing, I would find a tree out of sight, face it, and place my palms against the bark. Trees had always had a certain magic for me. Or if I'd already gone to bed, I would turn to the wall and do likewise. It didn't comfort me much, but I would almost cry in my need to touch something. I don't know why a wall or tree became the object of this expression. They must have seemed safer than another person.

All in all, during my Graceland years I cycled back and forth between anxiety and depression. I experienced suicidal bouts from time to time depending on the direction of my awareness. During my junior and senior years, I began to wake up to horrifying possibilities. Nothing could make me freak like the mention of homosexuality. The degree of my reaction spoke volumes from which I couldn't hide. I fought so hard. I just couldn't be one of "them." I didn't match the image or profile I had been fed, except perhaps in the sad-and-depressed department. I felt somewhat comfortable with and liked women; I didn't like most guys. I wanted to marry and have a family. I didn't think I was effeminate—at least, I screened my behavior constantly to be sure nothing looked "strange"; but I admitted that I was terrified anyone would think so. I just couldn't be one of "them."

Yet if this horror could be true, why? Why, me? What had I done? What could I do? Who could I look to for support? Certainly not the church! I had never really heard much preaching against homosexuality; nevertheless, the attitude was plain. Could I seek support or clarifying explanations from educators at the college? The ringing silence said it all: "There is no one here for you, Michael. You are alone."

Where could I seek a positive and contemporary role model? As Brian McNaught asked the audience at that conference, "How many famous and accomplished gay, lesbian, or bisexual people can you name? Can you name ten? Five?" Where could I look to find a role model—someone to show me that I could also be happy, successful, and openly loving? Where could I find this healthy image?

In the slow work of affirming myself, I began to separate from the church. Initially I resisted. I even started offering excuses for the church's blind spots and inadequacies. The ideals of love and truth remained unsullied and beneficial, as long as all had access. But did I? As a homosexual, was I loved? Did the truth of my orientation mean anything to the church? Didn't my very existence challenge long-held, socially accepted views? By the time I was able to provisionally claim my sexual orientation (not yet my sexuality), I felt such betrayal that I could no longer discuss it, much less associate myself with the body of Christ. I wasn't just enraged by the "true" church; I tossed in all of Christianity.

Years later I am still working through the detritus from my rejection of what I saw as an institution that rejected me. Some scars are very deep, and healing is slow. I still find it somewhat difficult to trust the church, but it is getting easier; and as I learn of the Community of Christ's efforts to be more inclusive of diversity, I am heartened. Intellectually, I now know the church isn't my enemy or even my assessor. And in the exercise of love, all things are possible.

I am trying to take responsibility for the direction of my life. In sharing my story, I am affirming myself and affirming my trust that being authentic with others will build understanding, respect, and love. I am building a bridge. And in doing so, each and every time I unlock the gates of secrecy and tell my story, I experience warmth and compassion that release me from the ravages of shame and that foster forgiveness. Sharing helps me heal the wounds and free myself to love as I was meant to love.

20

ON BEING GAY AT PARK COLLEGE

Brian E. Sadler

In the spring of 2006 Brian Sadler resigned as a pastoral team member for the Basileia Congregation of the Community of Christ, citing fundamental differences with World Church official policy on gays and lesbians in the priesthood. He currently lives in a spirit-led, monogamous relationship of nineteen years as of January 2007. He maintains his spiritual connection by volunteering for the United Methodist Church as a staff member for the "Strength for the Journey" retreat program, as well as other volunteer programs.

I WAS BORN in a fairly average family in Kansas City, Missouri, the last of four sons, with a sister three-and-one-half years younger than I. I always knew I was gay from age five, and so did my parents. I revealed my feelings to them when I was in my first year of college and simultaneously told them I was engaged to be married to a girl I had met. My father quickly assured me that he loved me, no matter what my personal feelings would be.

My mother suggested counseling and asked my fiancée what kind of future she saw with a man who might be exclusively homosexual.

My fiancée knew I was gay, as I'd always seen it as a matter of personal integrity never to hide my feelings from her. She felt that she could change me, over time, and it was on that basis we had become engaged. My mother's question cut through our naivete, and I ended our relationship.

My father had always lived his entire life in strictest harmony with his priesthood office in the Community of Christ. So it was natural for me to assume that the church had a similar supportive approach to homosexuality. I had been very vocal, seeking answers from my Church family, but I never got answers—only more questions. I quickly transferred to Park College, moved into the dorm, and began classes, feeling that this would be a safe place for me to live out my sexuality as an adult Christian in an open and loving atmosphere. After all, Park College was affiliated with my church.

I received a prompt and ugly awakening. Other students nicknamed me "Swiss Miss." I was the target of open ridicule and public jokes. My car was vandalized. My laundry was ruined by vandals who put crayons in the dryer. I was baffled. How could these "Christians" openly exhibit such non-Christian, intolerant behavior? I made an appointment with the campus pastor, seeking guidance on how to forgive the ignorance and intolerance of my fellow Christians. Instead he told me that these hatemongers' reaction was completely understandable. He also said flatly, "The church isn't willing to recognize the fact that you are gay, let alone attempt to take a stand on the issue publicly." I took the same stand with the church as it took with me, and I withdrew from church participation and from Park University.

I could not fill the void in my heart that was left by the church and God's people. After we had been ignoring each other for nearly twenty years, I felt called to return to the church when I heard about GALA from relatives who also felt empowered toward revival by women's call to the priesthood within the Community of Christ. I remain active in the church as an Aaronic teacher through the Basileia congregation in Orange, California, where I serve on the presiding team and am committed to the call of looking "beyond the horizon."

Shalom.

21

LEARNING TO LOVE THE UNLOVED

Mark D. Dixon

Mark D. Dixon, M.D., is a native of Michigan and a graduate of Graceland University and the College of Human Medicine, East Lansing, Michigan. He has served as treasurer and member of the board of GALA. He and his partner, Guillermo Salazar, M.D., a native of Peru, shared in a service of commitment in 2001. Mark is affiliated with the Community of Christ Health Ministries and served on missions to Honduras and Guatemala. He serves as financial officer and counselor to the pastor of the Clearwater, Florida, Community of Christ.

MY MOTHER HAS told me that angels seemed near at the time of my birth. She said the attending physician remarked, "This is a unique experience." In spite of all that, my journey has been very difficult, yet along the way I have experienced God's spirit gently guiding my life.

I was born in 1964 and grew up in the small village of Farwell in rural Michigan. The Community of Christ congregation there had a strong influence on my life. I had many good role models, including

my parents and my grandmother. I attended youth camps and reunions, and had many friends in my home congregation.

At a young age, I had experienced same-sex attraction. Soon I
began to see references to gays on television with which I could identify. At the same time I began to understand that it was not "cool" to
be gay. Gay children were being rejected by their families, ridiculed
and sometimes tortured by their classmates. Gay persons certainly
had no place in a small rural town. At age eleven, I heard a mother
tell her sons that, if one of them ever announced that he was gay,
there would not be a place for him in her home.

When I was twelve, my Aunt Gail returned from serving a year
as a nurse at La Buena Fe, Honduras. The slides she showed in the
basement of our church bore a powerful testimony of God's love for
all persons. This made a tremendous impact on my young life. I felt a
definite call to pursue a career in medicine and become a physician.
My parents were supportive, though others doubted that I would succeed, coming from our small school system. My heart told me that I
would succeed. I knew that my journey would take me from Farwell
and I continued to long for a life of acceptance and love.

My teenage years were pure hell. I wrestled with my thoughts
and feelings. I feared that I would lose the love of my family if they
learned the truth about me, but my trust in God grew. I prayed ear-
nestly every night for the next four years for God to remove the burden of my sexuality from me. Many nights I cried throughout the
entire night, without once falling asleep. I remember looking into the
eyes of person after person, secretly asking, "If you knew I was gay,
would you accept me?" Gay jokes and gay bashing were a way of life.
It seemed I had no place in our small-town society.

At age sixteen, I found myself at the top of our barn with a large
chain around my neck. I pleaded with the Lord for over an hour. I
was more afraid of living a life unloved than I was of death. Strangely,
I recalled the words of the same mother who had issued the warning
to her sons when I was eleven. Another warning she had given was,
"It is a sin to take your own life!"

I was furious with God. Why would God make me this way? When would God help me to change? How could it be a sin for me to end my suffering?

My life was not easier after that day, but I decided that, if I continued to live I would need to change my focus. I immersed myself in preparing for college and medical school. I had studied piano since age seven and excelled in music, which provided an outlet for my internal struggles.

I entered Graceland College in 1982. I had been at the top of my chemistry class in Farwell, but my small-town education had not prepared me for college. I worked hard to catch up and shared many joyous experiences with my Graceland friends. During those years, I served as an accompanist for music students, was an assistant to the biology professor in the anatomy lab, and was a house president. I graduated in 1986 with a major in chemistry and minor in biology. Unfortunately, I did not feel free to share the truth about my sexuality during those four years at Graceland.

The following year I entered the College of Human Medicine at Michigan State University in East Lansing. During my studies there I continued to attend a Community of Christ congregation. I was engaged in clinical study in Grand Rapids hospitals and attended the Grand Valley congregation. I found a true friend during my third year of medical school when I met Beth at church. Beth was a soloist, and I accompanied her on the piano. We grew to be as open and honest with each other as we understood ourselves. Our Christian love for each other and our love for God enabled us to learn to love ourselves.

Just prior to my graduation from medical school, I traveled to Zorzor, Liberia, in West Africa and worked in a mission hospital until we were advised to leave the country due to civil strife. The *Herald* printed my account of that adventure, "God Has Not Forgotten Liberia" (January 1991). I learned that I could make a difference in the lives of the less fortunate and a great love for the people of Africa grew within my heart. My life was enriched, and I experienced an even greater call to the healing ministries.

After serving two years in a surgery residency in Wilmington, North Carolina, my life took a new direction. I decided to resign from my surgery residency and enter an emergency medicine residency in Los Angeles. I vividly remember the first Sunday I attended the Orange Congregation. The painting of Jesus with outstretched arms drew me close.[1] His eyes seemed to speak to my heart, "Why wouldn't I die for you and all persons? I love you so much!" I wept and knew I had found a welcoming congregation. I was introduced to GALA (Gay and Lesbian Acceptance) and learned I was not alone.

In August 1996, I was called to the office of elder in the Greater Los Angeles Stake. I was aware of the church's current policy on homosexuality and priesthood; however, I could not deny the call. My call was processed with the full knowledge on my leaders' part that I was an openly gay man. I contacted my uncle in Michigan and asked him to ordain me. I revealed my sexuality to him. His response was that he didn't understand about my sexuality; but he had experienced God's spirit speaking to him on more than one occasion, saying, "I want Mark in my priesthood." As a result, he said, he would be happy to officiate at my ordination. I was ordained on January 7, 1996. Among those attending were my parents, my two brothers, Beth, and several GALA friends.

During my residency in South Central Los Angeles, I had a wonderful opportunity to serve many people who lived in dangerous situations and often died there. In 1996 I received the Dedicated Resident Service Award from the Department of Emergency Medicine, Martin Luther King Jr. Medical Center and Charles R. Drew University of Medicine and Science. That same year I received the faculty's award, the Theodore L. Jackson, M.D., Memorial Award for Best Outgoing Resident. I was also presented with the "Attending [Physician] of the Year" Award, 1996-97. During 1995-97 I made eight trips with LIGA International (the "Flying Doctors") to San Blas, Mexico. After my

---

[1] The artist, Rosemary Hardy, painted a first version of this painting in Nauvoo, and there turns out to be a GALA connection. Gail Biller, whose story also appears in this volume, told me that her daughter married Rosemary's son, Doug. Gail's mother saw the Nauvoo painting, fell in love with it, and commissioned Rosemary to do a copy, which she donated to the Church at Orange.

residency, I remained at the medical center for nearly two years as assistant program director of the emergency medicine residency training program.

On Solidarity Sunday, October 6, 1997, members of the Orange Congregation presented a diversity program with the goal of helping people more fully understand what it is like to be gay or lesbian in the Christian community. Due to my work schedule, I was not able to attend the service; but some of the response was negative. Several members of the congregation became angry and pressured church leadership to limit the congregation's acceptance and tolerance.

As a result of the divisions that were deepening within our congregation, the church leadership organized several Saturday meetings with a mediator from the World Church to help with dialogue concerning these issues. One Saturday, we sat in a big circle, each person speaking in turn on the various issues that came up. One of the gay persons in our congregation commented that heterosexual couples, whether married or dating, often hold hands in church and sometimes even kiss. He asked how the congregation would respond to a gay or lesbian couple behaving in a similar manor in church. As we went around the circle, my heart was broken. Some said, "Our children don't need to see that!" Others stated, "Why do you have to bring that to church? Can't you leave it in the bedroom where it belongs?"

I sat there in my chair weeping. This was a congregation in which I had invested a great deal of myself. I was the music director and played the piano and organ regularly. I was called and ordained an elder, even preaching in this congregation. It was not that they did not know I was gay. I had stood before them on the day my call was voted on and had told them I was gay. I had been bringing my boyfriend to church for several months. I was so hurt by their lack of understanding. And this was Southern California, an area known for its openness! I was filled with grief and turmoil. How could this happen here? What am I to do or where am I to go within the church if my life can't be lived out with love and acceptance here?

When it was my turn in the circle, I said, "I am not just Mark the piano player. I am also gay. If it were pasted on a sign on my back while I played the piano, why would it make a difference? You all already know this about me. God knows, too."

These were painful experiences for me. I felt I could no longer offer my gifts in this congregation and that I could be loved and accepted only when I met the congregation's expectations of who they wanted me to be.

I decided to leave Los Angeles and join my brother David and his wife, Heather, in Florida. They were totally supportive of me, and I needed my family's support at that time. My family had never given up on me in hard times past, and I knew they could continue to be there for me.

I moved to Florida in March 1998. I decided to travel to Guatemala where I met the late Ed Guy, a well-known and well-respected Community of Christ missionary, and studied Spanish at Antigua for six weeks. I visited with church members in Guatemala and my broken spirit began to heal. Once again I knew I loved the Lord, that I loved the church, and that I could love myself.

When I returned, I began my work in the emergency department at Tampa General Hospital. Very quickly I grew to love the staff, and I have developed close friendships with some of my coworkers. It is a great privilege to be able to care for those in need. I have listened to the last words of an elderly woman dying with pneumonia and delivered her message to her children who had not yet arrived. I have laid my hand upon the cheek of a young man less than twenty years of age as he drew his last breath, dying of a gunshot wound to the chest during gang violence. I have been blessed to see a middle-aged man named John enter the emergency room for the third time in one week—foul-mouthed, smelly, and intoxicated, yet I have been able to view him as a child of God, worthy of my best love, compassion, and kindness. Being gay has blessed my life. I have learned to love the unloved and to accept those who are different from myself.

In March 1999, I met Guillermo Salazar from Lima, Peru, at a medical conference in Tampa. He was completing his residency in pediatrics at University of Chicago. As we talked, we discovered many things in common. Our friendship grew; and over the next year, we fell in love and desired to share our lives together.

At midnight of the new millennium, we announced our engagement at a party in my home in Tampa. My parents and a few of our friends attended. On February 17, 2001, a little more than a year after our engagement, Guillermo and I were joined in a union ceremony at the Community of Christ in Clearwater, Florida. Many members of the congregation attended, as well as many friends and coworkers.

We are both part of the Clearwater congregation, where our relationship is understood as a committed, monogamous relationship of great importance to us. When one of us is not present, members ask, concerned, "Where's Mark?" or "Where's Guillermo?" It seems like such a small thing, but to us it communicates the unconditional acceptance of a loving church family.

My dream is that one day all persons, including those who are gay, lesbian, bisexual, and transgendered, will walk in dignity and love, serving as they are called to serve, with full acceptance within the Community of Christ.

22

KEEPING MY INTEGRITY AS A GAY MAN

Ron Turner

Ron Turner of Vassalboro, Maine, is a clinical counselor providing behavioral therapy services to children. In the spring of 2006, he petitioned the First Presidency to be reinstated in his priesthood office of elder. The First Presidency refused his request, but Ron continues to remain with the Community of Christ because of the loving relationships he has with many people within this expression of Christianity. He has been happily partnered with Jerry Morrell since 2003.

W HEN I WAS five years old, a neighbor invited me to attend a Christmas party at her church. From then on the Community of Christ became my church. When I was eight, some other children were being baptized. I also wanted to become a church member. My parents consented, and the church gradually became the center of my life. Participation brought many years of meaning and joy in my life. Attending Graceland College and graduating with a degree in social work in 1974 had a major impact upon my life.

However, the portion of me which was gay kept screaming to come out. When I finally started to deal with my gayness, I was thirty-one, married with two children, and pastor of my local congregation in Maine. From then on, it was a battle within myself about which side of me would prevail.

During this time of struggle, I accepted a call to eldership from the Maine District president, served as a counselor to the district president, and was invited to consider a calling to the high priesthood of the church. My wife Donna was also called to the eldership, and our two children were baptized. All of these blessings came at a great emotional price, because I knew what would happen if I told the truth about myself. However, God was most real to me and still remains so.

In 1984, after a number of months of seeing a counselor I confided in Donna about my sexual issues. Of course, this came as a shock to her. We mutually went to a counselor and somehow found a bond in friendship that extended over the remaining years of our marriage. In 1986 Donna and I decided to move to Augusta, Maine, an area without a Community of Christ congregation. I found a job as a psychiatric social worker at a state psychiatric hospital. In retrospect, this move was a means of diminishing my connection with the church. However we found several families who were members of the church who lived in the Augusta area, and through mutual exploration, we started to hold church meetings in our home. This was partially fulfilling; however, I was back to my old question of, "How would you feel if you knew the real me?"

The year of 1986 was a significant one for me. I finally decided that I had to act on my emotions and started to have same-gender sex at age thirty-four. Donna and I again started to see, over time, several counselors who basically shared that I was "okay" and that I had to deal with my homosexuality.

In 1990 Donna decided upon divorce, realizing that I could never be converted to heterosexuality. This was a painful decision for both of us. It represented the death of a relationship that we had mutually pledged at our wedding in December of 1976. Donna took the children, and moved to Bangor, about seventy-five miles north of Augusta. Later in 1996 Donna married a man who has been a blessing in her life. Our children were able to accept Ray into their family and have received the benefits of another family member in their lives.

I was no longer married, but I was still in conflict about how I viewed God, my relationship with the Community of Christ, and what I felt I needed to do to live honestly with myself as a gay man. It was certainly a tricky piece of maneuvering. In retrospect I was not terribly effective either to the church, my family, or to myself. I stayed in Augusta and continued to hold church meetings in my home with the small group of Community of Christ members. Every Saturday for the next six years, I drove to Bangor to be with our children. Although relations between Donna and me and, to some extent, our children were strained, we were able to successfully co-parent our two children until both were through high school and into college.

I attended the 1992 World Conference when the church adopted a favorable resolution toward people of alternative sexual orientations. I remember thinking that the church people were quite pleased with themselves about their "progressive" thinking toward "queer folk." However, to me the resolution was mostly a rhetorical statement as it did not actively deal with the question of priesthood of gay members or to extended issues such as gay marriage or recognition of same-gender partnerships. I remember returning home from that experience feeling quite confused. On one hand, the Community of Christ was beginning to deal with the "gay question." On the other, would real acceptance of gays as fully recognized members ever happen within my lifetime?

By this time our small group of Augusta church members had disbanded, and we merged with the Freeport congregation, about forty miles south of Augusta. Our district president asked me to be the pastor of the Freeport congregation. Although I had previously shared my homosexuality issues with the district president, I felt that I could not refuse and thus once again became a pastor to the larger congregation of the Freeport church. There were times of joy in working with some fine people. However my long-term issues were always there to haunt me.

In November of 1993, upon an invitation from a coworker, I decided to go where Christianity began. My son and I toured Israel with this hospitable group of local Episcopalians. In the Holy Land, I was exposed to a much larger view of Christianity and experienced a paradigm shift within myself about how to do my relationship with God.

I returned from Israel in December of 1993; and by January 1994, I had decided to sever all functional connections with the Community of Christ. Due to a lack of local leadership, this decision regrettably caused the temporary suspension of the Freeport congregation. I greatly struggled with my decision. However, due to emotional and spiritual considerations, I felt that I could not return to status quo activities within the church as I had previously done. I believe the promptings of the Holy Spirit encouraged me to take the steps that I did.

Later that year, I met a man who became my life partner for the next seven years. For thirteen years, Bill had been a United Methodist pastor. He had recently "come out" and was in the process of becoming a Metropolitan Community Church pastor in the Augusta area. We had seven happy years of companionship, traveling to such places as China and Ecuador. Our separation in early 2001 due to disagreement over sexual issues in our relationship was a mutually painful experience.

Bill was emotionally supportive of my decision to officially withdraw my name from the rolls of the church in November of 1996. I realized that the Community of Christ was beginning to grapple with the issue of gays within the church; but my conflict was much closer to home (my congregation and district) where I perceived that the prevalent attitude toward gays among the church membership would be one of nonacceptance.

Presently I have retired as a psychiatric social worker from the Maine Department of Mental Health and am in private practice as an independently licensed mental health clinician. I had completed my graduate degree in rehabilitation counseling from the University of Southern Maine in May of 1981. I am the grandfather of two wonderful grandchildren who are now the center of my life. My children have accepted me as their gay dad, and I trust that my grandchildren will likewise accept me as they grow to an age of understanding.

Following the end of my relationship with Bill and after having had essentially no contact with the Community of Christ for about eight years, I learned about GALA on the internet. I attended the GALA retreat in Excelsior Springs, Missouri, in September 2001 and felt very warmly affirmed by that gathering. That was a significant experience in rethinking my nominal relationship with the Community of Christ.

During this gathering, I met a man who would become a dear friend of mine. We initially mistook this friendship for a partnership and had to learn that platonic friendship worked best for us. However, from this friendship, Richard encouraged me to return to my local congregation in Freeport, Maine. For several years, Richard lived with me in my home; and as two gay men, we attended the local Freeport church and contributed what we could to the betterment of the congregation.

As I write this story I have recently returned from attending the 2004 World Church Conference for the Community of Christ. I am hopeful that the church will one day accept gay people into the full life of the church. I know that this will come at a cost to the church. Various people will feel that the church has compromised itself by accepting gays into the full fellowship of the church. However, I am convinced that Christ is asking nothing less than full acceptance of all his children. Based upon this hope and growing conviction, I have recently decided to take the risk to return to official, active membership status again. I have my human doubts but also have sufficient trust in God that this portion of his church will do the right thing.

23

NURTURED BY THE SPIRIT IN THE COMMUNITY OF CHRIST

Kevin Currie

Kevin Currie lives in Buffalo, New York, and works at a home for people living with HIV/AIDS and substance and alcohol abuse. He and his partner, Ray Mosser, are active in the Buffalo Community of Christ. Kevin is a former chaplain for GALA.

My JOURNEY BEGAN with turmoil, conflict, and strife one evening when I was just five years old. I was in bed for the night but not asleep. I could hear my mother and father in their bedroom screaming at each other.

Suddenly, my bedroom door burst open. My mother stormed in, took me from my bed, and led me into their room. On their bed, on his hands and knees, was my father, lunging about like a wild animal, his face scarlet and distorted with rage. As my mother brought me to the bedside, he propelled himself at me and, only inches away from my face, roared, "Who do you want to live with? Answer me! Choose her or me!"

Trembling with terror, I whispered, "Mama."

Within a few minutes, my mother and I were dressed and on our way out the door.

It was 1959. My father had caught my mother in the embrace of a woman friend, Anne. Later that same year, my parents briefly reconciled. My sister, Kim, was conceived, Anne returned, and my parents separated permanently. A divorce followed. I never lived with my mother again. Kim and I visited my mother and Anne on weekends between 1965 and 1970; but although their relationship lasted nine years, there was much conflict between them, and both of them drank. For those five years, Kim and I struggled to survive in the care of our father, relatives, friends, and strangers. Our nuclear family had detonated, crippling our opportunities for nurture and stability.

By the time I was fourteen, I had spent the previous nine years being shuttled among three states, five cities, and ten schools. Socially unskilled and emotionally exhausted, I tried to end my own life.

I was living with my father then, and it was not a happy experience. My emerging sexual desires conflicted with the rites of passage through junior high. My school was in a rural setting. Being the new kid, I was having trouble with a few members of the student body. I told my dad I wanted to leave New Jersey and move to Niagara Falls, where I had lived until I was in fifth grade. He got mad and said he never wanted to see me again. I believed he actually meant what he said. So, over the edge I went.

Failing to meet expectations at home and school, I took an overdose of a prescription medication and topped it off with an industrial cleaner. My father put me on a plane alone to Niagara Falls. I didn't remember much of the trip. Expecting to die in New Jersey, I found myself alive in a hospital in Niagara Falls.

I never did tell anyone what I tried to do. Funny thing, the hospital prescribed tranquilizers to help me "relax." They must have thought I had some kind of breakdown. Anyway, I didn't get many of them. My caregiver kept them for herself. I did get to rest for a few days, than it was off to continue the ninth grade.

Despite the struggle I was having with my emerging identity, I tried to fit in by dating girls, but I couldn't conceal my interest in having a male partner. This situation quickly deepened my internal polarization. I was existing in fear and ignorance. I hadn't discovered the intrinsic worth of my own being, nor had I seen the oppressive nature of the customs and beliefs I was taught through familiar faith centers.

Well, eight years of conflicted passion passed. In 1974, I was in the U.S. Navy. Thankfully, I there began a journey of reconciliation. Simply put, I had a spiritual experience, an awakening, the opening of a door into a place of eternal brightness, a brightness which began to illuminate my conflicted soul. This occurred while I was visiting one of my shipmates and his wife. They were sharing the gospel of Jesus Christ with a thirsty young soul. I was edified and soon thereafter baptized into their faith community. Ironically, this couple were Jeff and Alice Lundgren, whose spiritual zeal took a terrible and murderous path. But I wonder if I would have joined the church without their compassion and freely shared knowledge.

In 1975, I met a young woman who lived just next door to the church. We were married in 1976. During the next two years, in addition to the normal difficulties of adjusting to marriage, my wife and I also struggled with my sexual orientation. Shortly after our marriage, I had confessed my doubts about my sexual identity. She cried, and I tried to comfort her by saying we could make the marriage work. Another heavy emotional burden for both of us was our struggle with infertility as we tried unsuccessfully to conceive a child. She had three miscarriages during our two years together. Despite my best efforts, still in the back of my head, relentlessly nagging me, was that old desire to find a male partner.

By this stage of my journey I had gained enough self-confidence to tell my part of the world that I was gay. Regrettably, my wife and I had to end our journey together. This is an awkward time in any faith community. I was a deacon but was silenced and excluded from my worship family.

I eventually moved to another state where I spent the better part of twenty years as a member of the gay community. It was a stark experience, contrasting with the nurturing I received in my faith community.

In 1991 I met Ray Mosser, a young man, full of life, who would prove to be my better half and would satisfy my desire for a life partner. Within three years, we were buying a house and making a home together. During this time, I began to study scripture again, and by 1997 I was once again active in the Community of Christ. In November of that same year Ray was also baptized.

We have now been together for fifteen years and active members of the church for nine. We have been graciously accepted and are therefore given opportunity to learn the values shared by the community. In the spring of 1998, I was presented with the opportunity to minister as a priest. In November that year, I was ordained a priest. Ray and I are blessed to be nurtured by the good spirit in our congregation. We have found understanding and opportunities for service in the Community of Christ.

24

TRYING TO BECOME A COMMUNITY OF CHRIST

David Swart

David Swart is an accountant who has lived in Houston for the past seven years where he is active in the Pasedena, Texas, Community of Christ. Dave was formerly the pastor at the Leavenworth, Kansas, and Fairbanks, Alaska, congregations. He voluntarily suspended his priesthood license twelve years ago but has requested reinstatement and is awaiting a decision on his request. He is the president of the Houston chapter of GALA, sings in the Gay Men's Chorus of Houston, and enjoys visiting his children and grandchildren in North Carolina and Alaska.

I WAS RAISED in Kansas City Stake where my father was a high priest and the pastor of our congregation. In the summer of 1963, at age thirteen, my family moved to Alaska. Talk about culture shock! But I survived. Most of our social life revolved around the church and church functions. After high school I attended the University of Alaska and lived at home. At nineteen I was ordained a deacon and soon after a priest.

I graduated from the university in May 1972 and, six weeks later, married one of the two "available" church girls in the congregation. After all, isn't that what you're supposed to do? I was following the American dream. I had my college degree and had started down my career path, so the next step was to get married. My wife was the first girl I'd ever kissed and only the second "serious" girlfriend I'd ever had. We were both active in church and held various positions of responsibility.

I was called to the office of elder and at the same business meeting was elected pastor. Life seemed pretty well on track. My career was progressing nicely. My wife became pregnant and we bought our first home. About a year after our first son was born, we moved to Leavenworth, Kansas, where I served as pastor for two years. I was searching for something but didn't know what it was. Our second son was born.

In the summer of 1983 we moved back to Alaska. I changed careers, still looking for something, but still not aware of what it was. This move was a mistake, I realized about six months after we returned to Alaska, but it was too late. We added my niece to our family when my sister died, and a year later we adopted a Korean daughter. The stress levels at home were mounting. I changed jobs again, returning to government finance, my original career. Life at home was so stressful I didn't realize my marriage was in trouble.

In July 1992 during reunion, my wife and I had one of our few "fights." I see it as the turning point of my marriage. That fall we began marriage counseling. I asked to be relieved of all ministerial responsibilities at church. The counseling was not helping. On our twenty-first wedding anniversary, my wife announced during a counseling session that she had moved out of the house and would not return until I moved out. I was suicidal.

I was already seeing a psychologist, trying to cope with the troubles in our marriage, and I began some very intense personal therapy. I told my therapist I didn't know who I was, and I couldn't remember the last time I was happy. The subject of my sexuality came up. My therapist asked if I was gay. Giving what I thought was an honest reply, I said no. It was only after he said, "If you're gay, it's all right," that I allowed myself to consider the possibility. Until then I had no clue that I was gay. I began to look at my life, and especially my sexuality. I realized that there were some signs going way back that I just had never seen.

I eventually had my first experience with a man, and it was overwhelming. Suddenly (well, it seemed sudden at least) things fell into place. I discovered what had been missing in my life. For the first time, sex became satisfying and wonderful. I knew without a doubt I was gay.

The next few years brought some pretty dramatic changes to my life. My wife and I finalized our divorce one month short of twenty-second anniversary. I stopped attending the Community of Christ because it was too painful for me to be there. I voluntarily gave up my priesthood license. I could not accept the church's official position that homosexuals were sinners in need of ministry. Even though I had no idea how my local pastor interpreted this position, I refused to be hypocritical about it. I came out to my kids and felt a great load lifted off my shoulders. I could not lead a double life, and it was important to me to be open about who and what I was.

For a number of reasons, I chose to leave Alaska and reconstruct a life without the baggage of a past history. I moved to New Hampshire. To my knowledge, there were no Community of Christ congregations in the state; and it had been six years since I'd attended services when I received a phone call one Sunday afternoon from a childhood friend from Kansas City Stake. He had chanced to meet the niece my wife and I had raised. When they realized they both knew me, he got my number. I had no idea he was gay when he called, but I quickly guessed. I'm sure he knew from my niece that I was gay. The short version of the conversation is that he told me about a "gay-friendly" congregation in Lexington, Massachusetts, only thirty minutes from where I lived and told me how to contact them.

It just so happened I was at a stage in my life when I felt the need to reconnect with the church. I called the officials there, and they immediately encouraged me to give them a try. Two weeks later I did and the saints there made me feel very welcome. Slowly I eased my toe into the water and soon was active in the congregation at a level with which I was comfortable.

But once again my life was about to take a sudden change. I decided to move once again because of a man I had met, this time to Houston, Texas. Bolstered by my reception from the saints in Lexington, I made contact with the church in Houston. I had been warned that Texas might not be as accepting as Massachusetts, so I kept my "status" to myself. A few weeks later, a local high priest gave a sermon that included a very offensive statement about homosexuality. I think I was looking for an excuse to quit attending, but God wasn't going to let me off that easily.

When I moved to Houston, I had also joined the Gay Men's Chorus. The chorus sang at a Gay Pride service at one of the gay churches in Houston, and I felt the overwhelming presence of the Holy Spirit. My reaction was, "I want my church to be like this." That's when I decided to become an instrument of change in my local congregation toward more openness and acceptance.

I contacted our district president and shared my experience with her. I also let the pastor know my status. Both encouraged me. I began with the Wednesday evening small-group meeting that I usually attended. I had become fairly close to several members of this group. After working up my courage, I came out to some of them. They were very accepting. The first time I was invited to lead the discussion, I chose the topic of diversity and used some of the Temple School material on homosexuality as part of my presentation. Eventually I shared with the whole Wednesday evening group that I was gay. Lightning did not strike. Along the way I learned that if we expect others to accept us as gay, we must also accept them as they are. We don't have to agree on everything, but we do have to be as open to them as we expect them to be to us.

In September 2001, I was privileged to attend the GALA retreat in Kansas City. It was a rich spiritual experience for me. It also confirmed my resolve to make a difference in my church, at least locally. I'm pleased to say that I am now the chairman of the Worship Commission, that I am a frequent vocal soloist, and that I have participated in various capacities during our worship services in sharing my testimony and offering prayers. I feel that I have had a positive impact on my congregation.

I do know that God accepts me for who I am and I'm thankful that I have found my way back to the fellowship of the saints. I think we are trying to live the new name of our church. My hope is that we may all someday be a Community of Christ.

25

THE STRANGER HAS BECOME NEIGHBOR

Paul Davis

Paul Davis lives in Kansas City, Missouri, with his wife, Jeanne, an artist, and teenage children Mike, Jake, and Julie. He is presently a counselor to the Presiding Bishop of the Community of Christ, and has served the church in Seattle, Los Angeles, and Boise. A 1981 graduate of Graceland, where he received the gold seal for scholarship, Paul worked as a software engineer for Hewlett-Packard for fourteen years before accepting appointment with the church.

IT SEEMS TO me that happiness today depends on the ability to suspend your powers of imagination. My daughter asks me, "Dad, can we go to McDonald's?" You might consider this a simple question deserving a straightforward answer. "Yes" and "No" are the two possibilities that leap to mind. Julie has the mind of a theologian, however, and her ten long years on this earth have prepared her for the eventualities that spring from simple questions.

She doesn't mind waiting while I process the question. In my mind's eye, I see a feedlot. In the feedlot are cows. The cows stand side-by-side, heads sticking through bars to eat feed consisting partially of ground-up leftover parts of their brethren. Their hides are streaked with their own waste. A truck pulls up. The cows begin to get a sense that the best part of their lives is over.

That's what I see. What I actually say to Julie is, "No." She is prepared for this answer and has constructed a fine counter-argument, complete with a philosophical exploration of how life would be if she had been born to people of means and reason. Her argument is undermined by the fact that I do not tell her the truth behind "No." I tell her that McDonald's is not good for her and costs too much. The truth is that I cannot look at a hamburger without thinking of a cow.

Inability to suspend one's imagination is precisely the character flaw that causes prophets to run amok. They see what is, and then they imagine that it doesn't have to be this way. They cannot see into the future, except in the sense that they see a better world there—"if only." The "if only" is the rub, of course. If only we could eat hamburgers without grinding up cows.

If prophets were really prescient, they would proclaim for their clients two futures: one, just beyond the horizon, in which waits the better world they so vividly imagine; the other, on this side of the horizon, in which waits a collision with the "if only."

In 1994 when I was pastor of the Boise Congregation of the Community of Christ, we invited a local congregation of the Universal Fellowship of Metropolitan Community Churches to share our house of worship. If only neighbors could invite one another in so simply! In the process of deciding to extend the invitation and, in the longer process of learning to live with the acceptance of our invitation, we who decided and lived with it sometimes referred to the MCC as "the gay church." It would have been more accurate to call it a church that happens by design to have a large number of gay, lesbian, bisexual, and transgendered members, who happen by design to be able to share the truth of their sexual orientation with their worship community.

207

What the MCC says about itself, on its current website is:

All are welcome in MCC ... an inclusive worldwide Fellowship of Christian congregations with a special outreach to the world's gay, lesbian, bisexual and transgendered communities.... For those of us who were raised in a religious atmosphere, homosexuality was usually associated with shame and guilt. As a result, many of us were cut off from the spiritual dimension of our lives. Metropolitan Community Churches provide an opportunity to explore a spiritual experience that affirms who we are. Today, as self-aware and self-affirming gay men and lesbians, we reclaim the fullness of our humanity, including our spirituality. We find great truths in the religious tradition, and we find that our encounter with God is transformational and healing.[1]

I pray that members of the Boise MCC found transformation and healing as they encountered a God who was miraculously present as they began a partnership with Boise Community of Christ members in 1994. I pray that the two congregations continue to find transformation and healing as they encounter a God who is, and will remain, miraculously present in their partnership. It was a miracle. It continues to be.

How did we decide to invite our neighbor/the stranger in? Well, we had a business meeting. Long-time Community of Christ members who have grown old pining for a lively discussion at a congregational business meeting would have been gratified. Of sixty people in attendance, nearly everyone gained the floor to make prepared, impassioned speeches, thankfully one at a time. The measure of my naivete is that I had, at first, imagined we could extend the invitation without a business meeting. It was the pastor of the MCC, Reverend Tyrone Sweeting, who suggested that he would prefer to know that our congregation was officially behind the invitation. His congregation had been looking for a sanctuary for five years, lacked the funds to purchase a building, and had lost several leases along the way. As Rev. Sweeting told the *Idaho Statesman,* Boise's daily newspaper,

---

[1] "Who MCC Is; What We Do..." mission statement, retrieved spring 2003 from http://www.mccchurch.org.

"There's a running joke that you'd better be there this Sunday if you want to know where we're meeting next Sunday."

So we met. At the end of two hours, having exhausted ourselves, we voted. The count was 31 to 24 in favor. The MCC congregation had its own business meeting and accepted the invitation. We signed a contract. The MCC congregation began worshipping in the building. That marked the end of the easy part.

I barely know how to describe the next part. I received two dozen personal letters from members of the congregation and the community. I have saved them. For eight years, however, I never reread them. Reading them now, I learn that I have not healed from that miraculous, prophetic, imaginative, divine encounter. Reading them now, I feel a certainty that I do not continue alone in my woundedness but am accompanied on my journey by those whom I have wounded. These are very personal letters! The first one I received, written even before the vote, by a dear sister now departed from this earth, begins, "Dear Paul, please do not let the MCC rent our church. My heart is aching because many of my church friends have left already and if the MCC comes in many more are going." After several deeply felt pages, she concludes, "I had to 'talk' to someone about my heartaches so I chose you, our pastor. I know you can't change everything, but some things you can change, and we pray you will. We love you and pray for you."

This sister's letter gets right to the crux of the matter: What is the church for? The church for her was the place she went each week to experience worship, love, restoration, and comfort in, with, and by her community of fellow saints. I testify to this woman's faithfulness. She writes, "We would never be unkind to the MCC members and would welcome them and offer forgiveness and a new Godly life free from guilt and death, but not an organized church doing their own thing that's against the laws of God." She meant what she said about embracing any MCC member who would join the Community of Christ fellowship. She would have been the first to meet them at the door.

She meant the second part, too, about breaking God's laws. She cited Romans 1 and Leviticus 18 and 20, finding them clear enough for her. Something vital was going to be destroyed in her house of worship if those laws were not enforced, and she could not see a way around her conclusion that inviting the MCC to worship on Sunday evenings in our building amounted to a public announcement that the law was to be ignored. Her sacred space was defiled. Her faith in her beloved church as an upholder of God's laws, as recorded in scripture, was broken.

On the other hand, among the speakers at our business meeting was a teenage girl who said, "I've never had any interest in a business meeting before. It didn't seem like anything important could possibly happen there. I'm just so excited to discover that our congregation could do something like this. This is what church is for! If we don't do this, we have no right to continue coming here to worship in this place." (These are her approximate words. No one was recording the proceedings verbatim, but her words have stuck with me.)

A letter signed, "Some members of the Community of Christ" was left for the MCC to find the first evening they met there. Despite the ominous anonymity, it took an amiable approach, reading in part, "It's very sad at our church these days and a tension fills the building so we are asking you to be 'good guys' and give us back our beloved church." It ended, "Thanks for whatever you do to save our break-up."

A favorable article appeared in the *Statesman* a couple of days after the vote, prompting a few letters from readers. One signed by "A *Statesman* Reader" and addressed to "Branch Pres. Davis," read:

> In response to your article in the *Statesman* this week. I am very distraught and angered to see your consent allowing [sic] the homosexuals to use your building. Don't you realize, that not only are you encouraging this terrible thing; but are inviting more and more of this type of living. Don't you realize how this will spread "Aids" and all manner of sexual disease in our midst? Is this what you want?? Please think this through rationally, we owe each other a debt to keep our people strong and healthy. Especially our children. The homosexual way of life is abhorred by our Heavenly Father and also should be with every living soul.

There was worse. I omit it here. The people who wrote it might read it here, and I want very much for the feelings they experienced as they wrote to be long forgotten. There was a cost to this decision, in case that is not abundantly clear; but the surprise for me in rereading these letters is how the cost to those who could not find a way to keep their church, if it must be shared with unashamedly gay people, is so much greater than I had accounted for in my memory. I knew the decision hurt them and, in some cases, made them angry beyond the limits of decency, but I had not seen that theirs was the greatest sacrifice, because it was without redemption. For them there was no gain, only loss.

I also received several letters from people encouraged by our decision. One woman who signed her name said:

Dear Mr. Davis,
    When I read that your congregation had voted to rent your space to the Metropolitan Community Church, my heart was filled with joy and hope. There are significant differences between your congregation and the Metropolitan Church's. Yet you reached out to them with love. You set an example for the rest of us who call ourselves Christians. I am sorry this decision has caused division among your members. Discerning and responding to Christ's command to help the downtrodden is not easy. My own congregation is struggling with a similar issue. I give thanks to our Lord for your caring example.

Several months after the decision, a member of one of our neighboring congregations wrote to me:

Dear Paul,
    I didn't know about the big brouhaha at the Boise church until my friend told me the other day. I have to be very thankful that there is someone like you who is willing to practice his Christianity the way Christ intended. You see, I am the mother of a homosexual son, and I've seen the hurts and the struggles that he has had to endure.

She described the process by which she and her husband first came to learn of their son's homosexuality and then to affirm it.

As I said, these are personal letters! But why? The decision to invite the MCC in was made by the congregation. As the presider for the business meeting, I was practically the only person in the room who did not make a speech. My contribution to the prophetic task had come a month earlier, when I read in the *Statesman* that the MCC was looking for a home. I called their pastor. He and I had lunch. I gave our congregation the required two weeks' notice for the business meeting, then posed the question: "Shall we invite the Metropolitan Community Church to share our building?" Then I hung on for dear life!

After the vote, the details of sharing sacred space with another group still had to be worked out and then lived out by both congregations. Everyone in these two congregations has had a hand in this prophetic task, including those who could not see it as prophetic and yet paid so dearly.

But, of course, it became personal. It is not possible to have a story without characters. People needed an address for their letters. If my address would not work, they would write to their apostle, or to the president of their church. We seem to need heroes, and we seem to need villains. The newspaper and the television needed a name and a face, too. I was interviewed; my face was in the *Statesman* and on the local evening news. I think now, Why didn't I get the whole congregation to sit in the sanctuary for that newspaper photograph? And the MCC congregation, too?

Accepting an invitation like ours required a certain biblical courage, as much as extending it did. To be the stranger, to journey in a strange land, to open yourself to encounter the divine in the person of strangers—that's what Jesus was doing when he met the woman at the well. That's what the traveler from Samaria was doing on the road from Jerusalem to Jericho when he found a man by the roadside who needed help, earning himself the title of the Good Samaritan.

But, of course, our congregation would not have answered my call to assemble in the sanctuary to have its picture taken. By that time, our congregation had been transformed into two or more disparate bodies. At best, only those who voted in the affirmative would have shown up, and the moment might have been frozen in time as: "Pictured from left to right, the good guys. Not pictured, the bad guys." Thank God that untrue picture does not exist.

Six months after the business meeting, we held a town meeting to discuss, without a vote, the question: "Should we continue to rent our building to the Metropolitan Community Church?" It was not my idea to have such a meeting. The angry letters and phone calls had eased off, and I did not want to probe the wound. Wiser minds prevailed, however; and nearly all the active membership of our congregation attended the meeting and spoke to the question. I had the impression that no one had changed his or her mind on the essential questions, but the edge had been taken off the most fearful statements by the reality that the MCC had moved in and life had gone on. Despite my own fear that people's anger would be rekindled, I was wrong. It seemed healing to have the opportunity to be heard, without the pressure of a win/lose voice at the end of the day. The comments recorded that afternoon are in the Appendix. You could call it a snapshot of how the prophetic task looks, half a year along.

One year after the first business meeting, the congregation voted on the question, "Should we continue to rent the building to the Metropolitan Community Church?" A few Community of Christ members who had been present for the first vote had taken their leave of the fellowship in the intervening year. (I was one of them, having left town for a change of careers. I was not run out of town.) Some had departed but returned. The measure passed again, not unanimously.

Two years after the first vote, the congregation voted again. This time it passed unanimously. In subsequent years, subsequent pastors (there have been two) have announced at the annual business meeting that he or she is renewing the contract with the MCC, unless there is an objection. There have been none.

Over the ten years since 1994, the MCC congregation and the Community of Christ have shared the building on Sundays. One worships in the morning, and the other worships in the evening. Occasionally, a member of one shares in the worship of the other. On special occasions, like Thanksgiving, Christmas, and Easter, the two congregations worship together. At annual work parties, both congregations show up and work side by side. Last Easter, the two came together to wash each other's feet.

After the terrorist attacks in Washington and New York in September 2001, the Boise Community of Christ congregation called a business meeting and voted to invite the children of a nearby Muslim school to use the Community of Christ sanctuary as a place of refuge if the need arose. The vote was unanimous.

Evidently, our encounter with God is transformational and healing. A miracle has occurred in our midst. The stranger has become neighbor, simply by moving in. I retain a longing for a miracle such that the question "Shall we invite the Metropolitan Community Church to share our building?" could have been framed so as not to polarize those who had to answer it into "us" and "them." I long for the loss of memory that will allow me to look on a footwashing and not see the faces of letter writers.

If only neighbors could invite one another in, simply.

APPENDIX

Six months after the MCC accepted the invitation of the Boise Community of Christ, our congregation held a town meeting to consider the question, "Should we continue to rent the building to the Metropolitan Community Church?" We planned no vote for the occasion, only an opportunity to speak and be heard. While someone else facilitated, I recorded each speaker's comments on a flipchart. Speakers had the opportunity to correct what was recorded. For those who were able to indicate whether they were speaking for or against the question, we alternated one speaker "for" and one speaker "against," and recorded them on separate sheets. Many comments were in the "neutral" category and were recorded as such.

Statements "Against"

- The Bible says homosexuality is wrong.
- The gay lifestyle makes me uncomfortable.

- Some Community of Christ people have left our fellowship, and more might in the future.
- We have commandments to love God, love one another, and lead clean lives.
- Out of kindness, we are overlooking what Christ's lifestyle was.
- If you saw the gay videotape that I saw, you wouldn't want them here.
- The MCC is smoking in the church, which creates a fire hazard.
- We are taking a chance of getting a disease.
- Members of the MCC smoke and drink.
- We are selling our souls.
- Does our church approve of same-sex marriages in our chapel?
- Income is down.
- Baptisms are down.
- The founders of the Community of Christ in Boise were conservative; liberals who moved here recently have disenfranchised them.
- Long-time members now cannot worship here.
- We turned over the church to people we don't believe in.
- After the vote, the losing side was insulted and not treated in a Christ-like way.
- Even if God did not destroy Sodom because of sin, God did destroy the whole world in the flood.
- There are other ways we can help gays.
- We will be branded.
- We need to be careful; we can destroy everything.
- An "us" vs. "them" mentality was a result of the original decision.
- Being against the MCC is not discrimination. It's a religious issue. They're sinners.
- The decision divided the church.
- Some of our members were inconvenienced.
- This was an external, political force which caused the problem.

Statements "For"

• I don't agree with their lifestyle, but letting them worship here is not the same as agreeing with their lifestyle.
• HIV is not spread casually.
• It's not fair to assume all gays have AIDS.
• We may be using stereotypes when we talk about gays.
• Our church has sometimes lacked relevancy by avoiding difficult issues.
• Scripture may be interpreted in ways other than that homosexuality caused the destruction of Sodom. The real sin may have been a violation of the hospitality the Hebrew people were supposed to show strangers.
• God loves gays.
• God wants us to be whole.
• Jesus came for people who are sick.
• We are all sinners.
• The church is redemptive. We have a mission to reach out to all.
• The gay community is harassed and suffers.
• Homosexuality is a spectrum, not a single type. Some in that spectrum seek to worship.
• The essence of Christ is love of God and neighbor.
• Love knows no boundaries with respect to people.
• We don't love sin, but we do love the sinner.
• Let God judge, not us.
• We can read anything we want into the scriptures.
• The health concerns that have been voiced are not valid.
• We did not get bad publicity, but quite a bit of good publicity.
• We did not get vandalized.
• The MCC is no "hate" group.
• The MCC members are sincere in their desire to worship.
• Some Community of Christ members have gone to MCC services and heard nothing objectionable or against the gospel.
• The MCC is not performing marriages, which would be illegal in Idaho. They have a public way of dedicating themselves to each other, which is preferable to promiscuity.

- Gays are among us, not just in MCC.
- The MCC is not smoking in the building, but outside it.
- Parents of gays are ostracized.
- The issue is not acceptance of homosexuality.
- Gays are real Christians.

Neutral Statements

- The "liberal" tag hurts, and it's not fair.
- We need to find common ground, and not let ourselves be divided.
- I would not leave if the vote went the other way.
- The church is too important to leave it.
- The original vote was handled poorly.
- Some didn't hear about the vote.
- There was two weeks' notice, as required.
- The vote occurred during the summer, when no one was here.
- The MCC is made up of individuals, not a lump.
- "Yes" voters have been hurt and rejected, too.
- Those who left the Community of Christ fellowship chose to leave; they were not run off.
- What would Christ have done?
- The people will vote to determine what to do.
- The original decision was by the voice of the people, not the leaders.

26

EVERYONE HAS A NAME AT THE TABLE OF THE LORD

Andy Shelton, M.Div

Andrew Shelton is the Hispanic Outreach Minister and Congregational Support Minister for the Sierra Pacific Mission Center of the Community of Christ. An elder, he graduated with a master of divinity degree from Brite Divinity School in May 2003. Previously he worked in politics in Fort Worth, Texas, and taught high school English in Saltillo, Mexico. Andy has been a supporter of GALA since 2000.

"ANDY, THIS IS the body of Christ, broken for you."

He said these words to me as he held out a loaf of bread. I tore off a piece and dipped it in the chalice of wine held by the person next to him. It was the first chapel service of my first semester at Texas Christian University's Brite Divinity School. I was just beginning the master of divinity degree there, and I hardly knew anyone yet.

The Rev. Dr. Stephen Sprinkle, who was holding out that bread, had never met me before, but he had taken the time to learn my name. What an astoundingly powerful thing it was for me to have my name spoken as I took communion! We never speak to one another while we commune in the Community of Christ. But what really cut me to the core was that I didn't even know who this man was.

I quickly made an appointment with Dr. Sprinkle to thank him for taking the time to learn who I was. He immediately asked me to call him Steve. We sat and talked for two hours, comparing and contrasting the seminary's sponsoring denomination, the Christian Church (Disciples of Christ), and my own Community of Christ. We were both fascinated by the similarities. Before I knew it, we were becoming fast friends.

Steve told me right away that he was an out gay man. He told me about the church he had founded several years before, called Angel of Hope. While it was affiliated with the Disciples of Christ, he told me, it was amazingly ecumenical, with fifteen denominations represented among the membership. He felt sure that I would feel comfortable there, given my penchant for justice.

I started attending. We met on Sunday evenings, which meant that lots of the seminarians who were pastoring their own churches like me could attend. The students I met there remain my closest friends from Brite. I started playing the organ and participating in worship.

But what made this church truly amazing and revolutionary was its sexual diversity. Steve founded the church with a straight friend of his, Victor. It was created, from the beginning, to be radically in-clusive of all of God's children. Imagine it: a church with two pas-tors--one gay, one straight. Angel of Hope truly sought to be a church in which all people were united in Christ Jesus. It was amazing to see what I can only describe as the power of the Holy Spirit flow through that congregation as we came forward together to partake of the bread and wine each Sunday. Finally, I thought, I had found the perfect church, a church that lived up to its call and allowed the Holy Spirit to show us the reign of God on earth as it is in heaven. It was a place where I could be "out," so to speak, as a straight ally for the gay and lesbian community.

By the end of the year—it was 1999—the time had arrived for me to find a way to complete the two-semester-long internship required of all master of divinity students at Brite. I began to talk with Steve about the possibility of working at Angel of Hope. He expressed a lot of excitement at the prospect but regretted that there wasn't any money in the budget to pay me. I knew that the Community of Christ had recently created an internship program for young adults interested in church work, and so I began to explore the possibilities of a shared-time arrangement between Angel of Hope and the Community of Christ congregation I was already serving as pastor, the Lewisville Christ's Church of Peace.

Several months later, the committee in charge of the internship program, agreed to an arrangement in which, in exchange for a stipend, I would be named Student Associate Minister at Angel of Hope while continuing my pastorship at my own Community of Christ congregation. I would also work for a summer in Independence at headquarters.

But at about the same time, what was to become the saddest period in my life began. Many—but by no means all—of the straight people at Angel of Hope began to complain that the church was "too gay." Most disappointingly, Victor was chief among them. Tensions began to rise between the two groups. Some of us supported Steve and wanted the church to continue its radical mission of full inclusion for people of all sexual orientations, cultures, and socio-economic levels. The group of Victor's supporters wanted to be less vocal about the diversity in the church and more "spiritual." They complained that Angel of Hope had become a "one issue church," forgetting that we were at the forefront of ecumenical and multi-cultural outreach in addition to being a church that celebrated sexual diversity. When they refused to call for new lay leadership elections, they effectively kept gay people out of the core group which made decisions about the congregation's vision and mission. Some of the gay members began to complain that they did not feel enfranchised in the leadership of the church. Some members of the lay leadership team, made up almost exclusively of straight people, responded that gay people were "just too wounded" to take on that kind of responsibility. It was as paternalistic as anything I'd ever heard.

SHELTON: *Everyone Has a Name at the Table of the Lord*

In March 2000, Victor surprised us by resigning with no warning. I was about to come on staff, and the meetings I had attended with him and other staff members were getting more and more contentious. I hoped that, with his departure, we could heal the differences of opinion and move on. His resignation meant that his pastoral responsibilities had to be divided up among the membership of the lay leadership team, but tensions continued to mount over gay inclusion in the church. Since Steve was preaching more regularly, complaints about the "gayness" of the church increased. The gay people who hadn't already left started to, and we were having trouble reaching out to anybody because of the internal strife.

Finally, about a month later, Steve had no choice to resign. Not only was he crushed to see the vision of the church being eroded by an entrenched power group, but the burden of leadership was beginning to threaten his job at Brite, his only income. There had never been enough money to pay him and Victor at the same time. I resigned soon after Steve's resignation because I assumed my continued presence in the congregation would only prolong the conflict. I also resigned from the Community of Christ program because there wasn't enough time to redesign it and wound up putting off my required internship for another year.

I suppose there are a lot of ways to look at what happened, but I think the most useful analysis is as a power struggle. Even though Angel of Hope was established from the start as a radically inclusive community, it was not exempt from the influence of our larger society in which straight people still have all the power, whether we want to admit it or not. At Angel of Hope, many of the straight people were willing to tolerate—even liked—a certain level of inclusivity, but they soon began to feel threatened by the increased voice of the gay and lesbian members of the congregation. The benevolence with which the straight people at Angel of Hope had previously governed turned into self-protecting conservatism. And in a move that surprised no one, they called Victor back to be their sole pastor shortly after Steve's resignation. With him as their pastor, they would not be constantly reminded of the sexual diversity of the congregation.

221

Although this community was fraught with problems, I do believe, deep down in my heart, that such a church can exist. But this kind of community cannot succeed unless people who have traditionally held power are willing to give it up—not just use it nicely but relinquish it. In such a congregation, straight people would have to take deliberate steps to move aside and let gay and lesbian people make decisions. A radically inclusive community cannot be governed by paternalism.

The people who remain at Angel of Hope are well-intentioned straight people who want to have gay people in church with them. It is the chic thing to do if you want to be identified as a liberal. But being en vogue is not the same thing as doing the work of the gospel. Doing the work of the gospel means recognizing that power corrupts us. We must surrender our power to God and to one another if we are ever to see what true Christian community looks like.

During the many dark days that followed the crushing end of an incredible church, I was able to imagine what Jesus's followers must have felt when they found out that their Messiah had been crucified. I could not avoid the telling parallels between the vision of Angel of Hope being undermined by its own people and Jesus being executed on a cross by his own countrymen—and I do mean men.

But I stand firm in the faith of the resurrection, because when God raised Jesus from the dead, God acted in solidarity with everyone to whom Jesus proclaimed liberation: the marginalized, the outcast, the unclean, the hated. I believe in the fullness of faith that God will find a way to resurrect the original vision of this amazing radical community. I don't know when, and I don't know where. In the meantime, I have come to believe that, even when the very worst has happened, God will find a way to save us. No one can tell God who to love and who not to love. I believe that the people who left Angel of Hope are living in anticipation of another radical community to rise up so that the work of Christ can be done until he comes again. We all continue to fight, in our own individual ways, for a day in which every son and daughter of God can find a church home that will celebrate them for who they are, a church where they will have a name at the table of the Lord's Supper, just as I did that January morning when Steve and I shared together as members of the living Body of Christ.

27

Conclusion: Christ and Culture in Conflict

William D. Russell

In the foregoing personal stories of homosexuals, it is clear that centuries of cultural traditions have produced an American society which regards homosexuals as abnormal and undesirable people who should be avoided. In the Christian tradition, homosexuality has been seen as a sin which requires repentance and a change of sexual orientation. Denominations which have taken a strong stand against homosexuality take the position that sexual orientation is a choice rather than a condition imposed by genetics or early environmental factors. Their theology requires such a definition because it would be immoral to condemn as a sin a condition over which the person in that condition had no free moral agency to choose or reject it.

It also seems clear from the personal experiences recorded in this book that these individuals did not choose that condition. Furthermore, it seems clear that, at least for this group, many homosexuals deeply desire to participate in the life of the church as people treated with equal dignity. Many of them are the kind of gifted, caring individuals that churches need, most especially churches that rely heavily upon a lay ministry.

I hope it is also unmistakably clear that the negative view of homosexuality our culture holds stands in moral and ethical condemnation when viewed in light of the life and teachings of Jesus of Nazareth. For Christians, the life and teachings of Jesus provide a lens through which we try to understand what kind of lives God would have us live. The four gospels provide the core teachings by which all other scriptures and traditions should be judged. Scripture must also be judged in the light of reason and experience and through the witness of the Holy Spirit.

Those who have opposed equal rights for homosexuals seem to see it as a matter of "Christ versus culture," that is, they think contemporary culture is pressuring the churches to give up their long-held moral principles about homosexuality to gain favor with a "politically correct" secular society. They are right in one sense—the moral judgment of homosexuality is a case of Christ versus culture. But the sides are reversed: It is centuries of cultural tradition, rooted in prejudice, that are being called into judgment by people who have a vision of what it means to be disciples of Jesus Christ. The negative attitudes and stereotypes about homosexuals result from centuries of cultural traditions, silence, ignorance, and prejudice. Cultural biases against homosexuality, like some other prejudices, are unfortunately found in some passages in holy scripture. However, if we regard the life of Jesus of Nazareth as a lens through which we get a glimpse of what kind of lives God would have us live, we cannot continue to treat homosexuals with less than equality and dignity.

In *The Precarious Vision* (1961), Peter Berger wrote: "The persecution of homosexuals is so vicious for very much the same reason that racial persecution is. While a persecutor in the latter case uses his victim in bad faith to bolster his spurious self-identification as a member of a superior race, the persecutor in the former case forces upon [himself and] his victim the confirmation of his own usually

225

shaking self-identification as a 'normal' male. One beats the Negro to feel white. One spits on the homosexual to feel virile."[1]

Another writer in the 1960s who was also far ahead of his time and who had a profound effect on me when I read him thirty-nine years ago was the Canadian journalist Pierre Berton. In his *The Comfortable Pew* (1965), Berton contended: "The homosexual is the modern equivalent of the leper. His very job, economic and social status, community position, and public acceptance depend on the successful concealment of an awful secret. And when his disease is discovered, he is relegated to the modern leper colony—the half-world of his fellows which, with great irony and great sadness, is called 'gay.'"[2]

It seems that we all inherit some terrible prejudices from our culture. There is probably not a single reader of this book who was not raised to believe that certain people are less worthy merely by virtue of their religion, gender, race, ethnicity, or sexual orientation. Retired Episcopal Bishop John Shelby Spong recalls that he learned these dehumanizing, unchristian prejudices in the church itself when he was growing up in North Carolina. Over a lifetime he has found that the humble carpenter from Nazareth, whom we call the Christ, has called him to love unreservedly, thereby breaking down those barriers.[3] My memory of that address in Ames, Iowa, is still vivid.

Christians who have defended crippling prejudices like homophobia and racism have often been forced to rely on obscure biblical passages buried in the midst of some of the most unchristian sentences ever written. But because those passages are in holy writ, we tend to accept them. Instead, we should condemn them in the strongest terms possible. An example of an extremely wicked passage of scripture is Deuteronomy 23:2: "No bastard shall enter into the assembly of the Lord until the tenth generation." This is a despicable rule which no

---

[1] Peter Berger, *The Precarious Vision: A Sociologist Looks at Social Fictions and Christian Faith* (New York: Doubleday, 1961), 198.

[2] Pierre Berton, *The Comfortable Pew: A Critical Look at Christianity and the Religious Establishment in a New Age* (Philadelphia: Lippincott, 1995), 92.

[3] John Shelby Spong, "Theologian-in-Residence Lecture," United Church of Christ-Congregational, Ames, Iowa, February 24, 2001. See also Spong's autobiography: *Here I Stand: My Struggle for a Christianity of Integrity, Love, and Equality* (New York: HarperSanFrancisco, 2000).

amount of rationalization can justify. Similarly, wicked is "If a man lies with a male as with a woman, both of them have committed an abomination; they shall be put to death" (Lev. 20:13; New Revised Standard Version).

We easily recognize that executing people for homosexual acts is immoral. But many people who would not put homosexuals to death still would insist that the "abomination" reference in the same sentence is valid. They also fail to recognize that neither Leviticus nor any of the other scriptural writers were referring to committed same-sex relationships. That is the issue before us, and the scriptures are silent on the matter.

The teachings of our churches—highly influenced by and contributing to the surrounding culture—often depict homosexuals as evil, as mentally diseased, as child molesters, as people to be avoided. The churches spoke from an abundance of ignorance. But the issue was rarely discussed in the popular press before the early 1960s, and mental health professionals thought of it as a disease. In 1962, the first policy statement of the Community of Christ's Standing High Council on the topic (reproduced in Appendix A) saw homosexuality as a condition clearly needing rehabilitation and recommended professional counseling.[4] Many Community of Christ members find that statement an embarrassment to read today.

What is usually missing in these "biblical" defenses of our prejudices is Jesus. Every consideration of what the scriptures say about a given subject should begin by looking first at what the four gospels have to say. I argue that all other scriptures and all of our traditions should be judged in light of the life of Jesus we find in the four gospels. The four gospels come before the other New Testament writings, the Old Testament, the Book of Mormon, the Doctrine and Covenants, and certainly before any statements by the General Authorities of any church.

---

[4] The 1962 Standing High Council policy was not published until it appeared in a "Question Time" column by Fred L. Young, the World Church Secretary at the time. Hence, most members of the church did not know that the church had an actual policy on the issue until 1971, since there had been no conference action. Fred L. Young, "Question Time," *Saints' Herald,* September 1971, 53.

In his brief public ministry, as portrayed in the four gospels, Jesus regarded the outcasts of society as beloved people of God. He accepted and loved lepers and other outcasts, associated with women who were so marginalized in society that they could not serve as witnesses in a court of law, and enunciated as the central theme of his ministry: "The Spirit of the Lord . . . has anointed me . . . to let the oppressed go free" (Luke 4:18, NRSV). Certainly, our homosexuals are a very oppressed people.

Love is the central teaching of the gospel of Jesus. Love is the most important objective in most human relationships. Human beings need to love and be loved; and while acceptance by the larger community is important, possibly there is no substitute for the emotional intimacy that two people can experience when they commit themselves to unconditionally love each other for the duration of their lives. Such intimacy is particularly important if partners' families of origin reject their relationship.

We can easily love our friends. Jesus tells us to love our enemies as well (Matt. 5:44). But he takes us farther than that. By his life, he told us to love those who are marginalized and forgotten by society. To be forgotten is worse than being hated. Elie Wiesel, the well-known survivor of the Nazi holocaust, has said that the Jews in the concentration camps were not hated by the Nazis. They were below that, not even worth hating.[5] Jesus loved the outcasts of society who were not even worth hating.

The power of love heals. Jesus's love healed people. Those who are loved are usually healthier and heal more quickly. Christians should realize that their love can have a healing effect in the lives of their gay friends, who after years of abuse need the healing power of Christ revealed to them by the love of Christ's disciples.

Jesus condemned many of the behaviors of his culture; but in the four gospels, he never utters a word of judgment against homosexuals. It is in that context that I weigh what value to give the few biblical passages that condemn homosexuality. Here is my position: I reject biblical condemnations of homosexuality for three reasons.

---

[5] "Facing Hate: A Conversation with Elie Wiesel," Interviewed by Bill Moyers, Public Broadcasting Service, 1991, videotape in my possession.

First, the scriptural record shows Jesus neither condemning nor approving homosexuality; but because it shows him accepting everyone who came unto him, I believe that homosexuals also received his love and grace.

Second, Jesus himself redefined, reinterpreted, and even rejected some of the scriptures which were, at the time, "the law and the prophets."[6] The law is filled with abhorrent rules and regulations. The Apostle Paul recognized this when he said that "Christ redeemed us from the curse of the law" and "All who rely on the works of the law are under a curse" (Gal. 3:10, 13). He knew that the Mosaic law found in the first five books of the Bible was a great stumbling block to the free flow of Christ's grace and love.

Third, the canon of scripture of the Community of Christ includes the Book of Mormon and the Doctrine and Covenants, works that came through our founding prophet Joseph Smith. These works are completely silent on the subject of homosexuality.

The second point—rejecting Old Testament passages that do not conform to Christ's teachings of love—merits a more detailed discussion. The Mosaic law in the Old Testament condemns many actions, including homosexual acts, as punishable by death, as any reader of Leviticus 20:13 knows. Many of the "capital sins" are what we would agree today are misdeeds (like profaning the Sabbath or cursing one's parents) but not capital crimes; many are not crimes at all. But the two passages from Leviticus (18:22, 20:13) and the other passages traditionally used to condemn homosexuality do not speak to the core issue as it is being debated in society today: whether homosexuals are full human beings or whether they are damaged, diminished human beings. If they are fully human, then the next set of questions must be asked and answered. It is wicked or virtuous for two people

---

[6] When Jesus refers to scripture, he refers to "the law and the prophets." The "law" is the "five books of Moses" (Genesis, Exodus, Leviticus, Numbers, and Deuteronomy) while the "prophets" referred to the historical books (such as 1 and 2 Samuel and 1 and 2 Kings) and the prophets (the major prophets being Isaiah, Jeremiah, and Ezekiel and the minor prophets being the twelve short prophets at the end of the Old Testament (Hosea through Malachi). The third category of literature in the Hebrew Bible, "the Writings," was not canonized until the Council of Jamnia, 90 C.E., approximately sixty years after Jesus.

of the same sex to have a loving, monogamous relationship with a lifetime commitment? Is it wicked or virtuous for human beings in such a relationship to be full members of a Christian community, offering their gifts in service and praise and having those gifts accepted and appreciated?

"I read scripture contextually," said W. Grant McMurray, president of the Community of Christ, in his 2002 World Conference sermon.[7] The totality of Jesus's message suggests that homosexuals are accepted in God's sight on an equal basis with all other human beings. The strong condemnation of homosexuality in Leviticus may have occurred because the fertility cults which ancient Israel condemned included cultic homosexual prostitution. And the injunction in Genesis, calling Israelites to "be fruitful and multiply" may have been a factor in the negative view of homosexuality (Gen. 1:22, 28; 8:17; 9:1, 7; 17:6, 20; 26:22; 28:3; 41:52; 47:27; 48:4.) A society that needs population is not likely to encourage intimate human pairings which do not provide the possibility of procreation. If this social condition was, in fact, a factor in Mosaic times, it has obviously decreased in importance in our own day in light of the planet's increasing overpopulation. Today many Roman Catholics and LDS members have reconsidered the biblical injunction and the traditional teachings of their church to make personal decisions about limiting their fertility.

How, then, do I treat those scriptural passages which treat homosexuality as evil? I consider them as reflecting their culture rather than as divine principles. The biblical writers, in many cases, did not question the assumptions of their culture. We rarely do. As a result, some biblical writers condoned slavery, approved of polygamy, and couldn't conceive of a society in which women weren't seen as the property of men.

Joseph Smith III was one of only six citizens in Nauvoo who voted for John C. Fremont, the presidential candidate of the newly formed Republican Party in 1856, and Joseph remained a staunch

---

[7] W. Grant McMurray, "Called to Discipleship: Coming Home in Search of the Path," *Herald,* June 2002, 17; also in *World Conference Bulletin,* 2002 (Independence: Community of Christ, 2002), 183.

Republican for the rest of his life.[8] Very likely he endorsed the 1856 Republican platform plank which condemned "the twin relics of barbarism"—polygamy and slavery. In short, the son of the founding prophet of my faith tradition who was also the first president of my own church recognized that polygamy and slavery were immoral even though both customs can be presented as acceptable in sacred scripture; and in fact, his father had embraced these "twin relics" at times. Regardless of what certain scriptures or his father had to say, Joseph no doubt knew that Christ's spirit of love and his sense of justice found both polygamy and slavery immoral.[9] It is therefore not surprising that he identified with the new political party.

At the Sunstone Symposium in August 1984, Marvin Rytting, a psychologist asked why, if the LDS Church believes in love and lifelong committed relationships, as it says it does, it then withholds its blessing on a relationship because those in it are of the same sex?[10] This was my first visit to Sunstone, and I still recall the impact that session had on me. Twenty-one years earlier, I asked the same question about interracial marriage in a letter published in the *Independence Examiner*: "If two people desire to be married and meet all the normal qualifications for marriage...; are mature enough, are able to provide adequately for children, and so forth... why shouldn't society add its blessing regardless of the race of the two involved?"[11]

It is a terrible injustice in a marriage for one spouse to realize after the fact that his or her partner is not heterosexual and cannot make the kind of wholehearted commitment that is foundation-

---

[8] Roger D. Launius, *Joseph Smith III: Pragmatic Prophet* (Urbana: University of Illinois Press, 1988), 106, 108.

[9] His abhorrence of polygamy also had personal roots in his loyalty to his mother, Emma Hale Smith Bidamon, and his lifelong efforts to protect his father's reputation from the repugnant practice of polygamy which he tried to ascribe to Brigham Young.

[10] Marvin Rytting, "A Radical Pro-Family Perspective," Sunstone Theological Symposium, August 23, 1984, Salt Lake City. In his abstract, he wrote that his concern was "to make marriage and family life as accessible as possible to as many people as possible."

[11] William D. Russell, "'Spirit, Mind and Body' Best Way to Judge a Man," *Independence Examiner,* June 14, 1963.

al in a marriage. Yet in the Community of Christ, hundreds of such marriages—a handful of them reported in the personal accounts in this book—have been contracted without full disclosure, sometimes in sincere but misguided faith that the marriage will "cure" homosexuality, sometimes in well-founded fear of rejection, sometimes in denial, sometimes in an earnest desire to meet social and family expectations, and sometimes as a deliberate attempt to provide the homosexual with a conventional "cover." In any case, deception is involved, inevitably bringing sorrow and suffering, not only for the marriage partners but also for their children, extended families, and society as a whole. If our society allowed and encouraged young men and women to be open about their sexual orientation, many homosexuals and their heterosexual partners would not have gone through untold agony during the peak years of their adult lives.

Some gay-rights opponents see such openness as a "slippery slope," allowing homosexuals to "recruit" others to their lifestyle and to "prey" upon children. While I fully agree that a community has both a right and an obligation to protect itself against predators, I utterly reject this argument. Pedophilia occurs among both homosexuals and heterosexuals. Equating pedophilia with homosexuality is both cruel and ignorant. Typical adolescent sexual experimentation often has deplorable personal and social results regardless of the gender of the partners, but that's because of the nature of sexuality, not because of the partners' genders. Any form of "recruiting"—seduction, rape, prostitution, sexual coercion, exploitation, or even marriage between partners of greatly mismatched ages—is equally wrong because it overrides free choice. It is not homosexual activity per se that is wrong but wrongful sexual activity that a community should prohibit and protect its children from.

In a culture that teaches us to despise homosexuals, sometimes the most thorough attitude-changer is coming to terms with the fact that a close family member or a good friend is gay. For example, my mother was a very loyal, traditional Community of Christ member. My father, who died in 1982, had been a full-time salaried minister for the Community of Christ. Mother was eighty-one and my brother David was fifty-two when he told her he is gay. Many parents surprise their gay child by accepting him or her without judgment. But others reject their child, often for religious reasons. Mother surprised us by supporting David; and from that time forward, she would speak up if someone at the Community of Christ nursing home where she lived said anything unkind about gays.

I will never forget my reaction when my wife, Lois, and I attended our first GALA retreat in 1999. Among those present at the retreat were six of the best students I had ever taught in my thirty-three years at the Community of Christ-sponsored Graceland College. They were also about the nicest human beings I have ever known. Old stereotypes fade fast in a settling like that. At our retreats we share our personal stories. As I heard fine, God-fearing, moral people tell their heart-breaking stories of loneliness, rejection, and suicide attempts, resulting from their awareness of being different, I resolved to do what I can to support the acceptance of people without regard to their sexual orientation. To paraphrase Dr. Martin Luther King Jr., I became convinced that people should not be judged by their sexual orientation, but by the content of their character.

Don Wiley reports (chapter 4) that his son Alan came out to them as his parents wearing his jacket, with his suitcase already packed. He was so afraid that his parents would reject him and expel him from the family home. Instead, his parents accepted him lovingly, only sorrowing that they had not understood sooner the source of some of his problems. Similar stories of acceptance are found in the stories of the Swalls, the Billers, the Irbys, the Swoffers, Allan Fiscus, and Mark Dixon. But not all stories are so affirming. I still remember how angry and sick I felt when I listened to a panelist at the Sunstone Symposium in about 1999 who told about a gay man who attempted suicide. His friends rushed to the hospital and notified his parents. They declined to visit him.

It appears that most parents eventually if not immediately accept their gay child. Families and friends don't want their loved one to be the victim of discrimination. The reason we don't want them to be victims of discrimination is very simple: we love them. And most of us who have experienced God's love, also know—however we may "explain" homosexuality—that God loves them as well.

233

As of this writing, the Community of Christ still has an official policy of "silencing" gay priesthood holders—that is, removing their priesthood status, if they are not celibate[12] or in a committed relationship. However, in his sermon at the 2002 World Conference, President Grant McMurray admitted that on some occasions he has ignored the policy, saying: "I had been present in conferences where persons I knew to be in long-term committed homosexual relationships were approved for priesthood in jurisdictions where their lifestyle was known and their ministry was accepted . . . . To enforce the policy would have required me to intervene and prevent the ordination of someone whose call to ministry I could not deny. This I could not do. This I will not do."[13]

When jurisdictions like those Grant referred to ignore this policy, we should appreciate such ecclesiastical disobedience. It is in the noble tradition of Thoreau, Gandhi, and Martin Luther King Jr. to refuse to abide by such cripplingly unjust laws. On two occasions I have heard an a appointee Regional Administrator for the church, John Billings (chapter 1), publicly vow that he would resign if he were ever required to take harmful actions against homosexuals.[14]

The views of Wallace B. Smith (church president 1978-96) and W. Grant McMurray (president 1996-2004) are compatible on this issue. In a 2002 interview, Smith said:

> Homosexuality is probably inborn. The church needs to be completely true to the best Christian principles. [We] probably ought to accept homosexuals, including priesthood. But to do that is going to tear the church down the middle again. It is once again one of those problems of the tension between the pastoral and the prophetic. At what point do you make your stand? My concern was that we can only take so many hits. I think there was a pretty good unstated consensus that we are compromising and that [what] we, the Standing High Council [1982],

---

[12] The 1982 Standing High Council policy (Appendix C) has not been officially rescinded.

[13] McMurray, "Called to Discipleship," 17; also in *World Conference Bulletin*, 2002, 182.

[14] The first occasion was during the discussion of a paper at the 1994 Theology Colloquy at Graceland College in Lamoni, Iowa; the second occasion was a prayer meeting at the St. Louis Stake Reunion in June 1997.

are doing was contrary to the best Christian principles. But it was the best we could do.[15]

In evaluating a person's fitness for the priesthood in the Community of Christ, we are asking whether she or he is a spiritual person, a high-quality individual of good moral character. We should not be concerned with his or her sexual orientation. Rather, if a question about her or his sexual conduct arises, we should be concerned about whether he or she conducts the sexual part of his or her life in a responsible, loving manner. Such an approach will yield a sexual ethic that is consistent for homosexuals and heterosexuals, benchmarks of which are love, mutual respect, lifelong commitment, and true partnership in monogamous relationships. On the other hand, we would clearly disapprove of any individual, of whatever orientation, who conducts his or her sex life in irresponsible, destructive, dishonest ways.

At both the 2002 and 2004 World Conferences President McMurray asked the delegates to defer action on a new policy to replace the 1982 Standing High Council policy until a later time while the church engages in serious dialogue and "listening circles" on the issue. The Standing High Council and various other committees have worked on the matter. Listening circles are now facilitating dialogue among members with various perspectives on the issue.

The personal stories in this book issue a disciple's call to us. As individuals and as churches we need to confess our sin of homophobia and repent from it. A justice on the highest court in Australia, Michael Kirby, said that when we treat gays as though they should be ashamed of themselves or are evil, we "carry a very heavy moral responsibility for the hate crimes, the bashings, the denigration, the family rejections, the shame, the suicides, the despairing exposure to HIV and the lonely denial that [we] inflict on other human beings."[16]

---

[15] Wallace B. Smith, interviewed by William D. Russell, the Temple, Independence, January 10, 2002.

[16] Michael Kirby, "Social Justice, the Churches, and Homosexuality," speech to students of St. Ignatius College, Riverview, Australia, February 24, 2000; email copy courtesy of Professor Warrich Sarre, Adelaide, Australia.

Our churches are not free from sin in this area. In 1992 the Community of Christ took a small step toward recognizing our sin of homophobia. The delegates at the World Conference of that year adopted World Conference Resolution 1226 (see Appendix C) which affirmed that "the gospel of Jesus Christ reveals the unqualified love of God and the inestimable worth of all persons." The resolution repentantly acknowledged that "we confess our own imperfections in attitude and action" and resolved "to strive continuously to eliminate expressions of prejudice and discrimination." Citing the kinds of groups that are often the victims of prejudice and discrimination, the resolution listed sexual orientation along with socioeconomic status, race, gender, age, size, and mental and physical disability. Referring to those often victims of discrimination, the resolution further affirmed that "all are called according to the gifts of God to them." It called for our congregations to create "a spirit of openness and peace . . . where all persons may find acceptance and the opportunity to share their giftedness."[17] The resolution did not specifically call for the ordination of gays, but it implied it by saying that "all are called according to the gifts of God to them" and noting that our congregations need to be places where all persons may have "the opportunity to share their giftedness." In that conference action, the Community of Christ took a small step toward recognizing our sin of homophobia and repenting of it.

The claim of truly being a "Church of Jesus Christ" on earth while simultaneously holding and enforcing homophobic, racist, sexist, or anti-Semitic policies or attitudes seems like blasphemy. No matter what denomination we are talking about, when we deal with the question about whether we accept homosexuals as equals in the church and before God, the question we are asking is, "Are we truly a Community of Christ?" If homosexuals are not treated as equals in a particular church, in that regard it cannot responsibly claim to represent Jesus Christ.

---

[17] World Conference Resolution 1226: "Affirmation of Human Diversity," April 10, 1992, Community of Christ, World Conference Resolutions, 2002 (Independence: Herald Publishing House, 2003), 86.

Finally, if I am to be a genuine disciple of Jesus of Nazareth and if I hope to help build a community that truly acts on the belief that, in Jesus, we have the best lens through which to see the kind of persons God would have us be, then I must do my best to eradicate those prejudiced feelings toward homosexuals that our culture has ingrained in my soul. And I need to see that to support loving, committed relationships—whether they be straight or gay—is part of Christian discipleship. It can be a healing ministry. And in the context of the Church, I must accept and appreciate the ministry that is brought to the household of God by men and women who happen to be homosexual. Indeed, their experience as persecuted homosexuals may give them resources for ministry that their straight brothers and sisters do not have.

APPENDIX A

1962 Standing High Council Statement on Homosexuality

NOTE: *The 1962 Standing High Council statement on homosexuality has never been published in full. In 1971 the World Church Secretary, Fred L. Young, published the last ten paragraphs of the 1962 statement in answering a question in "Question Time," a regular column in the official church publication,* Saints' Herald *(September 1971), 53. Young omitted the first six paragraphs. The full document is published below and can be found at the Community of Christ Library/Archives in a "Manual on Marriage" file (Community of Christ Archives, 1967, f249 Acc #7784 RG27). The citation style has been standardized to match that used in this volume, but no changes have been to the text.*

18 October 1962

MEMORANDUM
RE: HOMOSEXUALITY AND OTHER SEXUAL PERVERSIONS

Pastors and other church administrative officers occasionally will be required to deal with problems arising from the practices of sexual perversion, the most common of which are referred to under various names, such as homosexuality, sodomy, or lesbianism. Medical terms for some of these practices are fellatio, pederasty, and cunnilingus. In order that one may minister effectively in these cases, he should not approach them with an attitude of prejudice, adverse emotions, embarrassment or social taboo, but rather he should attempt to handle them objectively, with a background of knowledge and understanding and with a sincere desire to help the individuals who are concerned in these matters.

The practice of overt homosexuality dates back to early antiquity. It was common among the cultures and civilizations with which the early Hebrews came in contact as they developed into a nation and is referred to with disapproval several times in the Old Testament. For example, there was the experience of Lot and the people of Sodom as reported in Genesis 19:1-25. A similar incident was recorded in Judges 19:22, 23. It was reported several times in the books of Kings that there were "sodomites" in the land. (See I Kings 14:24; 15:12; 22:46; II Kings 23:7.) The laws of Moses contained specific prohibitions of this practice. (See Leviticus 18:22; 20:13 and Deuteronomy 23:17, 18.) Similarly, it was part of the Greek culture with which the early Christian church came in contact as it extended its missionary program, and the Apostle Paul makes several references condemning the practice, among which are Romans 1:24-28 and I Corinthians 6:9, 10, 13. There seem to be no specific references to this subject in either the Book of Mormon or the Doctrine and Covenants.

A parallel situation exists in the modern world and in the culture with which the church young people are thrown in contact during their adolescent and youthful years. While accurate statistics are not available in this matter, several research studies have been made on a sampling basis which indicate that the problem is much more widespread than most people realize. This purpose of this memorandum is not to argue about or vouch for the accuracy of such figures but to use them as illustrations of the nature and extent of the problem. For example, these studies show that among adolescent boys and young men (which are the age periods during which most homosexuals start these practices) as high as thirty-five percent of those included in some of the samplings had at some time engaged in homosexual activities. This is in harmony with the common knowledge that a large amount of sex play and experimentation is carried on in these age groups, which is not discovered because it is done clandestinely, and does not have the outside consequences which follow from intimate relations with the opposite sex.

On the other hand, it is significant to note that even in the samplings with the highest percentage of homosexuality before age 21, a large number of persons later made the adjustment to normal heterosexual (man-woman) relations. There was, however, a residue of approximately four percent who had become so conditioned or habituated or were so susceptible to these practices that they were exclusively homosexual during adulthood.

The percentages among women homosexuals in the samples studied were about one half of those among men.

In recent years the problem of homosexuality has been studied very thoroughly by psychologists, psychiatrists, and social scientists and there is a large amount of information available.

It is recommended that anyone who has need of dealing with any of the aspects of the problems of homosexuality should read the most up-to-date reports and references available.

Inasmuch as the young people of the church may come in contact with these influences in the society surrounding them, it is to be expected that some of them will have engaged in homosexual practices and that some of them may have continued these practices into their adult life. The pastor should be prepared to give ministry to young people in making adjustments from these experiences to a normal way of life, and also be able to counsel adults who may come to him for help in seeking to overcome such habits which may have become imbedded in their personality. The pastor cannot be expected to be a psychiatrist or psychotherapist, but he should know enough about the problem to discuss it intelligently and give suggestions as to where remedial treatment may be obtained, either from a private psychiatrist or from the psychiatric division of some general hospital or mental health clinic.

Attention should also be called to the very real need for ministry to parents and leaders of young people, in order that they might be advised on how to counsel their children or young people in their charge, at appropriate times, on the dangers of continued homosexual practices and the possibility that one may become so habituated to the homosexual pattern that in later adult years he may not be able to enjoy normal family relations. To give effective counsel at this time is an application of the old proverb: "An ounce of prevention is worth a pound of cure."[1]

The concern of the church in connection with the practice of homosexuality is to set up safeguards against it, to protect the innocent and unsuspecting against enticements to it, and to reclaim those who engage in it.

In discharging responsibilities in the area of homosexuality the church should support those teachings and relationships which promote normal and healthy Christian associations, and should provide guidance for local leaders who must perform our chief preventive and remedial ministries in the field. It should be remembered that the essential requirement in effecting a cure is that the individual shall himself have a strong desire to be cured. It is in this area that ministry can be most helpful.

Any person found to be practicing homosexuality should be removed from any position as leader or teacher which may provide opportunities for this practice or teaching but should thereafter be given ministry, or referred to those who can give ministry, with a view to rehabilitation.

Members of the priesthood found to be practicing homosexuality, and persisting therein, should be placed under silence until the responsible administrative officers have all reasonable assurance that the practice has been abandoned.

When individuals molest children or young people or refuse to refrain from their solicitation of others, they should be reported to the civil authorities. Where such persons deny the practice complained of, administrative officers should take the greatest possible care that

---

[1] Dr. Evelyn Hooker (research associate in psychology at the University of California, with support from the National Institute of Mental Health of the United States Public Health Service) summarized studies made in this field, giving a brief outline of the problem, together with a bibliography of more detailed references for further research. See Evelyn M. and Sylvanus M. Duvall, eds., *Sex Ways—in Fact and Faith* (New York: Association Press, 1961), 166-83.

the available evidence supports the charges before they identify themselves with these charges.

To practice, solicit, teach, or incite others to indulge in the practice of homosexualism is a sin and all ministry in situations involving this sin, including any court action which may be taken should be directed toward repentance and reformation. In harmony with these principles, offenders should be labored with kindly and privately. If they do not repent, charges based on the facts may be preferred against them in the church courts. Should excommunication be decreed, the member involved shall not be readmitted to fellowship except upon evidence of repentance and stable readjustment. Any person excommunicated for this cause and later readmitted to the church, who is again found guilty of homosexual behavior as listed above, after appropriate court action, may be expelled from the church.

It is hoped that the above information will be helpful in assisting church administrators in dealing with the various aspects of this problem and minister in these situations in harmony with the general ideals of the church for the development of higher Christian life and better family relationships.

APPENDIX B

Standing High Council Statement on Homosexuality
18 March 1982

NOTE: *This document is the Standing High Council's 1982 policy state-ment on homosexuality, published in part by the* Herald *but in full in the* World Conference Bulletin, *2004, 143-45.*

Since the adoption by the Standing High Council of the memoran-dum entitled, "Homosexuality and Other Sexual Perversions" (Octo-ber 18, 1961), there has been a profusion of social, psychological, and medical studies pertaining to the issue of homosexuality, and with it has come debate, reflection, and confrontation, both within and outside the church. Other denominational bodies, through special task forces and in their legislative assemblies, have in recent years attempted to address this pressing problem which exists among many of their members, families, and friends. The church feels under ob-ligation today to restate its position on homosexuality for the guid-ance of administrative officials, and out of a genuine concern that a responsible, reconciling ministry be developed in relation to this difficult problem.

In June 1978, the First Presidency appointed a Human Sexuality Committee composed of representatives of professional disciplines and World Church divisions and quorums. This committee was charged with the task of exploring the area of human sexuality and recommending to the First Presidency ways in which the church can be ministerially responsible and responsive in this aspect of human life. Two years later the Human Sexuality Committee forwarded its final comprehensive report to the First Presidency. It contained formal papers which explored a wide range of issues and problems in the vital area of human sexuality, and concluded with affirmations and recommendations which it hoped would aid the church in developing an ethical and theological framework to strengthen the teaching of the church in matters of sexual behavior.[2] Subsequently, the church convened a task force to continue the process of developing and sharing insights in this area.

One of the aspects of human sexuality which the task force studied with a view to making recommendations to the church was the subject of homosexuality. The concern of the church is to provide ministries and develop the kinds of values that will lead to better understanding concerning homosexuality and encourage a regard for justice and a respect for dignity which both the church and society owe to all human beings.

While we seek always to keep faith with the moral perceptions of the restored gospel, we recognize that theology is dynamic and needs to be interpreted in light of changing cultures and times. Nevertheless, a position statement on this issue will likely produce tension and controversy on several bases—strongly held traditional attitudes, varying interpretations of scripture, insufficiency of our present knowledge, and the present varying inadequacies of the church's ministries in helping members understand the meaning of sexuality in human relationships. These, among others, are reasons why judgments about homosexuality are, of necessity, open to further review.

We call attention to the statement on homosexuality as printed in the *Leader's Handbook,* copyright 1980, 1981. "The church leadership continues to explore ways and means of ministering to homosexuals. The emphasis should be placed upon Christian values in all sexual behavior. An attitude of love and understanding should affirm the worth of every person."

---

[2] These affirmations were published in the *Saints Herald* for March 1, 1981, in the first of six articles dealing with a review of the work of the Human Sexuality Committee.

The purpose of the present document is to update our under-standing of current scientific data, address ethical implications, and make recommendations which will be helpful in assisting church ad-ministrators in dealing with the condition and activity of homosexu-ality.

Current Scientific Data

Although there are many theories, there is still little agreement as to the roles which genetic, glandular, cultural, or psychological fac-tors play in the cause or origin of sexual orientation. In regard to homosexual orientation, all available evidence points to this being an extremely complicated phenomenon for which there seem to be multiple causative factors. Among these may be an inherited predis-position, or an inappropriate identification with the parent of the op-posite sex. Cultural overemphasis on the stereotypes of "masculinity" and "femininity" producing feelings of inadequacy in those not able to fulfill these expectations, and a rigid dichotomy of male and female social roles with no allowance for any variations in personality devel-opment also are cited as possible contributing factors.[3]

Scriptural and Ethical Considerations

While the sacred writings of the scriptures provide us with in-sights into the pattern of God's redemptive and reconciling activity in all ages, they rarely provide final or complete answers. Effective preaching and teaching must always include interpretation relative to changing times and cultures. While the basic witness of scripture holds true for all time, virtually all aspects of humankind's relation-ship with God, including sexuality, are related to the cultural norms and traditions of the times. For example, it is not possible to interpret correctly the Leviticus Holiness Code without taking into account its historically conditioned context; many scholars suggest that the

---

[3] The label of homosexuality is often misunderstood. The word "homosexuality" denotes a condition, a state of affairs; it does not denote a course of conduct. A distinction must, therefore, always be made between homosexual orientation and homosexual activity, between the categories of "being" and "doing."

specific sexual prohibitions are related more to idolatry and other practices of the pagan populations around the Hebrews, rather than to intrinsic deviations.

Any adequate Christian position on homosexuality must regard the authority of scripture. The biblical passages primarily cited in relation to this issue are Genesis 19, Leviticus 18:22 and 20:13, Romans 1:18-32, I Corinthians 6:9, and I Timothy 1:10. All of these indicate that heterosexual relationships are part of God's plan for humankind. Nowhere do any scriptures offer support for or condone homosexual relationships. Our understanding of scriptures affirms that heterosexual marriage is God's will for men and for women. The teachings of Jesus also are clear with respect to marriage—he affirmed heterosexual marriage to be God's original and enduring will for men and women. Specific references to homosexuality are lacking in either the Book of Mormon or the Doctrine and Covenants.

The principles of the gospel apply equally to heterosexuals and homosexuals. Repentance implies the act of being personally responsible for choices; Christian freedom never allows one to live as he or she selfishly pleases. The love of God and the evidence of Christ's earthly ministry always make a distinction between the sin and the sinner. The power of the Holy Spirit constantly seeks to free each individual from acts of disobedience and alienation.

In summary, the issue of homosexuality is demanding increased attention in Western society today. Though the church is faced with changing attitudes about the existence and expression of homosexuality, it continues to hold to the norm of heterosexuality and exclusively sanctions heterosexual marriage. In doing so, the church recognizes that homosexual Christians and heterosexual Christians are all brothers and sisters and share in common the love and grace of God.

In addition, the church is aware that anti-homosexual bias has long existed in Western cultures in general, and that homosexuals have been and still are denied social justice.

In light of the preceding, the following guidelines should be noted by administrative officials in carrying out the teachings of the church and performing ministry involving cases of homosexuality.

246

Appendix B

1. The church recognizes that there is a difference between homosexual orientation and homosexual activity (defined as sexual acts between persons of the same sex). The former is accepted as a condition over which a person may have little or no control; the latter is considered immoral and cannot be condoned by the church.

2. The church affirms that Christian marriages is a sacred covenant relationship, ordained of God between a man and a woman. The sacrament of marriage has a long theological and ecclesiastical history, and the symbolism is exclusively heterosexual. Homosexual unions are not and should not be considered marriages in the sacramental sense.

3. The church affirms the worth of all persons. Homosexuals as well as heterosexuals are children of God and have full claim upon the acceptance and reconciling ministry and care of the church. That is, individuals with a homosexual orientation who refrain from homosexual acts should be fully accepted into the ongoing life of the congregation. Those persons who engage in homosexual acts should be dealt with in terms of redemptive ministry and/or church law procedures in the same way as those who engage in heterosexual acts outside of marriage.

4. In the critical matter of ordination, the church should not admit a practicing homosexual to the priesthood. It cannot sanction homosexual acts as morally acceptable behavior any more than it can endorse heterosexual promiscuity. If a member of the priesthood admits to, or is found to be engaged in homosexual behavior, the administrative officer having jurisdiction should institute procedures for silencing according to church law.

5. There will be instances in which those in leadership positions will become aware of individuals who are non-practicing homosexuals and who are seeking help in the area of sublimating their sexual impulses. For such persons, the possibility and opportunity for ordination should be kept open.

The concern of the church with the practice of homosexuality is to provide ministries which encourage the development of wholesome heterosexual attitudes.

When the practice of homosexuality comes to the attention of the church officials, advice as to appropriate ministries should be sought from the First Presidency. Counseling resources which are available in community agencies should be used when possible.

The church leadership continues to explore ways and means of ministering to homosexuals. The emphasis should be placed upon Christian values in all sexual behavior. An attitude of love and understanding should affirm the worth of every person.

APPENDIX C

World Conference Resolution 1226:
Human Diversity

NOTE: *The church's most authoritative statement on prejudice and discrimination is the resolution on "Human Diversity" adopted at the biennial World Conference on April 10, 1992, published in Community of Christ,* World Conference Resolutions, *2002 (Independence: Herald Publishing House, 2003), 85-86.*

W HEREAS, THE 1988 WORLD CONFERENCE requested that the issues of prejudice and racism be studied and recommendations developed as guidance for church members and jurisdictions; and

Whereas, The Human Diversity Committee was asked by the First Presidency to continue this study and to develop a policy statement for use by the church in dealing with issues of prejudice and racism; and

Whereas, The Human Diversity Committee has developed an "Affirmation of Human Diversity" which is included in its report to the 1992 World Conference; and

Whereas, This statement expresses valued principles of the RLDS faith and provides positive guidance to church members throughout the world in understanding and combating prejudice and racism; therefore, be it

RESOLVED, That the 1992 World Conference endorse the following "Affirmation of Human Diversity" and encourage its use in educational materials, worship resources, and leadership training:

Affirmation of Human Diversity

The gospel of Jesus Christ reveals the unqualified love of God and the inestimable worth of all persons. An awareness of God's love and of the love of others is essential to human fulfillment. For these reasons, we celebrate the rich diversity of human life.

However, human beings often fear, hate, and abuse each other because of ignorance about such factors as socioeconomic status, culture, race, gender, age, size, sexual orientation, and mental or physical disability. Such prejudicial behavior undermines the personal and spiritual development of both abuser and abused, and denies the mutual benefits of shared giftedness.

As persons of faith, we confess our own imperfections in attitude and action. Nevertheless, we accept the responsibility to resist fear and hate in all forms and to strive continuously to eliminate expressions of prejudice and discrimination.

We declare our belief that "all are called according to the gifts of God to them." We therefore acknowledge and affirm human diversity by creating a spirit of openness and peace within our congregations where all persons may find acceptance and the opportunity to share their giftedness.

We commit ourselves to work with all persons of goodwill to promote mutual respect, appreciation, and peace in all relationships.

APPENDIX D

NOTE: *After President W. Grant McMurray's comments on homosexuality in his World Conference Address on April 7, 2002,[4] he and other church leaders received a considerable amount of criticism from members opposed to liberalizing the church's policy on the issue. Some church members were especially upset when McMurray admitted that he had known of priesthood calls of persons in committed same-sex relationships and had done nothing to enforce the existing policy, choosing to allow the ordinations to proceed. In response to the volume of criticism that many church leaders had received, the twenty-three-member World Church Leadership Council met on September 19, 2002, and approved the policy statement below, published as:* World Church Leadership Council, "Community, Common Consent, and the Issue of Homosexuality," Herald, *November 2002, 28.*

Community, Common Consent, and the Issue of Homosexuality

[Introductory statement:] *The World Church Leadership Council met in a retreat setting September 19, 2002. During that time extensive attention was given to implementing the sharing goal, interquorum functions and relationships, review of budget projections, and a variety of other significant issues. The council also participated in a discussion of the church's processing of the homosexuality dialogue since the 2002*

---

[4] W. Grant McMurray, "Called to Discipleship: Coming Home in Search of the Path," *Herald,* June 2002, 8-21.

World Conference. From those reflections the council developed the following statement as further guidance to the church on this sensitive and important matter.

THE CHURCH HAS been called to a loving and respectful dialogue on the difficult and often divisive issue of homosexuality. We have traveled to scores of camps and reunions this summer and are aware that many people are troubled by the questions and conflicted over how to handle them. We are saddened by the pain and confusion that some are feeling. As church leaders we are determined to both grapple prophetically with issues before us and yet process them in a way that honors our community and the principles of common consent that govern us. Such challenges have confronted the church in every generation.

If the church is to be faithful to the demands of the gospel it will often be called beyond the boundaries of certainty to explore its implications in a complex world. We are deeply committed to seeking God's direction and embodying the life and ministry of Jesus in our own personal ministry and in the lived-out witness of the church. Even while doing so, God's people are also called to live together in love and to embrace the rich diversity of our global family. A creative and challenging tension will always exist between the desire for unity within the body and the need to press the limits of our understanding. We embrace both those principles in exploring the issue of homosexuality within our community.

In terms of policy we are aware that some are concerned that a few exceptions have been made to the 1982 Standing High Council statement guidelines that have governed us in the matter of homosexuality and ordination. That discomfort is shared by all of us in leadership, even in our awareness of the exceptions and the human and pastoral issues surrounding them.

As indicated by President W. Grant McMurray in his 2002 World Conference sermon[,] we are asked to seek issues on which we can agree and shape dialogue in areas where we do not agree. As we continue this exploration we want the church to know that we will follow the provisions of the 1982 guidelines regarding calling and ordination. This will not affect those ordinations that have been pre-viously provided for, even if they were exceptions to the guidelines. We will not make further exceptions to the guidelines on calling and ordination unless they are adjusted through the common consent of the people.

In terms of further processing and dialogue, we understand very well that various areas of the church need to approach the matter dif-ferently. In some nations it is not possible to even discuss it because of cultural and legal issues. In other places, regardless of how indi-viduals may feel, the question is very much a part of the culture in which the church is ministering and we have no choice but to talk to-gether about it. Each field apostle, in consultation with local leaders, will be responsible for determining whether that field will participate in the dialogue and what methods will be used. The World Church staff specializing in conflict resolution is designing a dialogue process that can be adapted to each area as appropriate. This process honors all viewpoints and provides abundant time and opportunity for each perspective to be heard and understood.

In our deliberations within the World Church Leadership Coun-cil we focus primarily on how we can effectively implement the two components of the sharing goal: "Each one, reach one" and "Hon-or God's call to tithe." This is fundamental to the fulfillment of our church's mission. There will always be issues upon which substantial disagreement will exist among faithful members of our community. Our task as a community of God's people is to invite all to share in fellowship, respect one another in our diversity, listen and learn from each other in love, and look beyond the things that may divide us to embrace our essential unity in Jesus Christ. The church has been counseled that "the path will not always be easy, the choices will not always be clear," but we have also been promised that "the cause is sure and the Spirit will bear witness to the truth, and those who live the truth will know the hope and the joy of discipleship in the com-munity of Christ" (Doctrine and Covenants 161:7).

As church leaders we live willingly in the tension between cer-tainty and the demands of faith. We proclaim the gospel of Jesus Christ and pledge anew to work tirelessly to build the communities of joy, hope, love, and peace that are at the heart of our mission. To do so requires openness and transparency, unconditional love and respect for one another, and a willingness to rely on leadings and assurance of the Holy Spirit in all things. We commit our personal ministry and our collective leadership to that end.

INDEX

NOTE: *Geographical locations, congregations, retreats, etc., are listed under their respective states, provinces, or countries*

A

Act Up, 35, 88

Adult Education (department), 12

adultery, unpunished case of, 156

Affirmation (LDS/RLDS), 27-29, 107-8, 113, 116

Affirmation/GALA News. See galaNEWS.

AIDS/HIV: awareness activities, 33, 40, 80, 92; committee on (1988), 37-38; conference resolution on, 37; death from, 32-33, 106-11; fears about, 198, 210, 235

AIDS Ministry Forum, 40

Alabama, 2004 resolution on homosexuality, 25

Alaska: Fairbanks Congregation, 201, 202

Alberta, GALA support in, 30

American Baptist Church, 50, 52 note 116

Angel of Hope, 219-22

B

Bacon, Mary C., 15 note 39

Baptist, Anthony, 33

Barry, Jim, 32-33, 40

Barwise, Leona, 14-15

Bauer, Roger, 12

Baux, David, 15-16 note 40

Beebe, Gary, 34-35, 38, 91-95

Berger, Peter, 225-26

Berton, Pierre, 226

Bible. *See* scriptures.

Biller, Gail, 78-80, 89-90, 93-94, 188 note 1; and Resolution 1226, 39-40; presentation at International Women's Forum, 16

Biller, Margaret, 87

Biller, Ted, 39, 78-79, 86-87, 89-90, 93-94; letter of, 90-91

Biller, Ray V., 78, 81-102; and GALA, 32, 35-36, 38, 81; and Human Sexuality Task Force, 16, 96-101; and March on Washington, 40; and priesthood ordination, 93-95; letter to *Saints' Herald*, 15, 16 note 40; ordination of, 39, 53, 79; resignation from Community of Christ, 81, 99-101

Billings, Sherry, 58-60

Billings, John, 53, 58-60, 92, 173; AIDS awareness activities, 36; and GALA, 38, 58, 92; and Temple School course, 98; and Welcoming Church Movement, 44, 58; refusal to silence homosexuals, 53, 234

Bischoff, Meredith, 42

Blue Hawks, Gwendolyn, 13

Boise State University, 54

Booth, Howard, 49

Booth, Lavanda, 37

Booth, Linda, 38, 42

Brite Divinity School, 218-20

British Columbia: District, 20, 23; GALA support in, 30

Brock, Carolyn, 16 note 41, 38, 92, 96

Brock, David, 25, 38, 92

"Bruised and Brokenhearted," 14

Brush, Merlene Swoffer, 37, 103-12

organization of, 36, 153, 158 note
1; retreats, 24, 34-36, 42-45, 59-60,
80, 88-93, 121-22, 152, 170, 174-75,
196, 204, 233; sponsored Temple
School course, 19; website of, 42
GALA (Gay and Lesbian Alumni of
Yale University), viii
*GALA: Gay and Lesbian Acceptance. See
galaNEWS.*
galaNEWS, 26 note 58, 29, 92, 125;
confidentiality policy of, 29; name
changes of, 31-32
Galusha, George, 51 note 115
Galusha, Yvonna, 52 note 116
Gay/Straight Alliance. *See* Graceland.
Gay/Lesbian Mormons, 26 note 58
Gay Pride movement, 8
Gay/Lesbian RLDS, 26 note 58
General Conference. *See* World Confer-
ence.
Ghandi, 234
Gilfillan, David, 27-28, 30-31, 35-36, 39
Gilstrap, Miriam L., 15 note 39
Gladden, Tim, 34
Glazer, Steve, 50, 52 note 116
Gochros, Jean Schaar, 120
"God Has Not Forgotten Liberia," 187
Good Samaritan Project, 33, 107
Grabske, Charles, Sr., 4, 7
grace, and human sexuality, 10
Graceland College/University: activities
related to homosexuality at, 45-53;
Affirmative Action policy, 46-47;
AIDS awareness activities at, 33-34;
Gay/Straight Alliance at, 47-48,
50, 62-63, 169-71; hate crime at,
48; domestic partner policy, 48-53;
newspaper. See *Tower.*
Graffeo, Everett, 38, 42
Graham, Duane, 11
Graham, Charlotte Willis, 13
Growing Up Gay, 175
Growing Up Gay and Lesbian, 18
Guy, Ed, 190

H

Hackett, Stephen, 27-28, 32-33
Hahn, Dick, 38, 92
Haiti: congregations in, 24
Hall, Laurel, 39
Ham, Wayne, 11
Hardy, Doug, 188 note 1
Hardy, Rosemary, 188 note 1
Hawley, Denis, 39
Hayes, Richard B., 18
Herald: articles on homosexuality, 5-6,
12-15; letters to the editor, 6-7, 15-
16; name change of, 23 note 51
Higdon, Barbara, 9 note 17, 11, 50, 52
note 116
High Priests/Seventies Conference, 12
Hines, David, 56
Hines, Elaine, 56
Hiles, Jeff, 37
Hiles, Orville, 50
HIV. *See* AIDS.
Hogue, Ray, 16 note 41
Homophobia in the Workplace, 175
homosexuality. *See also* priesthood. as
activity, 12-13, 245 note 3, 247; as
blessing/gift, 66, 88; as illness, 74; as
orientation, 12-13, 245 note 3, 247;
as youthful experimentation, 239-41;
rejection of, 69-70; stereotypes of,
226-27
Homosexuality and Social Justice (1982),
viii
Homosexuality and the Church, 17-19
and note 43. *See also* Temple School.
Homosexuality in Our Faith (work-
shop), 159
Hooker, Evelyn, 241 note 1
Hose, Alan, 90
Howard, Barbara, 38
Howard, Richard, 38
Hughes, Richard, 9 note 17, 11
Human Diversity Committee, 13; text of
resolution of, 249-50

McKain, Hal, Jr., 15, 16 note 40, 61-65, 169-70
McKain, Martha, 62
McKain, Rozie, 15, 16 note 40, 61-64
McKevit, Margaret, 9 note 17, 11
McKiernan, Larry, 135-36, 143-44
McKiernan, Rogene Smith, 133-47; and Carol, 140-41, 146; and Kathleen, 146
McLaughlin, Ken, 38
McLaughlin, Sue, 16 note 41, 20, 38, 96
McLean, Gary, 15, 16 note 40
McMurray, Grant, 24, 80, 97, 159; and GALA, 38, 40-41, 43; criticism of, 251-52; ordination of homosexuals, 22-24, 234; resignation of, 44; statements on homosexuality, 17, 20-22, 41-44, 127-28, 230, 235
McNaught, Brian, 18, 175, 181
Menzies, John, 53
Mesle, C. Robert, 46-47 and note 109, 48-49, 170
Mesley, Blanche Edwards, 1-2
Mesley, Cyril George, 1-3
Metropolitan Community Church. See Universal Fellowship of Metropolitan Community Churches.
Michigan: GALA activities in, 30, 34, 92; Gay and Lesbian Ministries in, 159; Lansing Congregation, 26 note 58, 153; priesthood ordination of homosexuals in, 53
Minnesota: GALA support in, 30; priesthood ordination of homosexuals in, 53; St. Paul congregation, 54-55, 150-51
Mississippi jurisdiction, 2004 resolution, 25
Missouri: Blue Valley Stake, 12; Columbia congregation, 65; GALA activities in, 30, 34, 92; Kansas City-Independence, GALA in, 26-28; priesthood ordination of homosexuals in, 53; Walnut Gardens Congregation, 125, 129
Moore, Barbara, 13

Morain, Bill, 50
Morain, Michael, 49
Morain, Tom, 49, 50
Morain, Sherry, 50
Morain, Vikki, 49
moratorium. See Standing High Council.
Morlan, Jack, 49
Mosser, Ray, 197, 200
Muir, Daniel T., 5

N

Naylor, Mathew, 16 note 41, 20, 38
New York: GALA support in, 30; priesthood ordination of homosexuals in, 53
Nissen, Merrill and Karen, 37
nondiscrimination. See Graceland.
Norman, Bill, 50, 52 note 116
North Dakota: GALA support in, 30
Nouwen, Henri J., 127-28

O

Oakman, Arthur, 105
Ohio: GALA retreats in, 34, 92; Jackson congregation, 43
Oklahoma: GALA activities in 32, 92
O'Neil, Denise, 33-34
Ontario: GALA activities in, 28, 30, 34
Other Side of the Closet: The Coming Out Crisis for Straight Spouses and Families, 120
Out of the Bishop's Closet, 26
Outward Bound, 136-37

P

Painter, Gene, 95
Parents, Family, and Friends of Lesbians and Gays (PFLAG): at World Conference, 80, 92; and GALA, 42; as support organization, 40, 78-80, 94, 120; conference, 175
Park College, 26
Passage out of Homosexuality, A, 18-19

Peace Corps, 105, 113-14
pedophilia, 232, 241-42
Peterson, Thomas, 13
PFLAG. *See* Parents, Family, and
    Friends of Lesbians and Gays.
Phantom of the Opera, The, 63
Phelps, Bobby, 36
polarized reactions to diversity efforts,
    43-44, 189-90, 207-17, 220-22
polygamous converts to Community of
    Christ, 19 and note 47
Porter, Duane, 15 and note 39
Precarious Vision, The, 225-26
Premoe, Dave, 38, 84-85, 92
"Presidential Papers, The," 9
priesthood. *See also* women. and celiba-
    cy, 54; and individual jurisdictions,
    53-56; cancellation of for homosexu-
    als, 90-91; ordination of homosexu-
    als, 4-5, 11, 13-14, 79, 105, 115-16,
    153-55, 188, 200, 234, 247; qualifica-
    tions for, 235; reinstatement to, 159,
    192, 201; withholding of, 76
Proposition 22 (California, 2000), 55

Q-R

Quinn, D. Michael: esteem for William
    D. Russell, viii; on Community of
    Christ policies on homosexuality, vii;
    personal experience of, viii-ix
racism, Resolution 1226 on, 249-50
"Reconciling in Christ" program, 45
Reorganized Church of Jesus Christ of
    Latter Day Saints. *See* Community
    of Christ.
Restoration branches: anti-gay rights
    activities, 50-51 and note 115; mem-
    bers of on Graceland faculty, 47
retreats. *See also* GALA.; Methodist,
    183
Ritchie, Karen, 11
RLDS. *See also* Community of Christ.;
    Auditorium, GALA booth at, 41;
    GALA's use of acronym, 31-32

Robinson, Kenneth N., 9-12 and note
    17, 16, 38, 42-43, 98
Rockwell, E. T., 15 and note 39
Rodriguez, Nilda, 40
Rohrer, Karen, 52 note 116
Rolfe, Rob, 51 note 115
Roman Catholic, viii, 10
Russell, David, 232-33
Russell, William ("Bill") D.
    and Gay/Straight Alliance, 170;
    and Lois;
        and GALA, xi, 233;
        wedding of, 39, 56;
    and Temple School course, 19;
    at 1996 World Conference, 17;
    letters to editor, 51 note 115, 52 note
        116;
    on Human Diversity Committee, 13;
    pickets lecture, 50, 52 note 116;
    D. Michael Quinn on, viii
Rytting, Marvin, 231

S

Sacry, Kathryn, 15 and note 39
Sadler, Brian, 183-84
Saint's Herald. See Herald.
Salazar, Guillermo, 39, 185, 190-91
Salt Lake Tribune, on commitment
    ceremony, 55
same-sex marriage, in Massachusetts,
    55
Sarre, Warrich, 236 note 16
Schaeffer, Roy, 9 note 17, 11
Schall, David, 16 note 41
Schow, Wayne, 18
Scott, Hazel, 13
scriptures, and homosexuality, 7, 15-16,
    226-30, 239, 245-46
Sears, Charlene, 11
Sears, Syndi, 16
Serig, Joe A., 6, 9-12 and note 17, 38,
    92, 96, 98
shame, experienced by homosexuals, 81,
    175-76

Thoreau, Henry David, 234

Toronto, Canada: Bathurst Congregation, and GALA, 27-28, 34; GALA
retreats, 34

Tower (Graceland student paper): and
Gay/Straight Alliance, 169-70; letters to editor, 51 and note 115

Troyer, Sharon, xi, 45

Turner, Donna, 193; and second husband, 194

Turner, Rod, 192-96; and Bill, 195-96;
and Richard, 196

Twomley, David, 51

U

union blessings/services. *See* commitment ceremonies.

United Methodist Church, 183

Universal Fellowship of Metropolitan
Community Churches: Boise congregation, 54, 207-17; mission statement of, 208

Urban Ministries Group, 41

V

VanAtter Nick, 36

vandalism, on GALA poster, 41

Veazey, Steve, 44

Velveteen Rabbit, The, 101-2

violence, against homosexuals, 47-48,
154, 184, 235

VISTA, 105, 113-14

W

Wallace, Jon, 51

Wallace, Nancy, 51-52 note 116

Washington: GALA retreats in, 34, 92;
Samish Island campground, 19

Watts, Parris, 9 note 17, 11

Weiss, Don, 36

Welcoming Church Movement/Pro-
gram, 44-45

Welcoming Community Network, 44-
46, 58

"welcoming congregation," 55, 150-51,
203

When Husbands Come Out of the Closet,
120

White, Mel, 120

Wiesel, Elie, 228

Wiley, Alan, 70-73, 233

Wiley, Donald J., 16, 69-73, 233

Wilkinson, Robert L., 15 note 39

Williams, Marjorie, 101

Windland, J. W. ("Larry"), 28, 34, 38,
58-59

Wintermeyer, Laverne, 33-34

women. *See also* priesthood. and D&C
156, 30; ordination of, 19 and note
47, 138-39; revelatory foreknowl-
edge of, 134

Women's Peace Conference, 80

World Church Leadership Council,
statement by (2002), 24, 251-54

World Conference: and AIDS ministry,
92; and PFLAG meetings, 92; GALA
activities at, 27-28, 34, 36-38, 40-42,
44; Jubilee (2000), 20-21, 98; 1954,
1-2; 1992, 194; 1996 report of Human Sexuality Task Force, 16-17;
2000, 20-21; 2004, 144; Resolution
412 (1896), on divorce, 3; Resolution 1034 (1962), on divorce, 3;
Resolution 1226 (2002), on human
diversity, 13-14, 18, 38-39, 80, 144,
236; text of, 249-50; Resolution 1279
(2004), on listening circles, 25-26

Spirituality Committee, 78

Y-Z

Yale University, GALA at, viii

Young, Fred L., 5-6

Zimmerman, Alan, 118-24; and Richard, 123

Zimmerman, Fran, 118-24

ABOUT THE EDITOR

WILLIAM D. RUSSELL recently retired after 41 years teaching American history, government, and religion at Graceland University in Lamoni, Iowa. He has written widely on religion and politics, with a special interest in issues of prejudice and discrimination. Bill was active in the civil rights movement in the 1960s, including being a co-founder of the Independence, Missouri chapter of the Congress on Racial Equality (CORE). He graduated from Graceland in 1960 and later received a M.Div. degree from Saint Paul School of Theology in Kansas City and a J.D. from the University of Iowa. Along the way he accumulated 75 credit hours in history. He is an active elder in the Lamoni Community of Christ and has served on World Church committees on racism, peace and justice, and human rights.

Printed in the United States
200987BV00004B/1-105/P